ERIC AND JENNY

RITA ELENA NIMPO

1

____

Eric Michael Barrett was one of the most powerful men in the world. He was a man of considerable wealth earned through many generations, dating back to the nineteenth century. The Barrett's come from old money and are the most coveted family in many arts and science communities. They have strong political and economic affiliations and attend functions all over the world, including the Oscars, the Cannes and Venice film festivals, exclusive opera performances, Broadway shows, fashion runway shows in Paris, Milan, Rome, and many others too exhaustive to mention here. The Barrett's are part of the New York, London, and European socialite circles, as well as quite involved in political and economic spheres. The Barrett's rub shoulders with the Waltons, Buffets, Gates, Bezos, Bloombergs and many other prominent, influential families. They are a family that receives lunch and dinner invitations from Royal families all over the world. Any function of significant importance worldwide included an invitation to the Barrett family. However, this is not a story of more wealth and power. This is the story of Eric and Jenny.

* * *

Eric had been preparing for a crucially important meeting. This morning he had skipped breakfast and was on his way to the office in an exquisite limousine that often felt like his office away from the office. As he completed making a few more calls and sent out crucial emails concerning the meeting, Eric realized he could use some coffee. He asked James, the driver, if he could stop at a coffee shop as he really could use a black coffee right about now.

"Which shop did you have in mind?" asked James. "I'm not sure any of these street coffee shops would be suitable to your refined tastes. There is a Starbucks coffee shop coming up. They claim to make great coffee and offer a wonderful experience," James continued with a silly smirk on his face.

"Wonderful, let's try that," Eric replied. James pulled the limousine into a Starbucks coffee shop and asked if he was to go through the drive-through. His face still had a hint of a smirk.

Eric laughed. "Well, since we're here, let's try the experience! I'll just run in and get one myself."

* * *

Jenny sat in front of her computer and was becoming tired of staring at her child development assignment. She'd decided she had far too many coffees and perhaps a cold glass of water was all she needed to refresh herself. Rather than standing in the lineup, she went directly to the counter.

"May I please have a glass of cold water?" she asked.

The barista obliged with a beautiful smile and gave her a huge glass. He watched for her every day as he secretly had a crush. Jenny was not someone you would quickly forget. She had the most striking blue-grey eyes that were akin to a husky's along with a soft voice that was quite melodic. She was extremely sweet, generous, and always polite. Jenny was fair-skinned, about five feet eight inches, and was physically well put together. She had light brown hair with blonde highlights that she often wore in a loose bun. When she walked into a room, everyone stared, which made her feel very self-conscious. She thought all the attention meant there was something wrong with her and made her very shy. She grabbed her water, said thank you, and quickly turned around to go to her seat. She ran right into a very attractive and well-dressed man who had just walked in the door.

"Oh my God! I'm so sorry. You just came out of nowhere!"

"Really? I thought I just came in from the front door!" The man responded, clearly annoyed as he had cold water all over his shirt.

"I didn't mean to do that. I can be quite inept. I am sorry," she said in a very apologetic tone.

The stranger just laughed and said, "well at least it wasn't hot coffee."

Jenny was mortified. She stopped trying to dry him off and finally looked at him directly.

* * *

Eric was dumbfounded. He had never seen a woman quite so beautiful, and her eyes were so striking he was speechless. Words were never something he struggled to find.

He put out his hand and said, "Eric. I'm Eric Barrett and you are?"

"I'm Jenna. Jenna Ali, but my friends call me Jenny," she replied softly.

"Well, Jenny, can I get you a rather large glass of cold water?" Eric said laughing.

"I feel awful," she replied. "You must be going somewhere extremely important and I've ruined your fancy clothes. I can take you to the Marshalls nearby and buy you a shirt. My car is just outside." She was trying to find a way to make the situation right.

"That will not be necessary. I have extra shirts at the office," Eric replied, smiling.

"Well, can I at least get you a cup of coffee?"

"No, thank you, but how about dinner?"

Jenny was starting to feel uncomfortable. "Umm okay ... look ... I am sorry about this, and I can pay you for your shirt," she said.

"No really, I just want to take you to dinner. It is not often I meet someone under very strange circumstances that captivates my attention quite like you have today. Please, just dinner?"

"Okay," Jenny said. "I'll pay for it though, to make up for your shirt."

"Alright, if that's what it takes to see you. How about tonight?" Eric insisted.

"I don't think I can tonight. I have a lot to work to finish," she said. "This child development assignment will be the end of me, but I have to get it done."

"Child development? Sounds interesting." Eric said smiling.

"It's only interesting until you take a course, then it goes from interesting to torture. But I have to take it because it's part of my program even though the material in the course is more geared to a psychology undergrad student." She stopped and said, "I'm sorry, I'm rambling, just stressed. I probably wouldn't be good company anyway," she said, looking very tired.

"Well, when would you be good company, do you think?" Eric asked as he stared at her with adoring eyes as if just starstruck.

"How about Wednesday night? This beast should be written by then and I will need a nice glass of wine just to calm down. Wednesday for a drink rather than dinner?" Jenny responded feeling a little more at ease with something less formal.

"Wednesday? It is a few days away, but okay. There is a restaurant downtown called Oasis, does that sound agreeable?"

"Sounds perfect. What time? I can look up the address on google."

"How about 8 p.m.?" he said.

"Okay," Jenny responded.

"I'll need your phone number of course; just in case anything changes," Eric said.

"Like what would change?" she asked.

"Anything, um, a meeting may run late, I get a flat tire, anything at all," Eric replied with a smile.

"Right," she said. She asked him for his phone and entered her number.

Just as she passed him back his phone, Eric quickly kissed her cheek and said, "goodbye for now, Jenny," with a huge smile on his face.

He returned to the car smiling, without a coffee and rather wet. James stared but said nothing other than, "Mr. Jones has called several times and seems to be rather agitated, Sir."

"I'll bet he is," Eric replied smiling. "Let's try to get to the office as quickly as possible, James."

Eric ran Barrett Industries, a telecommunications conglomerate. He was a corporate lawyer, like his father and grandfather before him, deeply involved in mergers and acquisitions. He had bright green eyes, red curly hair, an incredible smile, and was about five foot ten with a lanky build. He enjoyed all the good things that life had continuously afforded him. He was the most widely sought-after eligible bachelor in his rich, high-society circles. The closest thing he had to family was David, a friend of his father who worked closely with him at the firm; Brian, who was also both a close friend of the family and their family doctor; and, of course, Thomas and Heather, who ran the household for Eric, which, given the size, was quite an undertaking.

Eric had a beautiful ten-bedroom mansion, complete with a large staff and incredible gardens located on two hundred acres of land. The house had several pools with magnificent spa areas, elegant saunas, hot tubs, and, of course, a resident massage therapist. The games room was equipped with pool tables, bridge tables, comfortable leather couches, dartboards, and an extensive bar. The library was stunning with burgundy leather couches, mahogany walls, crystal chandeliers, and a large array of bookshelves with every topic imaginable, including art, philosophy, history, politics, and literature, many of which were written by internationally-acclaimed authors throughout history. It was an incredible room with two beautifully decorative Queen Anne-style desks and warm area rugs. The house also had a stunningly beautiful living room and dining room all complete with Louis XVI-style furniture and a large life-size painting of Christopher Matthew Barrett and Susan Marie Barrett, which Eric had commissioned to be painted the year after they had passed on. There were also impeccable statues, crystal accent pieces, and beautiful art on the walls. The art collection comprised precious originals and awfully expensive pieces the family had collected over the years.

The kitchen had a small dining area, elegantly decorated, where Eric preferred to eat. The dining room was so large, he hated being in there alone. He often complained to Thomas that unless he and Heather chose to eat with him, he could hear his own echo. Next to the kitchen was an exquisite solarium. It was quite large and had often been converted into a dining and dance area for the many parties his parents held. It was his mother's favourite room. She had beautifully decorated it with plants, floral couches, ornate chairs, and coffee tables. It also had a massive, elaborately decorated, white marble fireplace; three similar fireplaces were in the living room, dining room, and master bedroom. She would often sit there with Eric's father and watch the stars in the sky as they made plans for the next event. Eric had hardly stepped into that room since their passing.

From the solarium, one could enter the many gardens that surrounded the house. The house also had an array of garages where Eric had his prize collection of expensive cars and various limousines that James and the other drivers would polish and keep clean until Eric decided to use them. Much further away was a helipad in case Eric had to get to Toronto in a hurry. Eric also had a hangar with six jets for travel located on the property but farther from the house. The entire property was surrounded by surveillance cameras, security systems, and beautiful wrought iron gates. A five-kilometre driveway lined with poplar trees separated the outside world from the Barrett estate.

* * *

Eric felt giddy, as if he were a teenager that had just kissed his first crush. He felt happy, something he had not felt in so long he didn't know how to react to his feelings. The elevator doors opened to his third-floor office. It was, of course, his dad's office and he loved it. The office is where Eric felt most secure. He could often feel his dad's presence there.

"What happened to you?" asked Eric's co-worker Brad as he saw Eric walking in. "It's not exactly your best look."

"Yes, I need a new shirt but honestly, probably one of the best days of my life," Eric replied.

"Eric, you're late! I am not going to ask what the explanation is right now. We have important clients waiting in your office," said David, visibly upset. "Is there some explanation for this wardrobe mishap? It doesn't matter, get changed, I'll stall."

"David, I met the most incredible girl." Eric replied smiling, unaware that David was both upset and anxious.

"Well, perhaps you can tell me all about it after the meeting that starts in five minutes in your office. Do you think you can make yourself present-able for it fairly quickly?" David asked. David was the only one who dared talk to Eric as if he were his father, and the only one that Eric would allow it from. It was an incredibly special relationship.

"Yes, of course, I'll get changed and meet you in my office," Eric replied.

Eric walked into a very intense corporate acquisitions meeting. He had studied the corporation's precarious financial situation and the fraud allegations that would need to be silenced. He had secured authentic information that indicated the allegations were quite real. Eric had prepared for this meeting thoroughly, leaving nothing to chance, and today he was both sharp and on top of his game. Four hours later, after intense deliberations, Eric had managed to secure another company takeover.

"That went well," Eric said smugly as he poured himself and David a scotch.

"Yes, thank God you were prepared. When you walked in, I have to say, I had my doubts. But, just like your father, you were remarkable in there." David gave Eric a smile.

"Thanks," Eric replied, quite proudly.

"Now what's this about a young lady?" David asked.

Eric looked at David, with a cheeky smile, and said, "I met her at Starbucks."

David looked at Eric with bewilderment. "Since when do you go to coffee shops, their coffee is horrendous. Your coffee is much better than that."

"Yes, well, I had been preparing for this meeting and skipped breakfast. On my way in I realized I could use a coffee, so I asked James to pull into a coffee shop." Eric replied.

"Must have been quite a sight, an elaborate limousine in a Starbucks parking lot." David was unable to contain his laughter.

With a goofy smirk on his face, Eric continued his story. "Well, I was on my way in to get a coffee and this woman ran right into me with a large glass of cold water. She was so apologetic and so sweet. She offered to take me to Marshalls to buy me a shirt so she could make up for her mistake. Marshalls, I have no idea what kind of clothing store this is; why don't I know about it? Anyway, when she looked up at me, I was speechless, awestruck. She had the most incredible eyes that went along with her soft, gentle demeanor. She was so kind, trying to wipe the water off my shirt."

"What did you say?" asked David smiling.

"I offered to buy her another very large glass of water." He laughed. "We agreed to have a drink at Oasis. She accepted only if she could pay for it to make up for her drenching me. I have never met anyone like her. That kind of girl just is not in my social circle. She has no idea who I am, and she is buying me drinks! Can you imagine that!"

"Does she know you own Oasis?"

"No, she does not," Eric replied. "I feel so drawn to the girl, and I don't know why. And the fact that she didn't recognize me when I introduced myself surprised me. It's not the usual response I get when I say I'm Eric Barrett."

"How old is this girl?" David asked.

"I don't know," Eric answered. "I think she's quite young. She's in a program at a university somewhere, which would place her in her early twenties, I assume. That's all I know about her. I expect to find out some more when I see her. All I know is that I feel alive, David, and I have not felt like this in years."

"I hope she's everything you're looking for because no one deserves it more than you do."

"Thanks, David. Can we keep this between us? I don't want news getting around. I just want to get to know her without prying eyes." Eric was quite serious as he said this.

"Of course. My lips are sealed," David replied.

Eric went back to his office and started working. His day was full and by the time he looked at his watch, it was 10 p.m. He quickly made a phone call.

"Hello, Heather. I'm deeply sorry I didn't call sooner. I've had a terribly busy day. I just looked at my watch and realized the time. Forgive me? I'm sure you had a wonderful dinner prepared."

"Master Eric, your mother, God rest her soul, taught you better than to call late with a sorry excuse. But because I loved her and God knows I love you, I'll accept your apology," Heather responded.

"Thank you, Heather. I'm sure Thomas can finish my portion, and nothing will go to waste."

"That's the problem, Master Eric, he eats too much already," she said with a laugh. "Will you be home tomorrow night, Sir?"

"No, I don't think so. I will let you know for sure when I know myself. I do have a lot of work to get done. I better get going now. Good night, Heather."

"Good night, sir. Anything you want me to arrange with Maria at the penthouse?" she asked.

"No, I'll take care of that, you take care of Thomas and be kind to him. I need you both so very much in my life. Tell him I said good night." Eric hung up the phone and smiled fondly as he thought of Heather and Thomas. They had been so supportive when his parents passed away, always checking in on him, looking out for him, and calling out his poor behaviour exactly when he needed them to. He loved them very much.

Eric left the office and went to the top floor of the building where he had his penthouse. He took a shower and then looked outside at the stars as he relaxed with a scotch. He remembered his parents at that moment and started feeling sad. He needed to feel that happiness he had felt earlier that day. He needed to call Jenny. It was 11 p.m. but, he thought, why not? He called her number.

"Hello beautiful, I know it's late, but I just got home from work, took a shower, and wanted to just talk to you," he said, wondering if that was a smart way to open the conversation.

"Wow, that is a long day. Did you have dinner?" she asked.

"No, I haven't. Not hungry for food anyway," he said smiling, even though she couldn't see him.

"I know that sometimes I get so tired, I can't eat and just want to sleep. But I'm not sure if that's what you mean," she replied.

"I felt incredibly happy after meeting you today. I enjoyed your energy. My day was just so busy that I had no time to call and the minute I had time I wanted to hear your voice. Get back some of that happiness."

"What kind of work do you do that keeps you busy for twelve hours a day?"

"I'm a corporate lawyer, and a very busy one at that."

"How old are you, Eric?"

"I'm thirty-five, Jenny. Is that too old?" he asked.

"Well, I'm twenty-three, so you are kind of a relic," she replied laughing.

Eric laughed heartily, enjoying the humour. "Yes, I thought you were young, but honestly, I love your innocence, Jenny. It's so refreshing."

"I'm not sure how to respond to that, Eric. Do I come across as some naive little girl that you can play with, have your way with, and then move on? Because if that's what this is about, you can forget my phone number and the drinks."

"No! Not at all. I mean that I love your innocence. I love your gentleness, empathy. In my line of work, I often see the worst, not the best, of society. Not to mention your beauty is unparalleled. I'm not the most handsome looking, but I think I'm decent and that is all I can offer."

"I think you're handsome," Jenny said very softly.

"Oh, you do. Well, that's good news for me. I can cancel the face transplant appointment I had scheduled for Wednesday."

Jenny laughed out loud. "You're so funny. I think you have nice eyes."

"And the fact that I have freckles all over my face and body with bright, curly, red hair doesn't bother you?" he asked smiling.

"No, I think your freckles are cute, like a Raggedy Andy doll, I guess," she said laughing.

Just then Eric had a funny thought. "Will you be at Starbucks tomorrow?"

"No, I'm studying at home tomorrow."

"May I ask you where you live? I'd like to send you something."

Jenny thought he was going to send her flowers and liked the thought. "I can give you my address as long as you promise not to show up at my door. My parents, especially my dad, are a little strict about guys at the door."

"No problem, I promise it will only be a delivery," he said.

"Okay. I live at 98 Greensborough Drive in King City."

"Perfect. You see? That's the innocence I'm talking about. You trust me to not show up. I love that! I love that you trust me to do what I said I would do, without really knowing anything about me."

"I don't have a reason not to trust you, Eric. Not yet. Not until you give me a reason."

"You will never have a reason not to trust me, Jenny. I promise you that. I wish you could just come over here and we could share a glass of wine and just talk all night."

"Not until child development is done. Do you live in King City?"

"Yes, I do, but I work in Toronto. My firm is at Yonge and Eglinton and often when I work late, like today, I stay at a condo that I keep here since it's a long drive home," Eric explained. "I was just sitting here with a scotch looking at the stars and thought of you. So, I called, even though I know it's late."

"No, not late for me. I usually stay up to three or four a.m. But your condo sounds genuinely nice," she responded in a soft, cheery tone.

"Well, do you go to a university in the city? Because if you do, maybe you can pass by my office and I can show it to you. Perhaps we can plan to have dinner here," he said optimistically.

"I don't know how comfortable I feel with that. I hardly know you," she replied cautiously.

"A woman of morals and integrity! The more I learn about you the more I like you, Jenny Ali."

"Well, sounds like you're planning for future dates, so I should tell you that I'm Muslim."

"Okay, why is this so important to tell me now?" he was unsure of where this was going.

"Well, there's a lot of misinformation about Muslims in the media today. They claim that we're messed up terrorists that hate the west and want to live in the Middle Ages. You know, you've heard it all before. They keep women subservient to men and force them to fulfill their sole purpose in life—to have babies," she said sarcastically.

Eric was confused. "Is that what you believe?"

"No! Neither do Muslims," Jenny responded. "What most people don't know is that Muslim women enjoy greater rights than most women in many parts of the world, including the west. They are encouraged by their men to be the best they can be, especially when it comes to education. Muslim women are highly educated and often run their businesses, work as professors in universities, or CEOs of large companies. They are not subservient, obedient, housewives." She said all this rather seriously to drive her point home.

"Thank God for that! I don't think a woman would be genuinely happy any other way."

"That is true. Most people feel extremely uncomfortable knowing that I'm Muslim, so if you want to run now, you can, and it was nice getting to know you. You are decent," she said casually, although she hoped he wouldn't just drop their friendship as had happened countless times before.

"Jenny, I don't think I'll be running, and if you'd let me see you right now, I would be there in a heartbeat," he replied, hoping that clarified his feelings for her.

Jenny, not knowing how to respond to him, said, "Eric, I'm really glad you called tonight, that was sweet. I'll talk to you soon."

"Well, although I closed a multimillion-dollar deal earlier, this is the best news I've heard all day," he replied.

"Wow that's a lot of money. Do you get a percentage of that? The money will come in handy for Christmas, I guess."

"Yes, something like that. Do you celebrate Christmas?" he asked, a little confused after their prior conversation.

"We put up a tree, buy presents for each other, and enjoy the gift of giving and family. We do recognize Jesus, but as a prophet, not the son of God."

"My parents were Christian by faith, but we weren't that religious. We loved Christmas because there seemed to be a wonderful presence in the air. People seem to be more thoughtful and caring during the Christmas season, more so than any other time of the year. Gift giving and family are joyful memories I will always treasure during this time of year."

"Are your parents no longer with you? You talk about them in the past."

"Yes, they passed away four years ago in a car accident," he explained.

"Oh my God! I am so sorry. It must have been extremely hard for you and your siblings," she said with a note of concern in her voice.

"I'm an only child, Jenny, so I was left quite alone. But I don't want to talk about that now. Now we can talk about getting you a nice Christmas present."

"Oh no, please, don't do that. I barely have enough money to buy something for my family. I wouldn't be able to get you anything unless you don't mind something like a mug." She started laughing.

"Well, that would be fitting, considering how we met!"

"Besides, you don't know me well enough to buy me anything. You might find there are things I do that you will hate."

"Yes, Jenny, and you will too, about me. But I think there are many good things about you that I'm sure will outweigh the bad," Eric said softly.

"Well, if I don't get back to work, I'm going to get an awfully bad grade, which I cannot afford to do if I want to eventually get into the Faculty of Education. So, I really should go, but thanks for calling."

"The pleasure is all mine, my dear. And don't forget to expect a delivery tomorrow. Sleep well, Jenny. Good night."

"Goodnight, Eric. Maybe I will call you tomorrow," she said playfully.

It was just past midnight and Eric should have gone to bed but instead, he sat up at his computer and looked for a Raggedy Andy stuffed doll. He found one and ordered it to be delivered to Jenny the very next day. He called the twenty-four-hour line and paid an extra hundred dollars to have it couriered to her directly. He attached a note and hoped she would get a good laugh out of it. It was 3 a.m. before he could fall asleep.

2

It was early afternoon when Jenny woke up. She had spent most of the night and the morning working hard on her assignment.

"Good morning, Jenny. Sleep well?" Her mother knew full-well that Jenny kept a very strange schedule that seemed to work for her.

"Yeah, I did," she replied softly.

"Eggs are ready if that's what you want," said her mother with a smile.

"Yeah, sounds good," Jenny replied, not quite talkative yet.

"Oh, before I forget, there was a package delivered for you today. I left it on the dining room table. I have to go to a doctor's appointment, so I'll catch up with you later."

"I hope everything is okay, Mom." Jenny looked at her mother with concern. "I love you," she said, kissing her mother on the cheek as she left.

Jenny walked over to the dining room table and wondered what it could be. "I guess we're not getting roses," she said out loud. She opened the package and laughed when she saw the Raggedy Andy doll with a note attached. She carefully opened the note and read.

7is was the only way I could be near you. Please hug me, I love hugs.
With love, Raggedy Eric.

She unwrapped Raggedy Eric and took him to her room. Jenny had a smile from ear to ear. She picked up the phone and dialed Eric's number.

At first, she got his voicemail, then a few minutes later, he called back.

"Hello, Jenny. I'm sorry, I was just in a meeting. How are you this afternoon?"

"Well, I just woke up as I went to bed at 10 a.m., and I found this lovely gift. I love him!" she said with childlike happiness.

"Did he put a smile on your face? That was the intention."

"Yes, it did, and he is now in my bed fast asleep," she responded playfully.

"Oh, how I envy him and would do anything to trade places with him right now," he said jokingly.

"Well, Raggedy Andy says there is no room for you."

"Hmm ... we will have to do something about that."

Jenny was noticeably quiet and didn't know how to respond. Eric broke the silence. "Well, as long as Raggedy Eric is with you, I won't be jealous."

"I'm sure you're terribly busy, so I'll let you go. I just wanted to thank you for the thoughtful gift," Jenny said a little awkwardly.

"Truthfully, I have a meeting in about twenty minutes and really should look over a few documents. Can I call you later?"

"Sure, how about at 11 p.m.? I'll be looking to take a break about then."

"Okay, 11 p.m. will forever be known as Jenny time," he said playfully. "I think about you a lot. I hope that doesn't sound creepy to you. I will talk to you later, bye for now."

* * *

Jenny had been seeing Eric for a while now. She had strong feelings for him but was also confused about these feelings. One thing was clear however, this was unbelievably bad timing. She had so much to do and did not need this distraction. *Put him out of your mind and get to work. She thought. He's not exactly a knight in shining armor. He's just a guy that works as a lawyer and spends a lot of time in the o$ce. He does say all the right things. More reason to be careful. No one is* **that** *perfect. I think I'll take this slow.* She was falling more and more in love with him with each passing day and was trying to rationalize her feelings.

She thought about the first night they had drinks together, an encounter that went very well. Then she thought about the several following dinners at various venues. What she did not know was that Eric had taken extreme measures to conceal his identity in those very same venues she attended. Jenny did have extraordinarily strong feelings for him. He was so charming, so endearing, so loving, and she was so afraid of being hurt.

He wanted to know everything about her, and aside from telling her he was an only child, he never spoke about himself, which Jenny found a little disconcerting. He never took her to his office or introduced her to any of his friends or family. *I wonder what I can find out about my charming lawyer.*

"Google, it's time you tell me what I need to know!" she said out loud. Jenny hated doing this because she believed that people were entitled to their privacy. But, since he would not reveal anything about himself and she had such deep feelings for him, she felt extreme measures were necessary. *"Desperate times call for desperate measures,"* she said out loud.

She began with his name and his law firm on Eglinton came up. But so did a lot more information that Jenny couldn't believe. *7is can't be my Eric,* she thought. She clicked his name and then clicked images. Well, there he was! Eric Michael Barret the billionaire. Pictures with very prominent people, celebrities, royalty, politicians, people from all over the world. *"Holy Shit! He has a picture with Beyoncé! What does he want with me?"* Jenny felt very confused and angry. *"Why hasn't he told me who he is? What game is he playing and why?"* Jenny made up her mind right then and there. *"He may have a lot of power and money, but he cannot play with people just because he thinks he's untouchable,"* she said out loud. Jenny was so torn. She knew her feelings for him were strong and real but now questioned if he had feelings for her at all. Her emotions quickly got the best of her, and she cried uncontrollably. *"Why did you do this? What do you want with me?"* She thought about calling her best friend or talking to her mother, but she was so hurt, felt so manipulated, that she was embarrassed to tell anyone at all. Jenny decided to take a shower and try to collect her thoughts. It was almost 11 p.m. and Eric would be calling her soon. How would she handle this? All she knew right now was that she needed time to sort out her feelings.

Jenny's phone rang and she looked at the screen. "It's my knight in shining armour," she said sarcastically.

"Hello, Eric. How are you?" Jenny asked.

"Hello, darling. I'm exhausted honestly. It's been a long day and I still have a lot of work to do."

"What are you working on?" she asked in a non-committal tone. "Well, I'm glad you asked. I'm a member of the International Lawyers Group, and this year one of our major conferences is in Paris. I am the scheduled keynote speaker," he said very proudly.

Jenny was impressed and interested. "Really? What will you be discussing?"

"I will be lecturing on current legal developments in European private mergers and acquisitions. As a corporate lawyer, I am very much involved in this both on a national and international level."

"It sounds very complex. I hope it goes well for you," she added, rather coldly.

"Thank you." There was a slight pause before he continued. "I was wondering if you might consider coming with me. All your expenses would be paid of course and I'm sure you can find quite a lot to do in Paris while I lecture. We would be there for approximately three weeks, maybe a bit longer. I'll be conducting business while I'm there as well. What do you think?"

Jenny was surprised. He wanted her to go with him to Paris but wouldn't tell her anything about himself. Didn't he think she would figure it out? Was this his way of telling her? She was confused and needed time to think.

"I appreciate the offer. I mean who doesn't want a free trip to Paris? But I'm afraid I can't accept. I have a lot of work to do, and I've been falling behind in my courses. A three-week break to focus on school might be a good thing right now."

Eric was disheartened by her response. He was hoping she would accept so they could discuss everything he'd been keeping from her. "I'm sorry to hear that, Jenny. I was hoping you would come. I can get separate rooms at the hotel if that's what you're worried about."

"No, Eric. I just have so much to do, and from the sounds of it, you will be quite busy yourself."

With a very dejected and disappointed tone in his voice Eric said, "Okay, I understand if you would prefer to get caught up with your studies. Education is important after all."

"When do you leave?" Jenny asked, a little concerned by the tone in his voice. *He sounds hurt*, she thought.

"In a few days. Would you mind if I call you each night at Jenny time? I just have to find some way to stay connected with you, Jenny. Three weeks is a long time away from you."

"Of course, Eric. That would be fine. I work late anyway, you know that," she said laughing a little.

"Jenny, I wish I could explain how I feel about you. I just can't seem to put it into words. But from the first time we met, I felt like I had reconnected with a long-lost love. Like we've met in a past life, as if our souls were meant to be one. For so long, I've been only half of that one. Am I making any sense?"

Jenny was in tears as she gave a feeble, "Yes, I know what you mean."

"I feel you, Jenny. Do you feel me too?"

Jenny had now begun to sob. "Eric, I can't have this conversation right now. I think it's best if we talk when you get back."

"Jenny, I know something is bothering you. I was hoping we would have some time to talk about things. There's something I've been wanting to tell you for a while now, and I thought I would get an opportunity to do that with you in Paris. It doesn't look like I'll get that opportunity."

Jenny didn't let him continue. "Eric, please, let's talk when you get back. I need some time to myself. Do you understand?"

"Yes, of course. Just please know that my heart is yours, Jenny. I wish I could explain this insatiable need to connect my soul to yours. I feel empty, like something is missing when I'm not with you," he said in the most earnest tone he could muster.

As tears rolled down Jenny's face, she said, "I know Eric, I feel it too. But we have a lot we need to talk about."

"I'll be back in three weeks. If I can make it back sooner, I will. How about we meet at Oasis for dinner when I get back?" He wanted to make sure he had a plan to meet with her before he left for Paris.

"Okay, Eric. Oasis will be fine. I need to go now, I feel exhausted."

"Good night, my love. I'll call you tomorrow."

"Good night, Eric," she replied, and hung up the phone.

Eric had no peace. He had tried to reassure her of his love, but it didn't seem to be enough. He knew he had to explain things to Jenny and could feel that she was in a lot of pain. Pain that he had somehow inflicted. Jenny could not even speak to him. He called his florist at 1 a.m.

"Eric," answered Alex, from A Scent of Heaven flower shop. "It's 1 a.m. Is everything okay? Has someone passed away?"

"No Alex," responded Eric, "but I need a favour, right now!"

"Sure, buddy. What's up?"

"I need you to deliver twenty-four of your finest red roses tonight, right now."

"Wow, this means that you either really fucked something up or someone means a lot to you."

"Actually, both. I'll pay you five thousand dollars if you deliver them in the next half hour. Please! It's important."

"You don't have to do that, Eric. I'll do it for nothing. You're a good friend and you've been there for me so many times, times when my family wouldn't even stand up for me. Text me the name and address."

"Would you please add a card saying,

I know you're hurting because of me, but please know it will all be explained, and it will all be okay. I love you! Eric.

"Of course! I'll deliver it myself, Eric, and I'll send you a text to let you know she got them," Alex said.

"Thank you, Alex. I owe you one! Good night." Eric poured himself a drink and stepped onto the terrace of the penthouse.

"Dad, I could use some help right about now. Not sure what to do," he said out loud. He finished his drink and decided to take a shower.

* * *

The doorbell rang at Jenny's house at 1:45 a.m. Jenny quickly ran from the den to get the door. *I look like a mess,* she told herself. *Who would be ringing the doorbell at this time?* Jenny opened the door to a man holding a long rectangular box.

"Jenny Ali?" the man asked.

"Yes," she replied, a little bewildered.

"These are for you, from someone who loves you. Have a good night." The man smiled and turned to leave.

"Thank you," Jenny replied. She turned off the lights and took the box to the den. Jenny opened the box to find twenty-four exquisite long-stemmed red roses. She reached for the card and cried as she read it. She didn't know whether to cry or laugh.

"He had roses delivered at 1:45 a.m. That's commitment," she said out loud with a smile on her face. She dialed his number.

"Hello, Jenny. Did you get the flowers?" asked Eric. "It was all I could think to do at this hour. I feel you're in so much pain, Jenny, and I wanted to make you smile."

"They're beautiful Eric," she replied. "I've never seen roses so beautiful."

"Did they make you smile?"

"Yes, but where did you find someone to deliver at this time?"

"There isn't anything I can't do, Jenny, not for you," he replied. "Anything you want, it's yours, I love you. Whatever is troubling you, we can work it out together. You're a little more at peace. I feel it."

"Yes, Eric, you're right. But it's also extremely late and you sound exhausted. You should get some rest."

"Jenny, do you feel me like I feel you?" Eric asked.

"Yes, I do and some days I wish I didn't because it distracts me from getting things done." She paused and then said, "I love you, Eric, now get some rest."

"Good night, love, sleep well."

"Good night."

* * *

Eric left for Paris and while he was away, Jenny followed the conference online. She was so proud of her man. He was all over the media, and quite prominently. She had been able to listen to some of his lectures online and was quite impressed with his delivery, presentation, and knowledge. He was so charming and knew exactly how to keep his audience engaged. *He definitely knows how to work the room,* she thought. Eric kept his promise and called at 11 p.m. almost every night. On the off nights that he didn't call, Jenny wondered if he was dining with an elegantly dressed, sophisticated French woman. In reality, Eric was working on the business deals he would be addressing once the conference had ended. For Eric, the three weeks in Paris felt like an eternity. He couldn't wait to get back home to be with Jenny.

A few days before he returned home, Eric took a hotel limousine to Place Vendome. He was headed straight for Piaget, the most expensive jewellery store in Paris. Nicole recognized him immediately.

"Eric," she said with a smile. "Comment allez-vous, mon ami? It is so wonderful to see you," she said with a French accent.

"Hello, Nicole. It's wonderful to see you too," Eric responded giving her a warm hug. "Nicole, I'm looking for a nice gift for a special young lady."

"Follow me to the private quarters. I will show you our new collections, arrived just today."

Eric followed her to the back and was seated in a very ornate, plush velvet booth. Nicole disappeared to pick out a few pieces while champagne was brought to the table. Eric smiled and graciously accepted. Once Nicole returned, she motioned to the service staff to please take the champagne away and return with their finest scotch.

"Eric, have a look at this piece. It's a favourite of mine. It's a beautiful, handcrafted Piaget rose gold and diamond bangle bracelet. It has a shimmering texture and eighty brilliantly cut diamonds, 3.6 carats that certainly catch your eye set against the fine gold. What do you think?"

"It's perfect," he said with a smile. "I think Jenny would like that. Nicole, Jenny has the most beautiful blue-grey eyes. I would like your finest diamond sapphire collection—earrings, bracelet, and necklace. I don't know her ring size, so perhaps we can order that separately at a later date."

"Eric, I have just the thing," she responded and went to retrieve the collection. "Have a look," she said as she opened the breathtaking sapphire collection.

Eric smiled. "Yes, that's exactly what I was looking for. Would you kindly put the ring aside for me and I will call you with the appropriate size?"

"Of course, let me package this for you right away, just give me a minute. Oh, is the scotch to your satisfaction? I can request something else if it's not," Nicole said playfully.

"It's perfect, thank you."

As Nicole walked away to package the gifts, Eric smiled at the thought of seeing the sapphire collection on Jenny. *She will look so beautiful,* he thought as he cradled his scotch. He thought of how wonderful it would have been if Jenny had been there to pick out the pieces she would have liked. Nicole walked back in with beautifully wrapped packages.

"Is there anything else I can help you with Eric?"

"No, Nicole. I found what I came for and knew it was you who would find it," Eric replied charmingly.

"It is always a pleasure to see you at Piaget, Eric," she said.

"Thank you, Nicole. Maybe next time my Jenny will be with me. A bientot."

Nicole arranged for a limousine to take Eric back to his hotel. Once he arrived, he had the jewellery locked in the hotel safe. He didn't want to take any chances with Jenny's gift. He couldn't wait to get home.

By the time the conference concluded and all his business deals were complete, Eric was ready to return home. He missed Jenny, Thomas, and Heather, and looked forward to seeing David. He made arrangements to have his jet ready for 10 a.m. the next morning and started packing his things. He couldn't sleep, but with the time difference, it was morning for Jenny so she would be asleep. She kept such a crazy schedule but it seemed to work for her.

Eric slept on the jet and arrived home around midnight. He was more excited than jet lagged. He couldn't wait to see Jenny and was pleased to see James waiting to drive him to the house.

"Hello, James," Eric said. "It's good to be home!"

"Hello, Mr. Barrett," replied James. "It's good to have you home, sir."

Eric walked into the house and was greeted by Heather and Thomas. Eric was grateful to have so many wonderful people in his life. He sat with Thomas and Heather and discussed his three weeks away, the conference, and his lectures, and Heather ensured he was all caught up on the latest gossip. He excused himself, saying he wanted to rest awhile, and made his way to his room. He laid down on his bed and slept for a few hours. When he woke up it was almost 2 p.m., and wondered if it was too soon to call Jenny, but he couldn't wait any longer. He picked up the house phone and dialed her number.

"Eric, you're home," Jenny said in her gentle way.

"Yes, Jenny, I'm home," replied Eric. "These three weeks have been the longest and loneliest of my life. I usually enjoy Paris, but not this time. I missed you so much. How are you, my love? All caught up in your studies I hope."

"I am. I made good use of my time. Cleared my head, focused on my courses. Tell me about Paris."

"No, not over the phone. I want to see you. We do have a dinner date, at Oasis if I recall correctly? I'll tell you everything and anything you want to know, at 8 p.m. tonight" he replied.

"I figured you would want to meet," she said. "You promised me a heart-to-heart chat, some clarity."

"Yes, I did. Can we just catch up first, before things get serious? I've missed you."

"Okay, we can catch up first. I'll see you at 8 p.m. at Oasis."

Eric hung up the phone and took a shower, then called David to let him know he was back and that he would discuss the business mergers tomorrow. He was meeting Jenny and wanted to focus on her tonight.

When Jenny arrived at Oasis, Eric was sitting at the bar nursing a scotch. He walked over and kissed her on the cheek.

"Can I take your coat?" he asked.

"Yes, of course," she said, and then asked Eric if his friend was doing okay with the restaurant.

"Why do you ask?"

"Well, every time I come here, or really any of the places we go, I notice that we are the only guests. Maybe business isn't going very well." Jenny said hoping to get Eric to open up about his restaurant. If he did, it would be a perfect segue into a serious conversation that had to happen.

"I think the owner is doing quite well," Eric responded uneasily.

"Maybe it's just an off day," Jenny said a little sarcastically.

Eric sensed that something was bothering Jenny. He was now sure she had found out his true identity. *She must have so many questions*, he thought.

Eric very much enjoyed planning dinners and outings with Jenny. He found that he had become extremely more productive, working early mornings and quitting at about 10 p.m. almost every day. The business was going quite well. He realized he was working extremely hard to distract himself from thinking of Jenny. He had taken Jenny horseback riding on his farm and they'd had several dinners in his private dining rooms, and Jenny had no idea. He hated not telling her who he was, but he enjoyed being with her. It was as if he were transported into a different world where he could just be himself without fear. He didn't have to read into every word that was being said or deduce the hidden agendas. He was not sitting with another woman who was more interested in his wealth than who he was, and who would do anything to get it. He loved his time with Jenny, but tonight, all of that would change.

They had a very pleasant dinner where Jenny told Eric that she was impressed with his lecture. She had not heard all of it but did find a good portion of it online. She told him she thought he was brilliant. Eric humbly accepted the compliment.

"The conference was divided over a series of several days," he said. "Do you have any idea how many times I had to deliver the same lecture to a different group of lawyers? I'm sure I repeated myself so many times, I could deliver it in my sleep. It's so good to be back here with you." He held her hands in his for a moment, then placed two packages in front of her. "I come bearing gifts. Open them. I hope you like them," he said eagerly.

"You bought me gifts," Jenny said smiling. "That was so kind of you, but you really shouldn't have."

"How could I go to Paris and not come home with a beautiful gift for the love of my life?" You're all I ever thought about. Please, open them."

Jenny smiled and began to open the wrapping. When she saw the box, her face went pale. She had heard of Piaget in Paris.

"You went to Piaget?" she asked almost in a whisper.

"Of course, where else would I find a gift suitable for you in Paris? Open it, please, there are two," he said smiling.

"I'm afraid of what's inside," she said. "It will be very expensive, I'm sure." She opened the diamond sapphire collection first and was speechless.

"Oh my God, Eric, I cannot accept this," she said. "I'd be too afraid to wear them, they're real sapphires and diamonds ... so expensive!"

This was not the response Eric had hoped to hear. "It's a gift," he said. "You can't refuse a gift."

Jenny could see that she had hurt him. "I'm sorry, Eric. I didn't mean to hurt or offend you. This is just too much," she said.

"I thought they would look beautiful with your eyes. There is a matching ring that is on hold. I will need your ring size," he said. Then Eric got up from his seat and put the necklace around her neck, the earrings on her ears, and the bracelet on her right wrist. He opened the second package and placed the bangle bracelet on her left wrist.

"Just as I saw it in my dream. But much more beautiful with you right here. It's just a gift, my way of giving you something to say I love you, and that you mean the world to me. Please, just accept it," he said very softly.

Jenny looked at him in amazement. At that moment, nothing mattered anymore. As she looked into his eyes, she heard Savage Garden's song "Truly, Madly, Deeply" playing in the background. It was her favourite love song about a deep love that transcended both space and time.

"Oh, this is a beautiful song," she said. "Let's dance, there is no one here anyway." Eric listened to the lyrics of the song, in which a young man professed his deep desire to have a new beginning in life with his one true love by his side.

He pulled Jenny closer to him and said, "The lyrics in this song ... well, truer words were never spoken. Why don't we leave and spend some time getting to know each other better. I have a place nearby."

Jenny kept her head in his chest and said, "I'm not ready for that."

Surprised, he looked at her curiously and then asked, "Have you been with a man before, Jenny?"

"No," she responded, still looking into his chest and not daring to look up.

"Why? Is it your religious beliefs, parents, social pressure, haven't met the right guy?"

"A little of all of that, I guess, but mostly because ... well ... you see ... I don't want to have short-term relationships. I only want one, with one person. Someone who will commit to me, have children with me, and grow old with me."

"That's what we're all looking for, don't you think?" Eric asked.

"Yes, but I want him to know that I loved him before I even knew who he was, that I love him so much, he'll be the only one to touch me. The only one I shared my soul with. I know that sounds old fashioned, but that's how I feel." Jenny was now holding back tears as she realized how much she loved Eric, even though he was not telling her the truth about himself and hiding so much from her.

"How do you know I'm not that man?" He said as he looked at her lovingly.

She smiled and said, "Because if you were then I would have a ring on my finger, and you would be my husband. You know," she continued, "so many girls are looking for huge engagement rings, a big rock as they say. I don't even want an engagement ring. Just a simple silver band that symbolizes his never-ending love for me, for us. It's not the size of the diamond that matters, it's the size of his heart, his love. Without that, there is just fluff, bling." She shrugged her shoulders.

Eric was blown away. He could lay the world at her feet, and yet, she didn't even want it. She just wanted to be truly, completely, honestly, and faithfully loved. Jenny could not seem to look at him, and he was not sure if she was upset or embarrassed.

"Jenny look at me," he said. She looked up and had tears in her eyes. Eric pulled her close and kissed her passionately. She had never been kissed like that. She was speechless.

"I love you, Jenny Ali, never doubt that." He said as he wiped the tears from her face.

"Eric, I have to go," she said. "It's getting late. Thank you so much for a wonderful night and these awfully expensive gifts. Eric, how much did you spend?" she asked.

"It doesn't matter."

"It does to me. Would you please tell me?"

"I don't know, about $350,000," he responded curtly.

"You spent that much money on me?" she said in shock.

"Of course, Jenny. I would spend everything I have on you. What do I need to do to convince you of my love?" he asked, disappointed and angry.

Jenny could see the pain in his eyes and felt he was both hurt and sincere. "I'm sorry, Eric. This is just overwhelming. It's not every day a girl gets gifts like these," she said with a smile.

He held her close to him and kissed her. "All I want is you in my life because I can't live without you," he responded.

"I love you, Eric, but it's late and I have a long drive home," she said, wanting to leave before she began to cry again.

"Let me walk you to your car. After all, where we would be without the Mazda three," he said laughing.

"Don't make fun of my car. At the very least, it brings me to you."

"Thank God for that. I will personally have to thank Mr. Mazda," he said jokingly.

Once Jenny left, Eric returned to the restaurant and called James to pick him up.

"Did everything go according to plan, Mr. Barrett?" asked Tony, the restaurant manager.

"Everything was perfect, Tony. Thank you. Can you send over a scotch please? I'm just waiting for James."

Eric thought of how extraordinary Jenny was. He wondered if she was real, but she wasn't faking it, her emotions, her tears, and her feelings were very real, raw. He finished his drink, was driven to the penthouse, took a shower, and went to bed. He tossed and turned for a few hours, then got up and made himself another scotch, hoping it would be enough to settle this restlessness. He realized it wasn't restlessness. He missed her. It was like an ache in his heart and he needed to at least hear her voice. At 3:30 a.m. he called Jenny.

"Eric, are you alright?" he heard her say, rather than the usual hello.

"I'm better now, Jenny. I couldn't sleep. I needed to hear your voice. I'm sorry if I woke you up, that was selfish of me."

"No problem, I couldn't sleep anyway. I feel so agitated, such a turbulent, unstable energy, and I'm not sure why," Jenny replied.

"Yeah, I know what you mean. I have an ache in my heart Jenny, and it seems to go away just hearing your voice. I want to see you," he said, quite emphatically. "I want to see you as often as you'll let me, Jenny. I have been with many women, Jenny, but I have never felt like this. I'm not proud of my past. Actually, after listening to you tonight, I felt rather ashamed of myself, but I can't change what has happened. What I do know is that I am yours, completely yours, faithful only to you. Quite honestly, I'll do anything for you, Jenny."

"Do you really feel that way, Eric?"

"Of course. I wouldn't say it if I didn't mean it. I've been trying to show you in every way I know how. I sensed there was something wrong at the restaurant this evening, Jenny. Is there something you want to discuss?"

"Is there something you want to tell me?" she asked in return.

He had told her he would explain everything. He just didn't want to do it the first time he saw her in three weeks. "What do you know?" he asked gently.

"Enough. Whatever Google is allowed to say about you."

"A lot of what's written on Google isn't exactly accurate, so don't believe all of it. However, some of it is accurate and this is not a conversation I would like to have over the phone. I need to see you to explain my actions and behaviour."

"That won't be necessary, Eric. I don't think we have much to discuss anymore. I don't like being made a fool of or lied to. We common people do have integrity," she said with a bit of anger in her voice. "I will return your gifts to you," she continued. "You understand why I can't accept them."

"The gifts are yours," Eric responded emphatically. "They were bought for you, only you. I will, however, need some time to explain. Would you kindly agree to meet with me for one more dinner on Friday night, at Midnight Blue? I'll explain everything and you can decide what you want to do about our relationship after that. I deserve at least one opportunity to explain myself, right?"

"Okay, Eric. I will meet you Friday night for dinner and you'll have your opportunity," she replied. "Good night."

"Good night, Jenny. I love you," Eric replied as he heard the sound of Jenny hanging up the phone.

3

Eric had a private meeting with David regarding a new deal on the horizon. Completing the deal would mean Eric would have to go to London for a few days.

"David, do you not feel comfortable taking this one? I was hoping to just hang around for a while," Eric asked.

"I'm afraid not, Eric. I don't feel comfortable with the size and scope of this deal. I can certainly come with you if you like, but I would rather not handle it myself. It's not my realm of expertise."

"Don't we have anyone up to the task, David? Jesus, what if something were to happen to me? Isn't there anyone that can be counted on to pull off a deal?" he shouted angrily.

"What's this all about, Eric?" asked David. "You never shy away from a deal or going to London. You have quite a few lady friends there that you enjoy spending time with if I recall correctly."

"It's not about that. Frankly, they're only there for my money anyway. They don't care if my name is Eric or George as long as there's money and a good time to be had."

"Something you want to share, Eric?" asked David, sensing both anger and anxiety.

"David, I value your opinion very much. You, Brian, Thomas, and Heather are all the family I have. You know I've been seeing a wonderful girl, and the more I talk to her, the more I'm mesmerized by her. I believe it's because she's genuine, kind, giving, innocent, trusting. Need I say more?" He threw up his hands. "She is everything I lack in my life. She energizes me in a way I cannot explain. I just feel her in my soul and when she's not with me, I feel broken, empty, incomplete. With her, I'm alive, and that hasn't been the case for quite some time, as you very well know."

"I was under the impression that something was going on. You were brilliant in our latest acquisitions meeting, and we secured another multi-million-dollar deal. It was as if I was watching your father in action. You were amazing and I thought to myself, what has happened in the last little while to motivate you in such a way. I miss the sparring between you and your father. He was so proud of you and would enjoy these moments. I felt as if he had come back to work. Now you say it's because of this young lady. What do you know about her?"

"Well," Eric began, "I know she's a student at a local university who hates her psychology course, has integrity, and has very high morals and values. She respects her family heritage as well as her religion and is not very wealthy. I get the impression that she works hard for everything she earns. Her education is very important to her, and she would like to become a kindergarten schoolteacher, which I think suits her soft gentle nature perfectly. She lives at home, and I was made aware that her father is rather traditional and that I shouldn't come knocking on the door. She loves movies, parties, dancing, the theatre, the opera, and various popular musical bands. She is very artistic and plays piano. I know she enjoys all kinds of sports and would like to go skiing this winter. She's the most caring and thoughtful person I've ever met. Always worries about other people and becomes saddened when she hears of their hardships, even people she has never met. She has a heart like no one I've ever known, except for my mother." Eric paused and then said, "I love her, David, but I made the mistake of keeping her in the dark about who I was for far too long. I did it because I wanted to get to know her and have her get to know me. I wanted us to have that time. Well, she knows who I am and has agreed to meet with me on Friday to discuss why I kept her in the dark, among other things."

"That's why you don't want to go to London," David replied.

"Precisely," Eric said.

"Well, I'm afraid you have to leave tomorrow morning. It's only Tuesday so you should be able to wrap things up by Thursday night at the latest and make it back for Friday night," David said trying to be encouraging.

"Yes, and I will look like death warmed over and have the personality of a cucumber as I will be totally exhausted, much less be able to think." Eric sighed deeply. "Alright then, while I'm away, would you please call Joey at Midnight Blue and tell him I'll need the private dining room for Friday at 8 p.m.?" Eric asked. "I just want to make sure the plans are in place for when I get back," he said.

"Yes, of course. I'll take care of it."

"I'd better go pack," Eric said, both angry and annoyed. "Jet arrangements and hotel accommodations?" he asked as he was walking away.

"Already done and the details sent to your phone," David replied.

"Alright, good night, David. I'll chat with you while I'm away and maybe we can meet on Saturday if that's not too much of an intrusion on Marie and Michael."

"That should be fine Eric. Drop by the house anytime, you know they love to see you. Good night."

Eric went to his penthouse suite and packed. He felt enraged at having to leave right now. He was already in a foul mood when his phone rang.

"Hello?" he answered.

"Hello handsome," said a very sexy female voice. "I hear you'll be in London tomorrow." The voice belonged to Charlotte, an ex-girlfriend who had never really stopped loving Eric. Charlotte had decided she would take Eric anyway she could have him. The on-again, off-again relationship had been going on for years. Charlotte was very much in love, Eric not so much.

"Well, bad news certainly travels fast. Yes, I will be in London tomorrow, but I don't think I'll have much time for anything but work. I will be leaving as soon as I'm done," he emphasized.

"Where are you staying?" asked Charlotte. "The usual hotel? I could meet you there and help you unwind."

"Not necessary," he replied. "Please Charlotte, I don't want to see you or anyone for that matter. Inform your friends."

"Why so hostile?"

"I'm seeing someone and am committed to her and her alone. So please, I'm sure there are a few other gentlemen in town who might be interested in a solid night of unwinding. Good night, Charlotte." Eric didn't wait for a reply, he hung up and quickly called Nancy, his personal secretary, at home.

"Hello?" Nancy answered.

"Hello, Nancy. Did you inform Charlotte that I'd be in London tomorrow?" he asked.

"Yes," she responded. "I thought you might appreciate having a friend while you're away, and you seem to enjoy her company."

"Never do that again or you will be unemployed. Is that clear, Nancy?" Eric said, angry and annoyed.

"Eric, I'm sorry. It was not a problem before, so I don't understand your aggression," she replied.

"Are we clear Nancy?" he shouted, emphatically stressing each word as he said it.

"Yes, sir," she replied almost in a whisper.

"Good. Change my hotel accommodations to something in the downtown corridor that isn't quite so posh. No one will think to drop in on me there," he said.

"Of course, I'll do that straight away and send the details to your phone."

"Thank you. Good night, Nancy," he said in a rather cold tone.

"Good night, sir."

Eric finished packing his bag and walked into the kitchen where his dinner had been carefully prepared. Chicken cacciatore with a side of fettuccine alfredo and a Caesar salad. He picked at it for a while, then poured himself a scotch instead. *One of the richest men in the world*, he thought, *and one of the loneliest.* He always had to find clandestine ways to move through society for fear of being recognized, camera shutters unceasingly aimed at him, trying to get the next story on the popular businessman. Yes, his behaviour had given them a lot to write about over the years, but once his parents passed on, he had become quite a different person. Now he thought of Jenny, so sweet and kind. They would devour her like wolves with an unsuspecting sheep. How could he protect her from all of it? How would she react when he finally told her why he kept things from her?

Would she look at it as deception? Lies? Would she understand that he kept her out of his high-profile life to protect her from a world she was completely ill-equipped to handle? That he wanted her to see him and not everything around him? He had a massive headache, but it was 11 p.m. and it was Jenny time.

"Hello?" Jenny said.

"Hello, Jenny. Just beginning your break?" he asked warmly.

"Yes, actually. I just made some hot chocolate; you know with the tiny marshmallows? I love them. I was just sitting down thinking about all the work I have to do. How was your day?"

Eric took a deep breath and said, "I'm afraid I have to go to London for a few days, but nothing between us will change. I promise to call at 11 p.m. every night until I see you Friday."

"London? You just got back! When are you leaving?"

"Tomorrow," he replied in a depressed tone.

"Well, then I think you should just get some rest. You sound tired, Eric. You obviously have a lot to deal with. We will meet on Friday. What time is your flight tomorrow?"

"It's at 10 a.m.," he answered, realizing she was distant and just being polite.

"How long will you be there?"

"Probably until Thursday, but I'm looking forward to seeing you Friday. I made arrangements for dinner at Midnight Blue, 8 p.m. Jenny, I love you. That has not changed. I sense the distant tone in your voice and it's breaking my heart. Please, you will understand why I did what I did, but do not doubt my love for you."

"Eric, you have a very busy schedule that, quite frankly, seems to be killing you slowly. Why don't we postpone this dinner until you get some rest?"

"Not for the world. I'm so anxious at that the thought of you leaving me. I need to see you as soon as I can."

Tears were running down Jenny's face. She sensed he was being sincere. She wanted to say something to reduce the tension between them. She didn't want him on a plane, stressed and worried. She wanted to say something to make him laugh, lighten his spirit but couldn't think of anything.

She felt his heaviness in herself.

"What will you be wearing to dinner?" she asked.

"I normally wear a suit. That's what I'm comfortable in," he replied. "What will you wear?"

"Not sure," she said. "Do you think this will be a dress, skirt, or pants occasion?"

"My preference would be a black dress, hopefully with the jewellery I gave you," he said in a loving, warm tone. "I'm going to miss you very much while I'm away. I just wish I could hold you right now, kiss you good night."

As tears streamed down Jenny's face, she felt that he was being truthful. He did love her in some way.

"I'll miss you too. But it's just a few days," she said softly. She heard a long sigh coming from him and she sensed Eric was crying.

"You know, you're right. I am very tired and need to sleep. Good night, love. Sleep well."

"Good night, Eric. Have a safe flight," Jenny responded.

Eric hung up the phone and cried. He had never wanted to be with someone so much. He poured himself another scotch, scheduled a wake-up call, and slowly drifted off to sleep.

He arrived in London as scheduled for his 11 a.m. meeting.

4

Eric had been preparing for the acquisition of Eaton Enterprises, a
mass media conglomerate that dominated the publishing, entertain- ment,
and news industries. His objective was to secure a majority stake in Eaton
Enterprises, which would allow Eaton to retain its name and legal structure
and continue to execute its current business model. He was well prepared
for the meeting and knew that negotiations would not be easy, however, he
did know that Eaton Enterprises was struggling, having met with logistical
constraints, which significantly depleted its resources. Eric's proposal
would allow Eaton Enterprises to grow in ways it had not fathomed. This
would be an amicable acquisition, of this Eric was certain. It was the
acquiring price that needed to be negotiated.

Eric met with the corporate lawyers of Eaton Enterprises and began
negotiations. Initially, Charles Eaton was trying to finagle some sort of
merger. Eric listened attentively but was not interested in a merger at all.
Eric made it clear that he attended the meeting believing an acquisition of
Eaton Enterprises was on the table and proceeded to outline his terms and
conditions. The next six hours were difficult and grueling, to say the least,
but by the end of the meeting, Charles Eaton saw the advantage of a
Barret-Eaton acquisition. It would boost growth and fend off the
competition. Charles needed some time to think. After reviewing financial statements, profits, debts, and other key components, Eric offered to
resume the meeting on Wednesday, allowing Charles Eaton the time to

think about the proposal and discuss it with the Board of Directors. Eric was confident that Charles Eaton would not receive a better offer. He left the office and went to his hotel room. David had left him a message. *I'd better call back*, he thought.

"Hello, Eric," answered David. "How are things going?"

"Eaton wants to think over the details of the proposal. Initially, he was trying to establish some sort of merger and you know how much I detest mergers. Anyway, I'm confident he'll call an emergency meeting of the Board of Directors and present the proposal for discussion. I'm hoping to be able to wrap this up Wednesday, Thursday morning at the latest. How are things in Toronto?"

"Everything is fine. Brad's up to his usual office tricks, but nothing to be concerned about. How are you feeling, Eric? You left in a very foul mood, which is not like you. I've left several messages in case you needed additional information for the acquisition deal. None of which you returned. Nancy also told me about the conversation that transpired between you, and I have to say I was a little bewildered. It's not characteristic. Do you want to discuss it? I mean if you want to and have the time. I don't want to pry."

"I've just been re-evaluating my life and realized just how empty it's been. Just work, massive takeovers, acquiring wealth, lavish business parties, conventions, and no relationships to speak of. I don't have friends other than you, Thomas, and Brian, and do you know why? Because I cannot trust anyone. There isn't a single person that doesn't want something from me, and every relationship I have is a fake friendship of sorts. Superficiality at its best. The only real thing I have in my life is Jenny and even there, I've had to hide who I am both for her protection and so that I have a real chance of finding someone who wants to be with me. What I'm afraid of is that once I tell her she will walk away. Not because she doesn't care, that's not who she is, but because I've had to lie to her about everything. So, yes, David, I'm feeling quite stressed and anxious right now."

"Eric, once you discuss this with Jenny, and she understands why you did these things, if she loves you, she'll forgive you. She will recognize that she had the privilege of getting to know the real you, the Eric that not many people are privy to know," David replied. "I don't think you need to worry."

"Don't you see, David?" Eric asked. "I fear I've lost her. I didn't get the opportunity to build a relationship that will be worth saving in her eyes. If she had fallen in love with the poor Eric, she may have forgiven the Eric that had to lie to protect her, but I'm not sure she does love me. Any idea what would happen to her if the news that I was seriously seeing someone was somehow leaked? She would be hunted like an animal and nothing would be off-limits. 'Billionaire pursues young girl twelve years his junior' would be a kind headline. Anyway, have you made the arrangements at Midnight Blue?"

"You are scheduled for 8 p.m. on Friday. All taken care of," David replied.

"Thanks, David, I should be home Thursday night and maybe we can discuss this deal at the penthouse. I'll text the details to your phone. Good night, David."

"Get some rest tonight, Eric. Eaton might still have a few tricks up his sleeve, and you will need to think on your feet."

David was right. Thursday morning was no picnic. The eight-hour meeting was brutal and exhausting, but Eric was successful in achieving his goal. He had acquired Eaton Enterprises for 48.5 billion dollars. It was 9 p.m. when he left the office, went to the hotel, and called his jet to be ready to leave in an hour. He packed his clothes and was just about to walk out the door when someone knocked. He dropped the bags and opened the door. Charlotte was standing there with a bottle of champagne and a big sexy smile.

"Hello handsome. Thought I would stop by. It took a while to find you. These are not the accommodations we're used to, but they'll do," she said in a very sensual tone.

"I don't even want to know how you found me," Eric replied. "I was just leaving so would you mind showing yourself out," he said quite icily as he walked away from her and back to his bags.

"Why so mean?" Charlotte responded. "I just thought—"

Eric interrupted her angrily. "I thought I told you to leave me alone. I thought I was very clear on the phone. What do I have to do to help you understand?" he said, practically yelling at Charlotte.

"Well, she must be quite something, this lady friend of yours. Anyone, I know?" she asked, angry at his tone.

"No. No one you know. She is not part of your circle of friends. She is the most amazing person I have ever met, and I really can't wait to get home to see her. Now, I have to leave, a car is here, and my flight is ready. Feel free to stay and finish your champagne, the room is paid for." He took his bags, walked right by her, and shut the door on his way out. Charlotte was stunned. He had never treated her like that before.

I wonder who this girl is, Charlotte asked herself. She popped open the champagne, lit a cigarette, and started making phone calls.

5

Eric took a nap on his flight home. He was more exhausted than he realized, but at least he would be home Thursday night to meet Jenny.

"Mr. Barrett, we'll be landing in about twenty minutes," said the pilot. "You have a call from David Jones. Can I put him through?"

"Yes, of course," replied Eric. He picked up the phone. "David, is something wrong? I thought we were meeting at the penthouse."

"Eric, fly straight to your house in King City and land there," David said with a tone of apprehension in his voice. "There is a barrage of reporters waiting for you at the airport. They all want to know who the mystery girl you're seeing is. Your worst nightmare is coming true, I'm afraid. To avoid getting on the news tonight, I suggest you land at home."

Eric let out a deep sigh. "Thanks David, I'll let the pilot know."

"He's already been informed. It's you I needed to tell," David responded. "I'll come over to the house early in the morning. We can discuss this new problem we have on our hands."

"Okay, good night, David," Eric replied in a monotone voice.

Eric landed on an airstrip close to his house. James was there to pick him up. Once inside the house, Heather and Thomas ran to meet him.

"Master Eric, are you alright sir?" Thomas asked.

"Yes Thomas. Why wouldn't I be?" Eric responded with a smile. "Well, because the phone has been ringing off the hook with people asking all kinds of questions about a young woman you're seeing,"

Heather responded.

"How have you responded?" he asked with concern.

"I told them there was some mistake as Master Eric was in London on business and there is no young lady here or anywhere else. I told them you are still available and not off the market in case any young lady was asking," Heather responded.

Eric leaned over and kissed her cheek. "Heather, you're brilliant," he said smiling.

"Is there a young lady, sir?" Thomas asked.

"There is indeed, and you will meet her in due time. Maybe sooner than I had anticipated. I'm really tired though, so I will have to say good night, for now."

Eric took a hot shower and wondered what to do. He might not be able to take Jenny to Midnight Blue after all, but how and where could they go? Where would they not be seen? The penthouse and restaurants would all be staked out as would his horse farms and cottages, hotels, and any of the homes he owned worldwide. He couldn't just fly Jenny to Europe. It would have to be someplace new. Someplace the media wouldn't look. Eric quickly called Brian.

"Hello?" Brian answered.

"Hello, Brian. I'm sorry for calling this late but I have a favour to ask."

"What is it that couldn't wait 'til morning, Eric?"

"I have a bit of a situation. I'm seeing a young lady that no one knew anything about until tonight, and although I have my suspicions of how this happened, I need a place that no one knows about where I can have a quiet dinner with her and not worry about the press. I need some time to talk to her privately and I was thinking that maybe I could use your guest house."

"Well, Eric, normally I would say that's fine, but my mother-in-law is in it now. She'll be here until Sunday. You're welcomed to use it after Sunday," Brain said.

"No, that will be too late," Eric said.

"Listen, my brother has a nice restaurant in Lancaster. I can call him and make arrangements. No one would look for you there. It's rather quaint and in the old town. What do you think?"

"Thank you, Brian, but that won't be necessary. It's quite a distance from here and I couldn't ask her to drive out that far," Eric responded.

"Can't James drive her?"

"No, she likes to drive herself. I'll explain later when I have the time. Sorry for waking you Brian and thank you for trying to help me." Eric hung up the phone and called Jenny at 2 a.m.

Hello, Eric. Are you okay?" Jenny asked.

"Yes, Jenny, I'm fine. I just got in and thought I'd give you a call. I'm afraid I'll have to cancel dinner. I feel awful about having to do this, but if there was another way, I would have found it before calling so late," he said, feeling both anxious and distraught.

"It's okay Eric. It's probably best. I'm sure you're tired. Maybe just stay home and get some sleep," she said.

"Jenny, please believe me that if there was any other way, I would be with you tomorrow night, but I can't," he said. "There have been some unforeseeable developments that prevent me from meeting at many of my establishments."

From the tone of his voice, she could tell he wasn't just sorry, he was hurting. "It's okay Eric. You're not running away, and neither am I. Maybe we can talk about our situation once you've sorted out your new issues."

"No, Jenny, I need to see you. You need to understand why I have been behaving the way I have. I'm sure you're questioning many aspects of our relationship right now. Wondering why I dated you, why I deceived you by not revealing myself to you. You must be hurting on so many levels and I need to clarify things for you." His tone was apologetic.

Listening to him talk, Jenny felt like she was talking with her Eric, her sincere, wonderful, loving Eric. The man she loved so much and wanted to be with but was so torn between an illusion and reality. "How about Saturday?" she asked.

Eric had a thought as he was speaking with her. "Jenny, do you want to go skiing tomorrow? I remember you said you enjoyed the outdoors."

"I'd love to Eric, but we don't have any snow," she said laughing.

"What If I can arrange for us to fly to Blue Mountain. Would you like that?"

"We don't have to fly," she responded. "I can drive us there."

Eric thought that was genius. With all the chaos caused by Charlotte's little prank, no one would notice him in a small Mazda. "Okay," he said. "I'll meet you at your house. I'll be nearby and won't knock on the door, I promise. Let's say 11 a.m. Saturday?"

"Perfect," Jenny responded. "Do you like to ski?"

"Not one of my favourite activities," he replied "I have been several times as you can well imagine, but from the time my parents took me as a boy, skiing was not something I enjoyed. To this day, I don't own a set of skis, so I'll have to rent them. However, getting back to our plans, a friend has a quaint, cozy cottage just outside of Blue Mountain Village. Would that be agreeable to you?"

"Yes, as long as it has two bedrooms, we're good," she replied laughing.

"Yes, I think it has four," he said, smiling. His tone was much happier, and Jenny could tell he was relieved. Someplace far away might be the perfect opportunity to have a heart-to-heart talk without distractions.

"Perfect, see you Saturday. Good night, Eric," Jenny said quite softly, knowing full well that he would call her with the details of where, how, and when they would meet.

"Good night, darling. Sleep well. I can't wait to see you."

Eric ran down the stairs and out the door. He knocked on the door of the guest house, where Thomas and Heather lived.

"Sorry to wake you, Thomas," Eric said. "Does your son still have that small cottage outside of Blue Mountain?"

"Yes, he does," Thomas answered half asleep.

"Eric is that you?" asked Heather.

"Yes, it is I'm afraid. I'm making some plans and need Thomas' help with them," Eric responded, sheepishly feeling like he should have called instead.

"What's going on, Eric?" said Thomas, a little annoyed.

"Can you please call Mark and find out if I can use the cottage for Saturday and possibly Sunday?"

"Right now? At this hour?" Thomas asked, confused by Eric's behaviour.

"Please Thomas, it's important to me. I'll pay him well for the accommodation." Eric replied. "I need to know the cottage is at my disposal, otherwise I'll have to come up with another plan and I'm running out of time."

Thomas picked up the phone and called his son. He explained the situation and asked him to keep it to himself. No one should know that Eric was in Collingwood. Thomas hung up the phone and looked at Eric.

"Yes, he'll have it ready for you and says it's not necessary to pay him any money," Thomas confirmed.

Eric breathed a sigh of relief. "Thank you, Thomas!" he said as he gave him a tight hug.

"She must mean a lot to you, this young lady," Thomas said, a little concerned by Eric's erratic behaviour.

"Thomas, I think she's the one and I need time. Quiet time, unseen and unheard."

"I understand sir," Thomas replied. "However, can we go to bed now?"

"Yes, of course," Eric replied with gratitude. "I know it seems quite out of character but thank you so much for your help."

"Love does make a person do crazy things," Heather said laughing. "Good night, Eric." She turned to go back to bed.

"Good night, Thomas," Eric said. "And thank you again."

It was almost 4 a.m. by the time Eric finally fell asleep.

6

Eric was at work by 6 a.m. He had two hours of sleep but thought it might be better to arrive early and get as much done as possible. He would be away for the weekend and needed to get a few things finished beforehand. Also, by arriving early, he could avoid any press wondering about the most eligible bachelor in town. David arrived at 8 a.m. and walked right into Eric's office.

"Good morning, David," Eric said with only a brief glance up from his computer. David was staring at him quite peculiarly.

"Good morning yourself. I didn't expect to see you here this early," replied David. "Were you able to sort out your little situation?"

"Yes, I will be in Blue Mountain for the weekend at Thomas's son's cottage. It is quiet, small, and very low-key. I'll be able to spend some quality time with Jenny and do everything in my power to make sure she understands. David, I can accomplish multimillion-dollar deals and steer my competitors straight into my arms. This, however, will be my most difficult task. Losing Jenny would destroy me," he said quite seriously.

"I hope things work out for the best, Eric, and you know I can take care of things here. Right now, I think we need to deal with this situation, put something out there to quell the dogs sniffing for information. They believed Charlotte's story and I have not been able to find out exactly what she told the press. I've tried to reach her, but she knows why and is avoiding any contact," David replied.

"David, what do you suggest I do?"

"Well, I was thinking we create some kind of story around a slighted ex-girlfriend who was seeking revenge and just wanted to make your life a living hell. That would give them something to write about and us some peace. We might be able to get some work done in here again."

"Alright, doesn't sound like a bad plan, I just hope it doesn't blow up in my face somehow. I will leave you to it. Does our PR team agree with this?" Eric asked.

"They should be in my office in an hour. We'll put something out and take care of this mess. Just stay low and out of trouble, please."

"I'm spending the day here, the evening in the penthouse, alone I might add, and then I'm having James drive me to a gas station near Jenny's house where I will promptly board a small silver Mazda and leave the city for a few days. Hopefully, it will be enough time, enough time to explain everything," Eric replied.

"Okay, I'll leave you to your work while I promptly clean up your mess," David responded with a laugh.

"What would I do without you, David?"

"Some days I ask myself that exact question," David responded with a smirk on his face as he headed out of Eric's office.

Eric worked until 10 p.m. and then went to his penthouse. Maria, his housekeeper, had left dinner ready for him, but he didn't feel much like eating. He took a shower, grabbed a scotch, and called Jenny.

"Hello Eric," Jenny said.

"Hello, beautiful," he replied. "Have I called a little too early, it's not quite 11 p.m. I just got home and thought I would check to see if you still loved me and are excited about tomorrow?"

"I am very excited about tomorrow and can't wait to go skiing!" she replied.

"So, you don't love me?" he asked, hoping she was just being playful.

"We have a lot to talk about, and the fact that we can do that, and ski is what I am looking forward to," she responded.

"I fell in love with you the minute you looked up at me while you were wiping my shirt. I'd never seen eyes quite so beautiful, matched perfectly with a kind heart and soft voice. I was so captivated by you and still am. The more I learn about you Jenny Ali the more I want to be with you, every waking minute of my life."

"Wow! Did you rehearse that or are you just able to talk like that at will?" she asked.

"Are you mocking my feelings for you? I mean it Jenny I mean every word!" Eric said rather angrily. "Why don't you believe me?"

"Because no one talks like that, Eric. No one," she said, realizing at that moment how much she enjoyed these late-night chats and how much she looked forward to them.

"Maybe not anyone you know, my love, but my feelings are real and grow every minute," he said.

"I don't want to make you angry, Eric. I've just never met anyone like you before, and there is a lot of uncertainty in our relationship right now. There are a lot of answers I still don't have, Eric. We are at different stages in life and run in vastly different social circles," she responded, painfully aware of her reality.

"Jenny, you're right. I am at a different stage in my life. I'm looking for the woman I want to spend the rest of my life with and honestly, I think I have. Do you love me, Jenny? Do you feel the same way I feel about you?"

The conversation had become quite serious. Jenny did love Eric, but they still needed to discuss the lies and deceit. *How can he even think about love or marriage*, she thought? She decided to answer a little light-heartedly to break the seriousness.

"That will depend on how well you ski tomorrow," she replied. "I love skiing, not good at it, but I love it."

"Well then, I guess I will have to do my best on the slopes tomorrow," he responded with a laugh.

"It's time to earn that love, my friend," she said playfully. "I need to get back to work so I'll be ready in the morning. How will I find you?" she asked.

"James, one of my drivers, is dropping me off. I took the liberty of looking at your neighborhood. There's a gas station on the northwest corner just up the street from your house. I'll be waiting there in a limousine. Just pull up and I'll climb into your car. Okay?"

"A limo? I'm sure I'll be able to spot that at the gas station! Good night, Eric."

"Good night, beautiful. I miss you and love you so much," he responded.

7

Eric was waiting at the gas station and making business calls. James had picked him up at 8 a.m. and they arrived at the gas station by 9 a.m. *No one will be looking for me here,* Eric thought. He used the next two hours to make calls and set up meetings. On Saturday morning, most of the world was shopping, watching or playing some sort of sport, cleaning homes or cars, or just enjoying a leisurely weekend, but not Eric. By the time James picked him up he had already put in two and half hours of work. He then completed phone calls and had several short meetings while he waited for Jenny at the gas station. While James was used to Eric working, it was never quite like this. Eric thanked James for putting up with him and encouraged him to take the weekend off.

"James," Eric said, "if I need you, it will be on Sunday afternoon or evening depending on how things go. I'll let you know. In the meantime, enjoy yourself. Go wherever you like and enjoy the car."

"Thank you, sir," James replied. "My son would enjoy a ride in a limousine, and I can have him pretend he's a wealthy lawyer," he said laughing.

"Let your son dream and enjoy," Eric responded. "When was the last time you took your family on holidays, James? I'm sure your wife and the kids would enjoy Universal Studios in California. You do so much for me and you never fail me, James. Please, call the office, speak to Nancy and she'll take care of it."

"That's not necessary, sir," James replied. "I'm just doing my job."

"Make sure you tell Nancy to include accommodations, I have a few properties there, choose one. No arguing with the boss! You are always here for me and I take you away from your family on weekends and late at night. It's the least I can do."

"Thank you, sir. You're very kind."

Just then, Jenny pulled up. Eric collected his computer and phone, threw them in his bag, and climbed into her car, carefully looking around to ensure he had not been seen by anyone.

"No tinted windows, I see. Not used to that," he said.

"Well, you can put on my sunglasses. It will give you the same effect. And you're welcome for the ride by the way," Jenny said smugly.

Eric was a little quiet, thinking of the meeting he had just finished and hoping no one would recognize him. It was so quiet that Jenny turned on the radio and softly began to sing along with a song.

"Wow, you have a beautiful voice," he said. "If teaching doesn't work out you can start a music career."

"You awake now? You were so quiet, I thought you were asleep," Jenny said.

"I'm sorry, I've been up since five this morning working and while I was waiting for you, I had a few business meetings, so my mind was a little preoccupied. I just need to learn to relax."

"Is that why you're always drinking scotch?" she asked. "I noticed that every time you call late at night, you're drinking scotch."

"It helps me relax and fall asleep," he replied. "I find that I'm so wired I can't sleep. So rather than taking sleeping pills, I have a scotch."

Once they were on the highway, Eric leaned closer to Jenny and started to kiss her neck as she drove. Jenny yearned for him, she loved him and wanted so much to be with him. But she had to stop living the lie.

"Trying to relax?" she asked.

"It feels so good to be close to you, love. And yes, I'm finally starting to relax." He couldn't tell her he was nervous someone would recognize him and take away his opportunity to explain everything to her. Or that she would be prey to camera shutters and microphones wanting answers to who she was and what she was doing with a billionaire like Eric Michael Barrett. He loved being invisible with Jenny. There was a peace in his heart that he never knew, and he so enjoyed it. He was going to keep it that way for as long as fate would allow. As they drove, they told stories, laughed, and sang songs, and when they stopped to get coffee or something to eat, he held her close to him, praying he would not be recognized. He hoped his casual clothes and sunglasses would be enough of a disguise.

"Eric, why is it that when you hold me, I feel like I'm being gift wrapped?" Jenny asked. "It's not a hug but a wrap."

"Well, that's because when I hold you it's like my soul is complete. It's our two halves uniting as one. I feel an inimitable peace. You're a part of me in a way that I wish I could explain, but I can't. So yes, it may feel like a wrap to you but it's a unification of two parts that can only function effectively as a whole. You know, my day only gets better at 11 p.m. when I make that phone call and connect with you. The rest of the time, I'm inundated with work and I'm thankful because it's a distraction. If I'm not working, I think of you, how I wish I could be with you. How much I just want to be in a quiet room and have you near me. Talking honestly, looking into those beautiful eyes, and losing myself in them, wanting so much to be with you. It's an ache I wish I could explain, but now, having you here, in my arms..." He sighed, smiled, and just enjoyed the moment.

Jenny looked at him, not knowing how to respond. She wondered if what he was saying was real. How could he talk honestly when he had been deceiving her for some time now?

"I think we should get some coffee and be on our way, otherwise it will be late by the time we arrive," Jenny said.

"Always so task-oriented on a road trip?" he asked.

She smiled and said, "let's gooooooo!"

As they arrived in Collingwood, Jenny asked Eric where they were going. Was she to drive to Blue Mountain Village?

"No," he replied. "Do you mind if I drive from here? Maybe you can take a break. It's just easier for me to drive rather than telling you which way to go," he said.

"Sure, I don't mind," Jenny replied as she pulled to the side of the road. "Just be careful with my car. Not even a scratch or you'll have to pay for it," she laughed.

"No problem, I'm a pretty good driver," he said as he smiled back smugly. They switched places and Eric called Mark.

"Hello, Mr. Barrett," Mark answered.

"Hello, Mark. I should be there in about five minutes," Eric said.

"Okay, Mr. Barrett, I'm on my way." Mark hung up the phone and left to meet them.

Jenny was enjoying the beautiful scenery of Blue Mountain with crisp, freshly fallen snow covering everything. They arrived at a quaint little cottage secluded in the mountain. Eric parked the car, popped the trunk to get the bags, and opened the passenger door for Jenny.

She looked around and said, "This is beautiful!"

"I'm glad you like it," Eric replied. Taken aback by how such a simple cottage seemed to fill her eyes with wonder and awe. He wondered what she would think of his house in Greece on the island of Crete, or his house in the hills of Tuscany surrounded by wineries. Just then, Mark pulled up.

"Hello, Mr. Barrett. I hope everything is in perfect order, sir," Mark said. "I was up here half an hour ago and started a fire so the cottage would be nice and warm for you both." Mark looked at Jenny, said hello, then looked away quickly. "I'll get your bags, sir," Mark said.

"Hey, it's okay Mark, we can get our bags," replied Jenny. "You've been nice enough to let us stay here. Thank you for that, it's a nice place." She kissed him on the cheek.

Eric went into the cottage and quickly drew the curtains on every window. Jenny and Mark brought in the bags.

"Thank you for helping me with the bags Mark," Jenny said a little annoyed. "Mr. Chivalrous must have forgotten about them."

Eric looked at Jenny apologetically. "Yes, thank you, Mark. That's great. And thanks for letting us stay here for a few days. It will be nice to get away for a while."

"No problem, sir. You've done so much for my family; I will forever be indebted to you. I never thought these accommodations would be suitable for your refined palate, but I am incredibly happy to help you, anytime."

Eric hugged him, said thank you, and walked him to the door. He gave him an envelope filled with thirty thousand dollars.

"No, sir, I can't accept this, please sir," Mark said as he shook his head.

"You have no idea how much this means to me. Thank you! Get something nice for your wife. I'll let you know when we leave," Eric responded.

"Not necessary sir just lock the door and leave the key under the front doormat. Enjoy your stay." With that, he left.

When Eric went back inside, he saw Jenny sitting by the fire. She looked over at him. "C'mon, come and sit down," she said. Eric took off his coat and his shoes and went to sit with her.

"You lied to me, you said this cottage had four bedrooms, but it only has two," she said.

"I didn't realize it had only two bedrooms. That doesn't seem quite enough. Mark has four children. There's not enough room for all of them," he replied. "But it is cozy."

"Hmmm, maybe this couch is a pull-out couch and two people can sleep here. That makes it like an extra bedroom for two children. I think it works perfectly," Jenny said. "Let's see, get up, I want to see if it's a pull-out couch." Eric got up and sure enough, it was a pull-out. She opened it up and carefully put the throw blankets from the couch on the bed.

"I'll sleep here," Jenny said. "Right by the fire."

He looked at her with a smirk on his face and replied, "It will be really cold in one of those rooms up there. I think it would be better if I slept by the fire as well." He had a silly grin on his face.

Jenny stared at him long and hard, and then said, "As long as you keep your clothes on, you can stay."

He smiled and said, okay. She smiled back at him and opened up her arms just like a child does, and said, 'hold me, Eric!" At that moment, she just wanted to forget all the lies and deception and just enjoy her time with him, for however long it would last. *7is may be the last memory that we share*, she thought.

Eric happily obliged, and as he held her close, he sighed.

"Why do you do that Eric, why the big sigh?"

"Remember what I told you about our souls coming together? It's the pleasure I feel when they meet and the peace it brings to my heart," he replied. "Now, no more questions, just hold me, kiss me, and love me as much as you are able."

Jenny took his face in her hands and said, "I love you, Eric," as she fought back tears.

They fell asleep in each other's arms, neither one wanting to let go. The fire went out long ago, but the fire within their souls passionately burned.

Eric woke up early. He was so used to an early schedule, he didn't know how to sleep in. He held Jenny close and gently kissed her lips good morning.

"I guess we're not going to be doing much skiing, but I don't mind. I love being in your arms and could stay here for a while." she whispered. Eric smiled and after spending a few hours enjoying the love of his life he looked at Jenny with a silly grin on his face.

"I have never done this for anyone, but today Eric Barrett will make a nice breakfast for the love of his life" Eric said.

"Sure, right after you start a fire because it's very cold in here," she said. He kissed her again, wrapped her in a blanket, and started the fire. Then he walked over and opened the fridge. *Perfect,* he thought. Mark had it stocked with juice, eggs, and bread and butter, all he would need to make a decent breakfast. He started with making coffee first, then proceeded to make food. Jenny met him in the kitchen and put her arms around him.

"Do you take such good care of all your girls? I'm sure you have many, Mr. hotshot lawyer. Your kisses have many years of experience on them," she said.

"Honestly, I usually have a lot of sex with women I don't care about. Now I have someone I love very much and no sex. Strangely, I'm okay with that. Something tells me it's definitely worth the wait. And the answer to your question is no. In fact, you're the first girl I have ever made breakfast for."

"Somehow, I doubt that, but the intention was nice," she replied.

"I'm serious, and one day when you meet the people I consider family, they will vouch for me that it is the truth," he said reassuringly.

"Well, I hope the eggs are good because I'm really hungry. I'm going to turn on the TV, see what's going on in the world." Just as Jenny reached for the remote, Eric lunged over to stop her.

"Don't!" he yelled. "Please don't! Let's just enjoy this beautiful day. Don't spoil a perfect weekend," he said, thinking the whole Charlotte story on the news channels would further complicate things.

"What's going on?" Jenny asked. "You couldn't relax in the car until we were on the highway. You left Mark and me to bring in the bags while you rushed in to draw all the curtains as soon as we arrived. Then Mark said these accommodations certainly don't match your refined palate. I'm guessing not your usual accommodations. What is going on and what are you afraid of? If you think I'm too dumb to notice these things I'm not. I'm very observant and not feeling comfortable right now. Are you ashamed to be seen with me? Am I not rich enough? Sophisticated enough?"

"Oh no, love, that's not it at all," he responded with a smile. "How about we finish breakfast and then I'll tell you all about it."

"No, I'm not comfortable with this. What would I see on television, connected to you, that I shouldn't see according to you? Do you want to answer this or do I turn on the TV?" Jenny asked.

"I don't know where to start and I don't know quite how to tell you. You would think all the wrong things and none of them would be true. But we did say we would discuss this. Can we have breakfast? You said you were hungry, and I went through all this effort. Please, one peaceful meal. That's all I'm asking for," he said with a loving smile.

"Sounds like the last supper," she said quite amused.

"Yes, and I'm quite certain I'll be crucified."

As they sat down to eat, Eric's phone started ringing while texts came through, one after another. Eric read the texts and slowly closed his eyes and took a deep breath. He hadn't told Jenny about Charlotte and how she had exposed Jenny to the media as his new flame. Somehow the story had erupted, people knew where they were, and he was not going to get the chance to explain. Suddenly, there were cars parked outside the cottage. Mark was at the door and people were taking all kinds of pictures.

Mark came in very apologetically and said he thought it would have been fine.

"What are you talking about, Mark?" asked Eric.

"From time to time," Mark began to explain, "people who know I have a connection with you ask if you'll be visiting. When I bought the groceries, I happened to mention that you were stopping by. I didn't think and didn't make anything of it because Mrs. Cole, the owner, is such a sweet lady. I didn't think that her husband would use the information to make some money."

"That's fine, Mark," Eric said. "It wasn't intentional, and you're not used to having to think about each step or word you say as I have become so accustomed to doing. There are already people on their way to help resolve this situation. Don't worry." Eric replied.

Mark tried to give Eric back the thirty thousand dollars. "Thank you for your very generous offer, but I'm afraid I didn't earn it. I've spoiled everything."

Eric looked lovingly at Mark. "Buy some nice gifts for that beautiful family of yours, after all it will be Christmas soon," he said.

"Oh sir, I don't think I can buy thirty thousand dollars worth of gifts. My conscience would not let me enjoy the money I failed to earn."

Eric gave him a warm hug. "If you can't spend it all then take a trip. I'm sure the kids would love Disneyland and you can certainly stay in my home there. Just call the office and my secretary will set that up. Now, I'll let you out and lock the door behind you. I'm waiting for a team of people that David has already sent. They just landed and should be here shortly. Thank you, Mark." Eric ushered him to the door.

Mark left and Jenny looked at Eric very intently. "Who are you? I don't know you at all, do I?"

"I'm afraid the answer to that question will have to wait until we get home. Please collect your things and make sure to leave nothing behind. I mean nothing. They will use whatever is at their disposal to get information. Please pack quickly as a car is on the way to pick us up. Do you have sunglasses? If not, use your ski goggles so you won't be recognizable," Eric instructed. "I know it sounds crazy, but you have to do as I say, and I'll make sure you get home safely. Please. I don't want them to know who you are. You will have no peace and people will be camped outside your parent's door just like they are here. Do you understand? This is for your protection Jenny and the protection of your family."

"Who are these people? Are you involved with the Mafia or something?"

Eric laughed heartily. "If I were, this would be a lot easier, and most likely no one would be here. No, Jenny, I will explain once we are safely at my home. From there I will make sure you are safely returned to your home. But right now, we're running out of time. Please pack everything, and don't leave any trace of who you are behind," he replied.

Jenny packed quickly and checked and double-checked everything to make sure she had not left anything behind. She was frightened. She had told her family she was going to Blue Mountain to ski with her girlfriends. If they were to see her on TV or in pictures anywhere, how would she explain? She was also stressed at having to be rushed off to who knows where by people she had no knowledge of and had no reason to trust. She put on her boots and coat and then went to the kitchen to stack the dishes in the dishwasher. Eric looked around knowing exactly what to do. This wasn't his first rodeo. He combed the place thoroughly. After a clean sweep, he came down the stairs and looked for Jenny.

"What are you doing?" he asked.

"I'm cleaning up for Mark. What would he think of us if we left the place in such a mess?" she said.

Eric just hugged her and said, "I love you, Jenny. You're in a strange place, surrounded by things you don't understand, a sea of vultures outside the door wanting to get a piece of you, and you're worried about leaving the place clean for Mark. Believe me, Mark will understand."

"You gave him thirty thousand dollars to stay here?" she asked.

"Yes, he has a wonderful family, and I needed a place that no one would find. So, I thought it was a win-win situation," he replied.

"That's a lot of money," Jenny said.

"Yes, and I hope they enjoy it. Are you ready?" he asked, trying to divert the discussion. "Sunglasses, goggles, anything?" She put on her ski goggles. He tied up her hair and put it under a hat.

"Where are we going? What about my car?" Jenny asked.

"I'll make sure it's picked up and delivered to your house without a scratch, I promise. Now, ready? Let's go."

Eric spoke to someone on the phone while Mark waited outside in his car to lock the cottage. Five men came in, took Jenny by the hand, and surrounded her as they put her into a limousine. Eric smiled at the press and waved.

"Thank you for ruining a wonderful weekend," he said both angry and forcefully.

"Is this the mystery woman you're connected to? Is she the one you're serious about? Where does she come from? Is she as wealthy as you are sir?

Is this a marriage that will increase your already vast holdings?" the press yelled back.

"In due time gentlemen, good day," he said as he entered the limousine. He looked and Jenny. "Are you alright?" She was shivering with fear and Eric took her in his arms. "It will be over soon, and no one will be chasing us, I promise. Do you want a drink, calm the nerves?" he asked. She shook her head indicating she did not.

He quietly held her close, wondering if she would ever forgive him for what he was putting her through. This was what he had been trying to avoid, but try as he might, it exploded anyway. He loved her so much. He knew that she was aware he was wealthy but how shocked would she be to find out that he was head of a vast telecom conglomerate, owned several corporations, homes all over the world, hotel chains, restaurant chains, and so much more? Would she forgive him, or would she think he had been lying just to fool around? All he knew was that the possibility of losing her was killing him right now. Not knowing how to handle his emotions, tears ran down his face.

Jenny felt a teardrop and looked up at him. "Is this a little much for you too?" she asked.

"Jenny," he said, "just promise me you'll give me a chance and that you won't walk away. Please. I can't lose you too!" He closed his eyes and held her close until it was time to board the jet.

8

As they entered Eric's jet, the couple continued to be accompanied by four gentlemen. Jenny wondered who they were and why they didn't leave them alone. She wanted answers but wasn't going to get them with everyone around all the time. The men spoke with Eric and then promptly sat behind him and Jenny.

"Who are these guys?" Jenny asked.

"Security," Eric responded.

"Why do we need them right now? I think we're pretty secure in a flying jet."

"They'll leave once we land and get into the limousine with James," he responded.

"Who's James?"

"I mentioned him to you, remember? He's one of my most trusted drivers."

"How many drivers do you have and why can't you trust all of them?" she inquired.

Eric just laughed. "I have different drivers for different events and occasions. It's a little complicated to explain but they all know who drives me to which location depending on the circumstances and specific engagements."

Jenny just looked at him with a confused look on her face. "If I had a driver, I'm sure I'd only need one," she said.

"Would you like a drink, Jenny? A glass of wine perhaps? We should be landing in a few minutes."

"No thank you, I'm fine," she replied.

They landed and climbed into a limousine with James the driver.

"Everything arranged, James?" Eric asked. James replied in the affirmative.

"What's been arranged?" Jenny asked

"You ask a lot of questions, you know that?" Eric said laughing. "I've arranged to enter through the back gates rather than the front or sides of the house. I don't anticipate anyone will be at the back gate. Not many people know of this entrance, which is quite hidden from the road. Then we'll drive up to the house but will have to enter from the kitchen or the delivery entrance. David thought it would be best since there are people all around the house."

"Who is David and why does he decide how things are arranged?" Eric smiled. "You'll have an opportunity to meet him. I grew up with David and his family. They were always around in our home. Holidays, birthdays, anniversaries, he was there. He worked with my father and was his closest friend. We all worked together until the accident. David is now the closest thing I have to a father," Eric replied. Just then, David called, and Eric decided to put him on speakerphone to show Jenny that from this point on there were no secrets.

"Hello, Eric, are you alright?" asked David.

"Yes, we're okay," Eric replied. "Tell me how this happened David."

"Well, apparently you were not very nice to Charlotte when you were in London. She was rather upset and informed the media, as you are well aware, that you were seeing someone."

"Yes, but we dealt with that before I left for Collingwood, so what happened?" he asked rather angrily.

"Didn't Mark explain what happened at the grocery store?"

"Yes, but even if they had been tipped off, the reaction should have been contained. That's what I pay people for," Eric replied with a very cold tone that almost scared Jenny. "Hire a new team. I will not have this incompetence interfere with my life again."

"Eric, you know what the media is like once they get wind of a story like this. They're like a dog with a bone. This was an incredible opportunity for them, and while they couldn't be sure it was true, the sheer thought of it was enough to send out the cavalry. You're a very prominent figure, Eric. I know you took the weekend to explain things to Jenny, and this whole situation may have escalated things a little. How did she take the news?"

"I didn't get a chance to explain, David. This is what I feared would happen no matter how hard I tried to contain it," Eric replied. "Get new people in the PR department. I want people that can anticipate these things. Are you at my house right now?"

"Yes, I'm waiting for you to help in any way I can," replied David.

"Good, we should be there soon." And with that, Eric hung up the phone.

Jenny just looked at him. She was seeing a whole new side of Eric she could never have imagined. She began to see the powerful Eric, not the kind and funny Eric she was used to seeing.

She looked at him with a hint of fear and said, "I don't know what is going on right now or what is happening. All I know is that I've never been in any situation like tonight and have never been so frightened for my life. I've been whisked away from one car to another to get to a jet. Not exactly what I'm used to. And, oh, let's not forget the disguises so no one would recognize me!"

"Jenny, everything I've done tonight has been strictly for your protection and the protection of your family. You see, if anyone had a photo of you or any shred of information, they would be at your parent's door asking all sorts of questions they would not have the answers to. Not to mention they would be harassed constantly."

"Who are you? Where is the Eric I know?" she asked in tears.

Eric held her face in his hands and very lovingly said, "I am the same person you've had wonderful dinners and conversation with, the same man that held you in his arms and danced with you, the same person who held you close all night long. The same man that watched you sleep and wished he could make time stand still. Jenny, I have not changed," he insisted. As Eric spoke, they arrived at a gate that was covered in green foliage. No one would ever suspect it was an entrance. As they drove up to the house, Jenny's eyes just about popped out of their sockets. It was a beauti- ful mansion, the likes of which she had never seen.

"You live here?" she asked.

"Yes, I live here," he answered, watching her every move.

"Alone?"

"Just Heather, Thomas, the staff, and I," he replied.

They arrived at the back entrance and entered the house. Eric was quickly greeted by both Heather and Thomas.

"Master Eric, are you alright? It's quite an ordeal you've endured," Thomas said.

"And you must be the reason for all the fuss," said Heather.

"Heather, Thomas, I'd like you to meet Jenny, the love of my life," Eric smiled proudly.

They both said hello and motioned to leave the delivery area and enter the house.

Once inside, Jenny was like a deer in headlights. She had never witnessed such luxury in her life. She had seen places like this in magazines and on television; Casa Loma was the largest house she had ever seen. She had never seen anything so elegantly decorated. Eric realized this was probably rather daunting, and Jenny might be feeling overwhelmed by it all.

Eric took Jenny's hand and said, "It gets smaller as you become more familiar with the house. I think David is in the library, it's just down this way."

The library was stunning and something Jenny thought her mother would die for. It was large with books from floor to ceiling, but the ceiling was two stories high. The room was covered with beautiful dark oak bookshelves that had sliding ladders to get books from the second story. She was in awe.

"Jenny, this is David," Eric said smiling. "The organizer."

"Hello," she said, almost in a whisper. She was so overwhelmed, shocked, and speechless.

"Would you like a drink? You look like you could use one," David said smiling. "What would you prefer?"

"Vodka, neat," she replied quietly.

Eric was still watching her. He could tell she was in shock. She had never had vodka, at least not with him. He wondered how she would take in everything he had to say to her. Being in the house must have given her some idea of who she was dealing with, the majesty of the mansion, the servants, the cars, the jets. At least she had by now concluded that he was very wealthy. But would she forgive him for lying to her, for the deception he had carried on for months now? Had it not been for Charlotte, he would have been able to do this in a way that would not have been so shocking.

"How's that vodka?" Eric asked.

"Good. Are you going to tell me what's going on now?"

Eric took Jenny by the hand and sat her down in a comfortable chair, then kneeled before her. He held her hands in his and began telling her who she was dealing with.

"Jenny, from your Google research, you know that I'm a billionaire. I am, however, a multi-billionaire who has inherited his considerable fortune from his father, who inherited it from his father; a sizable fortune dating back generations. I'm a corporate lawyer who owns a vast telecommunications conglomerate. I own several luxury hotel chains, high-end restaurants, many corporations, and have homes in many parts of the world. There is so much more, but maybe I'll leave that for later. I have a lot of power and influence and people both fear me and respect me because of that. There isn't anything I cannot give you, Jenny." Eric looked up at her lovingly.

"Except the truth," Jenny replied. "You lied to me for months, not knowing that I knew, and if this Charlotte woman hadn't been pissed because you didn't sleep with her, you would not have told me. You just wanted to enjoy yourself with an innocent girl because that's something you've probably never had, something different for you. Why not date a girl twelve years younger, have some fun, and move on?" Jenny was angry, distraught, and afraid.

"Jenny, it's not like that at all," he said quite sternly and seriously. "I can sleep with anyone, that was never my intention with you," he said.

"Really? Is that why we went to Blue Mountain, so you wouldn't try to sleep with me?"

Eric laughed a little and replied, "Jenny, I won't lie. I wanted to love you, but that's because I am truly in love with you." He looked at her adoringly.

"You asked me what I wanted in a relationship. I said that no relationship can exist without a secure foundation. Do you remember that conversation, Eric?" Jenny asked, visibly upset.

"Yes, I do," he responded.

"Oh, so when I said that a relationship must be based on trust, respect, truth, and honest communication, where two people *don't* lie to each other and *don't* keep anything from one another, but share everything," she was now in tears as she spoke, "you agreed with me and did the exact opposite. After months, you still couldn't trust me with the truth! This whole relationship is based on a lie."

"No, Jenny, it isn't," Eric responded desperately. "Work complicated the many times I tried to tell you everything. I love you very much and I honestly cannot see my life without you in it. I was trying to figure out how to tell you all of this. Initially, I didn't want to, because I wanted you to see me, not all this. Then, I enjoyed you, not having to read into every word you said because your words were true and honest. You love me for who I am, not for what I could give you. I went to London and stayed at the Holiday Inn, imagine that, just so Charlotte wouldn't find me, but she did and I told her very clearly that I was in love with the most wonderful person on Earth, and that I was so fortunate to have found such an angel. I meant every word I said, and I couldn't get back soon enough just to be with you."

"Eric, you've lied to me about everything, the dinners, the restaurants, they were yours!" she said.

"Yes," he replied.

"And all those stories you told me about clients, giving you a night on the house, or wanting to thank you for work well done, all lies. The horse farm is yours too?" she asked.

"Yes," he replied again. "Jenny, I'm not proud of what I've done, but I did it for us. I wanted to have a normal relationship without the nightmare that is my life. I wanted to protect you from the vultures who would stop at nothing to hurt you, but most importantly, I wanted you to see me, the real me, without all the money. Right now, you don't see me anymore, you see all of this. But I am the man you fell in love with, the one that held you in his arms wanting so much to love you. When we're apart, there's an ache in my soul that I can't appease in any way except to be with you. Jenny, I love you and want you to be my wife." As he said this, he held her close to him. "Please believe me!"

Jenny was in tears, not knowing what to think or to believe. She didn't fit into his world, and after what she had seen tonight, she wasn't sure she even knew anything about him. All she knew was that it was all based on a lie.

"Eric, I want to go home now," she said emotionless.

"Don't do this to us, Jenny, please don't. I have lost so much in my life, I cannot lose you too. Jenny, don't! I know you love me, I feel it, that's why I'm certain. You wouldn't be crying if you didn't love me," he pleaded.

"I do love my Eric and I always will. But you, I don't know who you are or if you're even sincere. I want to go home. I need time to think about all of this," she said.

"Fair enough," he said. "Take a few days to process all of this, and I'll call you then. We'll talk about how you're feeling and hopefully make some plans to at least keep seeing each other, even if you don't want to marry me."

Jenny looked at David, who had been standing silently this whole time. "Would you mind taking me home. You're the organizer from what I'm told, so you'll make sure I get home without any of these people taking pictures."

"Of course, it would be my pleasure," David replied.

Eric held Jenny close to him, kissed her passionately, and said he would call her in a few days. He smiled and kissed her again, then sat next to her in David's car for a moment.

"Jenny, please understand I did it to protect you, not to lie to you. To give you a chance to spend time getting to know Eric, the real Eric. The Eric who is not surrounded by money. I did this to give us chance away from the nightmare that is my life, surrounded by unforgiving chaos that must be managed. Everything must be vetted, analyzed, scripted, managed. I do not have the luxury to be free as you do in your world. I enjoyed being invisible and basking in your love. Please, Jenny, come home. You don't need to leave," he pleaded with her.

Jenny looked at him with tears in her eyes. "You sound so sincere, so honest, but you're not. You lied and deceived for no reason. I didn't want your money, power, or influence. I just wanted you to be decent, but you couldn't be. I don't know why we ran into each other that day. It was a mistake. Normally, you would never go to a Starbucks. You should have just bought a coffee and left me alone. I would have been able to say, hey, I know that guy. I met him once. Instead, now I can say hey, I know that guy, he broke my heart because he couldn't speak the truth, he couldn't be sincere, honest, just took advantage of a situation because it made him feel good," Jenny said, lashing out from the pain she felt in her heart.

"No, Jenny, it's not like that. I didn't know I could feel the love you have given to me. I know now that I can't live without it. My soul is bound to yours Jenny, by whose design, I don't know. What I do know is that I can't be apart from you. That I feel broken without you and that I didn't know how broken I was until I met you. You made me whole. You saved me in so many ways. Please promise me you'll come home," he said in tears.

"To this? This isn't my home."

"No Jenny to me," he said. "You are my home, and I want to be yours." Tears were streaming down his face.

"I need to go now, Eric. I need time, please?" she said in tears.

"Okay, Jenny. I'll call you in a few days, give you a chance to think things through," he replied apprehensively. He shut the car door and gave David a feeble smile as he waved goodbye.

9

The whole ride home, Jenny sobbed like a child. David was quiet because he knew what it meant. They arrived at her house and David parked in the driveway.

Jenny looked at David and said, "Please look after him. Check on him every day and make sure he's alright. Please make sure he's alright," she begged him. "I need to know that you'll make sure Eric will be okay," she said distraught and almost hysterically.

"Jenny, it doesn't have to be like this," David said. "He loves you. He is a mess when he doesn't get a phone call from you. He didn't want to go to England because he had promised you dinner. Can you imagine a man of his stature and caliber not wanting to fulfill his business obligations because he promised a young girl dinner? Then he tried to find a suitable place for you to go, because he intended to come clean and ask you to marry him. He told me so and told me he couldn't live without you."

"There's been so much deception," she whispered. "Tonight, I've seen an Eric I don't know. The Eric I know is so different. David, I don't know who he is. You and I both know that I don't fit into his world. I am not what he needs. He needs someone strong, elegant, and refined. Someone who won't trip on her own two feet and embarrass him. He needs someone who understands his social, political, and economic worlds and can func- tion within them. I just want to be a teacher and teach kindergarten. I'm not that person."

"Did Eric ever tell you about his parents?" asked David.

"No, not much. Just that they were killed in a car accident," she replied. "Let me tell you a little story then. Christopher Barrett, Eric's father, was sitting in the library reading the paper when he came upon an advertisement. It was a fundraising ad to launch a literacy program for underprivileged children. Susan McClelland, a librarian, had paid for the ad in the hopes of collecting enough money with which to start the program. Christopher was quite taken, not with the cause, but with Susan. He thought she was the most beautiful woman in the world. He decided to visit her. Well, Susan was quite surprised when Christopher showed up with an entourage of security and people to do his bidding. She quickly asked if she could help him with something as he had disturbed just about everyone in the library with his entrance. Chris smiled at her and said he was here to see her about her advertisement. He asked if there was someplace, they could talk, and she led him to her office. Well, Susan was hoping for the best and fearing the worst. She was quite shaken up by his commanding presence. She showed him into her office and had a cup of coffee in her hands. As she shut the door, she tripped on the carpet pouring coffee all over the bottom half of Christopher's pants and his shoes. She was very apologetic, of course, and Christopher made no mention of it. He reassured her he had other pants and shoes he could wear. He asked her about her program and how much money she would need for such a noble endeavor. She said she was trying to raise twenty thousand dollars and knew it would take some time, but she wasn't giving up hope. He told her he would give her the twenty thousand to start her program, but that she would have to come to the house to collect it. Susan looked at Christopher and said she didn't know who he was, but he couldn't come in and expect she would do anything for money. She would find an honest way to raise it. He told her not to flatter herself, gave her his address, and said she would have to do nothing more than come by and collect her cheque.

"Susan went to the house. Much like you, she was quite stunned and speechless when she entered. She told the butler she had an appointment to meet Mr. Barrett and had arrived at the agreed-upon time. She was then shown into the library and was in shock when she saw it. He had the cheque in his hands and walked over and gave it to her, and then returned to his desk. She looked at the cheque and as she was walking back towards him to tell him that the amount was incorrect, she happened to tip over an antique lectern and broke it. You see, Christopher's cheque was for fifty thousand dollars. She apologized profusely and said she would repair it for him. He told her it could not be repaired as it was an antique. She offered to pay for it then and he told her he paid eighty-five thousand dollars for it. She looked at the cheque and said she had fifty thousand and she could work off the rest. Maybe she could catalog his library. He told her that it would not be necessary, but if she would accompany him to a gala and at least pretend to like him, they would be even, and she could keep her fifty thousand for her literacy project. She asked if there was anything more to this evening. He said there was not, he was not looking for an escort service. He gave her the card to a clothing store and told her to pick out a dress, shoes, and a coat for the evening. She should ask for the woman on the card and tell her that he had sent her. She could keep everything at the end of the night. Well, the rest, as they say, is history. They fell in love that night. They danced the night away and made arrangements to see each other again. A few months later, they were married.

"Christopher couldn't see himself with anyone else. He, the richest man in town, with a lot of power and influence who was relentlessly chased by many women of high society, wanted his librarian. He was the hap- piest man alive. Eric is not that different from his father. You see, what Christopher fell in love with was what he called Susan's purity of heart, and that's what Eric has found in you. When he told me how you met, I thought to myself either history repeats itself or the apple doesn't fall too far from the tree, but either way, Eric had found his angel, that's what he calls you, with purity of heart. I tell you this because Eric loves you. After all, you are everything he is looking for and everything he is not surrounded by. Please think about it and call him in a few days. You will not regret your decision."

Jenny thanked David and repeated that he should take care of Eric, then left to go home.

10

————————

Two days had passed. Eric waited until 11 p.m. then called. Jenny did not pick up. He thought maybe she was working extra hard on her studies and had gone to bed early. He would try in the morning. He arrived at the office and began working, knowing that she probably wouldn't be up until 2 p.m. He called in the afternoon and left a message. He called again at 5 p.m. and left another message. She wasn't picking up. Eric called and left messages for the next three days. What he didn't know was that Jenny was sitting on her bed listening to all of his messages and cried at each one. She was unable to focus on anything and exams were just around the corner. She was a mess and wished he would stop calling because her heart couldn't take much more. Eric was relentless; he called every day, eight to ten times a day, and left pleading messages for her to please call him. Jenny was unable to get out of bed, she was exhausted, couldn't sleep, didn't eat, and spent most of her time in tears.

Eric wasn't doing much better. He spent his nights trying to reach Jenny and drowned himself in scotch so he could sleep. He had lost a considerable amount of weight and was working more hours than he ever had, as it was his only distraction. After two weeks of trying to reach Jenny, working nonstop, and drinking to fall asleep, Eric broke down and cried. He shut the door to the library for privacy and spoke to his father out loud.

"Dad, I miss you so much right now. I have been working hard to maintain and improve the Empire you left me. I know how much you valued it and how much work you put into it, but I can't see a way to go on. I love her dad, she understands me. I know she loves me but because I didn't tell her the truth from the outset, things just got out of control, and she left. I've lost her, Dad. God keeps taking all the things I love away from me, and I wish I knew why. I just can't see any reason for continuing. She has my heart and my soul dad. I feel empty without her and my soul aches to hold her in my arms. I know you probably think me weak right now, but I can't do it anymore. If she doesn't want me in her life, I don't want to live. What's it all for, Dad? I have an empire, I'm one of the wealthiest men in the world, and am completely and utterly alone. I saw my life in her, Dad. I saw my children, my family, my whole world, and it's all over. I think it's time I came home to you and mom. I don't want to be here without her." Eric reached for the scotch and a medicine bottle. He didn't see what the medication was, but he didn't care. He took a considerable amount of both, and then fell onto the floor minutes later.

* * *

David had been trying to call Eric, but to no avail. He was now really worried. He called Thomas and asked him to check on Eric. Heather had made a pot of tea and was on her way to the library to sit with him for a bit. As Heather opened the door, she screamed and dropped everything. Thomas heard the shriek and ran to the library.

"Call David and Brian," Thomas said to Heather. "Let them know what's happened and let Brian know we are on our way with the helicopter." With the help of other staff, Thomas put Eric into a limousine and drove to the helipad where the pilot, who had already been informed, was standing by, ready to move.

Brian was not only Eric's doctor but a well-respected cardiologist who worked in the hospital and especially enjoyed working in Emergency. He believed that the Emergency wing was where he could make a difference. Thomas and Heather were following the instructions Brian had provided over the phone. Once they arrived, Brian was there to meet them. Eric was placed on a stretcher and immediately brought into the hospital through the Emergency wing and to a private room where no one would notice the billionaire. Eric's vital signs were very weak. Thomas told Brian that he found medication in Eric's hands and that it appeared he had taken it with scotch. He gave Brian the vial he found in Eric's hand. Upon seeing it, Brian took a deep breath and shook his head. He had given Eric a prescription for sleeping pills. Eric had requested them to help him get some rest. Within half an hour of arriving, Eric was rushed to the ICU. He had suffered a heart attack. Brian was able to stabilize him, but his condition was precarious. News spilled out of the Toronto General Hospital that Eric Barrett, the multi-billionaire, had been rushed to the hospital and was in critical condition in the Intensive care unit.

* * *

Jenny went downstairs to make a cup of tea. Her mother was pleased that she was in better spirits. It had been a horrible few week, and Jenny preferred to keep everything to herself. Jenny's mother had been doing everything possible to support her daughter through this terrible situation that she knew very little about. She tried to get her to eat and was only able to get protein shakes down her throat. Jenny looked a little better this morning. She had taken a shower and dressed well. She was very pale, had lost weight, and was still quite weak.

"Mom, do you want to go for a walk?" she asked.

"Sure, Jenny, why don't we do that. The fresh air will feel good. Let's take a walk through the park. I know how much you enjoy that."

Jenny smiled and went to get her coat. They spent the day together, had lunch at their favourite spot, and even did a little shopping together. It would be Christmas soon and her mother was grateful that Jenny seemed to be turning a corner. They arrived home and ordered a pizza. While they waited for the pizza to arrive, they sat at the kitchen table and Jenny's mom recounted funny stories of her childhood. The pizza finally arrived, and they decided to eat in the family room as they watched TV.

"Oh, this poor young man," said her mother. "He was rushed to the ICU yesterday. He's a multi-billionaire, had everything he could want, and decided to take his own life. Apparently, his housekeeper found him, and he was rushed to the hospital. Had she not brought him his tea, he'd be dead," Jenny's mother explained. Jenny looked at the television in horror, trembling.

"Mom, did they say what his name was?"

"Yes, Eric Barrett, or something like that."

Jenny started to cry and said in a very shaky voice, "Mom you need to drive me to Toronto General. This is all my fault." She began crying hysterically.

Her mother looked at her in disbelief. "Jenny, how could this be your fault? You know this man?"

Jenny tried to explain the situation through her tears.

"He wanted to marry me, said he loved me. But he lied to me about everything. He said it was for my protection. When I saw him in his world, I wasn't even sure I knew who he was. I thought that even if he did love me, I could never fit into his world. So, I left. He's been trying to call me for weeks and I have not returned any of his messages. He begged me to call him and to come home. Oh, Mom, I never thought he would do something like this! I never thought ... Please, drive me down now, please," Jenny begged her mother. They hugged as Jenny trembled.

"So, this is what has been going on these past few weeks?" her mother asked. "Honey, you're weak and can hardly stand, you're not up to this! He is in very good hands, I'm sure."

"Please mom, not now, we need to go to the hospital. I need to see Eric. Please! I would drive myself but I'm shaking. Please Mom," Jenny begged.

"Okay, Jenny let's go."

Jenny arrived at the hospital and went straight to the ICU. She could not possibly get to Eric. He was surrounded by heavy security. Photographers and the press were all being contained in an area of the ICU wing. Jenny had to see him. How was she going to get to Eric? Between the police and heavy security, it was impossible to get through. She pushed through the crowd of reporters and ran past security towards the Intensive Care Unit nurses' station

"I need to see Eric," she pleaded with the nurse.

"How did you get here young lady?" asked the nurse. "Reporters are to remain in the contained area assigned or they will be asked to leave the premises."

"I'm not a reporter! Please, just let me see him," Jenny begged the nurse.

"Miss, if you don't leave voluntarily, I will call security."

Not knowing what else to do, Jenny started screaming. "Eric! Eric, where are you? Eric!. Eric!" Jenny was hysterical. The nurse screamed for security.

David, hearing a distraught woman crying out his friend's name, left the ICU room to see what was going on. Jenny saw him and yelled out his name.

"David! David, please, please let me see him!" David motioned to security to let her through.

"My mom too please?" David nodded. She ran to him, and he stared at her.

"You look just as bad as he does. Why are you torturing each other Jenny, why?" David asked.

"Where is he David?"

David led her to a nearby room, and as she entered, she grabbed David's arm, frozen in disbelief. Eric was attached to so many machines and had lost so much weight, she hardly recognized him.

"This isn't Eric, there is some mistake," Jenny said.

"I'm afraid it is Eric," responded Brian, who had just walked in to check on his patient.

"Are you his doctor?" Jenny asked. "You have to help him," she screamed through her tears. "You have to save him!"

Brian looked at her with a very stern look in his eyes. "Jenny, is it? I am doing everything possible. He's like my son. I'm doing all that is humanly possible right now."

"It's all my fault," she said as she put her hands on her head. "He called me today and told me he understood that I wasn't coming home. He said I was entitled to my feelings and that he would not call anymore. It's my fault. I never thought he would do this."

"Don't start the blame game, Jenny. We are all to blame," responded David. "I should have never let him go early, Heather should have brought his tea sooner, Thomas should have checked on him more frequently, and Eric, Eric should have known better. It serves no purpose Jenny. Right now we have to somehow convey to him that we care, that we are all here for him, especially you Jenny. He was a mess, yes, but honey, so are you. I can see this hasn't been easy for either one of you and I hope and pray that he comes out of this alive so we can see you both flourish together. Now, let's focus on Eric, okay?" David said as he gave her a big hug.

"Yes," Jenny nodded. She walked over to Eric's bedside and took his hand. She held it tight and whispered in his ear, "I'm here Eric. If you still want me, I'm here."

"Brian, how long has he been like this?" she asked.

"A few days. When we brought him in to the ICU, he had a heart attack, caused by taking a significant amount of sleeping pills with a considerable amount of scotch," responded Brian.

Jenny still couldn't believe Eric would try to take his own life.

"He has suffered a lot of loss in these past four years," Brian explained. "I have seen him through difficult times, but he never felt so hopeless as to take his life."

"I noticed he was working himself to death," David added, "taking on a lot, but what I failed to see was that he was using it as a distraction. I often dropped by the house and stayed until he went to bed. He would call you several times, leave messages, and then drink until he would pass out. That was the only way he could get any peace. I caught him talking to his father and asking him to please provide some relief to the emptiness and the pain he felt in his soul. I waited outside for a few minutes, collected myself, and then knocked as if I had just arrived. He was in so much pain. I've never seen him like that. I took him in my arms and just hugged him while he sobbed. A thirty-five-year-old man sobbing like a child. It was at that point that I should have come to see you Jenny, but I waited until the next day and it was too late," he said, fighting back tears.

Tears rolled down Jenny's face as she listened to Brian and David.

"He does love me," she whispered. Then she continued talking to Brian and David. "I just wish he had included me in all of it instead of hiding things from me and trying to control every situation. I thought he was lying to me. I couldn't understand why he would want to be with me, Jenny, a nobody, when he could have his pick of any woman in the world. I had no idea that he was sincere. He was telling the truth. He wanted to be with me because our souls are bound in a way that neither one of us can explain. He was right when he said that I loved him and that he knew because he could feel it. I feel him too, and I don't know how, I just do."

David walked over to Jenny and hugged her. "Jenny, you will quickly learn that Eric leaves nothing to chance, especially with the people he cares about. Eric wants to ensure that the people he loves want for nothing. So, to do this, he thinks of everything possible and makes sure he has the situation in hand. He wanted you to get to know him, who he is at his core. Not the person he is in public, not the person surrounded by opulence and power, the real Eric. To do so, he went to extraordinary lengths to ensure the two of you could be alone to discover each other. Do you have any idea how hard that was to pull off?" David asked. "I can tell you from personal experience, he had to anticipate everything that could go wrong and have a contingency plan in place in case it did, and let me tell you, his plan- ning was impeccable. Nothing was going to go wrong. The only thing Eric had not anticipated was Charlotte's reaction, and that's because they had stopped seeing each other years ago. He had no idea her feelings for him were that strong. You will learn that this is who he is and that's why he must control every situation, but he did it with the absolute best of inten- tions for you. The Eric you were able to get to know is the Eric no one will ever see; except the people he considers family," David said with a smile.

Jenny walked over and stood at Eric's bedside. "Oh my God, Eric. I've been so wrong about everything, and I am so sorry," she said to him. Then she took down the guard rail on the right side of the bed, took off her coat and shoes, and climbed into bed with him. "I love you," she whispered into his ear, putting her arms around him and closed her eyes. The nurse came into the room and said she could not stay in the same bed with him. She could arrange for a cot if necessary. Brian made sure Jenny didn't move an inch. He was willing to try anything to help Eric.

A few more days passed and there was no change to Eric's condition. Jenny had been with him day and night. She had not eaten and survived on protein shakes her mother brought for her daily. She was looking rather ragged. Her eyes were swollen from crying, she was exhausted from stress, and worried that Eric was not improving. She prayed and cried and passed out from exhaustion. David wanted to take her home to get some proper rest, but Jenny would not leave. She instead encouraged David to go home and get some rest. He went home, took a nap, and came back at approxi- mately 2 a.m. to check on Jenny and Eric.

David had been managing the press, photographers, and anyone else that wanted a piece of Eric. He had been holding down the fort at the office and had delegated many of his responsibilities to Michael, his son, a recent graduate from Osgoode Hall Law School who had started working with the company in September. It had been baptism by fire for Michael, but, like his father, he was a quick study.

As David came in, he saw Jenny. She was weak, but she smiled and said hello.

"How is our boy doing? Has he moved anything at all?" David asked. Tears ran down Jenny's face as she shook her head. David sat down in the only chair in the room. Several nurses came by, checking vital signs and making sure Eric was receiving his fluids. A few more hours went by and Eric moved his arm. Very slowly and weakly, he hugged Jenny. He whispered her name as he attempted to open his eyes. Jenny was so thrilled she shouted his name.

"Eric! Please open your eyes," she said. And he did, giving her a feeble smile.

"Did you see that David?" she asked.

"I sure did," he replied, overjoyed. "I'm calling Brian."

Within minutes, Brian was there, shining a light in Eric's eyes and talking to him. Eric responded appropriately to each of his questions and made a very weak attempt to pull Jenny towards him. Then he let out a huge sigh.

"Is there peace in your soul, my love?" Jenny asked with tears in her eyes. Eric smiled weakly, replying in the affirmative. It didn't last long, however, as Eric faded back into a deep sleep. Jenny was disappointed and began to cry, but Brian was encouraged.

"Jenny, no need to cry. He'll come out of this very soon. Just keep doing what you're doing because it isn't medicine that's bringing this boy back. It's love," Brian said with a smile.

All night, Jenny waited for some sign that he would come out of this state, but she was sadly disappointed. Eric didn't move a muscle. At about 2 p.m. the next day, while Thomas and Heather were visiting, Eric reached for Jenny's hand. She gave it to him and held his tightly. He smiled. The joy that Heather and Thomas felt at that moment brought tears to their eyes.

"The Lord has heard my prayers," said Heather. "We're going to take him home, he's going to be okay. I just know it."

Jenny smiled. "Keep praying for him, Heather. He needs all our prayers."

Jenny called David to give him an update. He had several meetings that day but would come by at around seven that evening.

"Hold him tight Jenny, we don't want to lose him again," David said, smiling as he hung up the phone.

Now it was a waiting game. Brian increased the dose of fluids being pumped into Eric, which would help him feel stronger. Eric opened his eyes from time to time but could not keep them open for longer than two or three seconds. He tried to hold Jenny's hand but was only able to hold it for a few seconds before letting go. Jenny held his tight regardless.

When David came by to visit, he saw what he had been seeing for the past week. No change in the ICU, Eric lying there, helpless, and David was powerless to help him in any way. After an hour, Jenny encouraged him to go home and get some rest. If there was any change, she would call him.

It was a very quiet night and Jenny prayed. She was on her knees in tears, begging God to give her one more chance to make up for her mistake.

"Please don't take him from me," she begged. "Please don't take him from me. I made a mistake and I'm so sorry. I just want a chance to make it right, please don't take him, I beg you, please!" She climbed up and lay by his side in tears. She put her arms around him and held him tight as she had every night for the past week. It was around 3 a.m. when Jenny felt someone holding her. She jolted and saw Eric smiling at her.

She kissed his lips ever so gently and said, "Am I dreaming? I missed you so much!"

He had tears in his eyes and said very slowly, "You look like hell."

Jenny answered, "That's exactly where I've been for the past three weeks, Eric." He reached for her and kissed her gently just as Brian walked in.

"Aren't you two a sight for sore eyes? Eric, son, it's so good to see you!" Brian said, relieved he was awake. "We were all so worried you might not make it. I have a long lecture saved for you, but not now." He hugged him and kissed his forehead. "I'm going to leave you with the best medicine of all right now." He nodded toward Jenny. "And I'm having you moved out of the ICU and into a private room." Brian left to make the arrangements.

He woke David, Thomas, and Heather to tell them that Eric was fully awake and doing well. David called Eric's cell phone and Jenny answered.

"You were supposed to call me if there was any change," David said.

"I was going to call but was too busy kissing the love of my life. David, I'm so relieved," she said.

"How is he? Is he weak? coherent? What have you noticed, Jenny? Just tell me the truth."

"He's weak but very coherent. I don't think there was any brain damage, if that's what you're worried about, and neither does Brian," she replied.

"That's great news," David responded, tears of joy streaming down his face.

"David, I have to let you go now," Jenny said. "They've moved him out of ICU. We're on the fifth floor in a private room and the nurses have just finished with him."

"I'll be there in the morning, Jenny," David said as he hung up the phone. Once everyone had left, Jenny climbed into bed with Eric, put her arms around him, and enjoyed feeling him hold her. She kissed him good night and they both fell asleep.

David arrived at 6 a.m. along with Heather and Thomas. Jenny's mother arrived as well. They were all pleased to see him awake and doing well.

David looked at Eric, smiled, and said, "It's really good to see you, son."

"Thanks, David," he replied. The expression on Eric's face told David he had something to say, something incredibly important.

Eric looked at Jenny and said, "Marry me?"

"Yes, Eric, I will," she replied as she kissed him gently.

"Today, right now," Eric said, straining from the pain he felt in his head.

"Eric, what's the rush? You can barely talk. Let's wait until you're better," Jenny replied. "We have a lot of time for this."

He looked at her and shook his head as he rubbed it with his hands. "Today. Please don't fight me, I don't have the strength. Whatever religion you want for the ceremony, Jenny, it's fine."

"Okay, but where will I find an Imam here?" she laughed.

Eric looked over at David. "Find an Imam ASAP and call Jenny's dad. Heather, call Helen. You know what to do," he said in a barely audible whisper.

"Of course," Heather replied smiling.

David found an Imam close by who would conduct the ceremony. Jenny's mother called her father, who by now was aware of the situation, and Helen arrived from Tiffany's with several wedding bands to choose from. All arrived within the hour.

Brian was concerned about Eric's headache and wanted to get a scan done ASAP, but Eric insisted it would have to wait until after he was married. The ceremony was performed while Brian arranged to have the brain scan done in the room. As soon as the ceremony was complete, Brian had the scanner brought in. Eric looked at him and asked if this could wait. Brian responded with a simple no.

The scan showed what Brian had suspected. Encephalitis. A bacterial infection that was causing the brain to become inflamed. Brian began treating it aggressively with antibiotics, which weakened Eric a bit. The next forty-eight hours would be very decisive. He explained his findings to everyone in the hallway outside and asked Jenny to monitor his headaches. If he didn't respond to treatment, they would have a real fight on their hands as this could be fatal.

Jenny did everything she could to make him comfortable. She monitored each time he complained of a headache and tried to comfort him. For the next twelve hours, he complained incessantly of the pain in his head. She reassured him that it would be better soon as the nurse had given him something to numb the pain and help him sleep.

"Hold me, Jenny," he asked. She climbed into bed and held him as tight as she could. He slowly fell asleep. Jenny cried.

Brian came by at about 3 p.m. Eric was feeling much better, a little weak, but his head didn't ache.

Eric smiled. "Brian, I feel good today. My head doesn't feel like it weighs three thousand pounds and it doesn't ache like before. Maybe I just had to get married for all my symptoms to go away."

"Eric, that's great news," said Brian. "I'm having some food sent up. It's about time you started eating. Mrs. Barrett, your husband is going to be just fine." Brian was smiling as he left the room.

It would be another two days of antibiotics before Eric would feel like him self again. He looked over at Jenny who had fallen asleep in a chair.

He got out of bed and took her by the hand. "Hey,

you're up," Jenny said. "That's fantastic!"

"Come here," he replied. "You need the bed more than I do. Jenny, you've gotten so thin, I'm going to have to order a lot of McDonald's food for a few weeks at least."

"I see your sense of humour is in full swing. If I'm to lie in that bed, you're coming with me," Jenny said with a huge smile.

"No argument there, my love. Not the best honeymoon in a hospital bed, but I'll take you any way I can," Eric said.

"Well hold on there, tiger, we're still not exactly out of the woods. You've had a heart attack that put you out of commission for weeks, and you're only just feeling better from encephalitis. I think we take it slow," she insisted.

"I'll give it a few days, but then you're mine. By that time we should be home."

"I hope so, Eric. I hate this place."

Early the next day, Eric woke Jenny at 5 a.m.

"Are you okay, Eric?" she asked.

"Yes, I'm fine. I'd like to take a shower, but I'm afraid I might get light-headed. How about you come with me?" He smiled.

Jenny was a little nervous, she had never been with a man. Eric had never seen her naked and yet she was his wife. He got into the shower and took her hand. She was shy and tried to cover herself with the other hand.

"It's okay," he whispered. "It's just a shower." He held her close and said, "Honey, nothing and no one will ever pull us apart again." He kissed her gently.

Jenny smiled. "I thought you needed to get washed."

Eric laughed, "I lied. I just wanted to hold you, naked."

"I think we should take this slow, please, Eric."

"Okay, Mrs. Barrett, I'll be a good boy, but only for today," he responded.

They were washed and dressed when Brian came into the room.

"Brian, I want to go home," Eric said.

"You can go home as soon as you pass a few tests. If you can walk up and down this hallway twice without falling or tipping, you can go home and I'll send a nurse with you," responded Brian.

"I love challenges. Let's do it," Eric responded with a smile. He successfully walked up and down the corridor three times instead of two, then looked at Brian with a cheeky expression on his face.

"Show off," Brian said, smiling at him. "I'll set up the discharge papers, I think home is just where you need to be. Call David and let him know you can go. He'll make arrangements to get you there. It will be nice to have the hospital back without all the security, photographers, and reporters," he complained as he left the room with a smirk on his face.

While they waited, Jenny said to Eric, "I didn't know David's son Michael worked at the office. You never mentioned him. I didn't even know he had children."

"Oh yes, Michael started working with us in September, fresh out of law school," Eric replied. "I didn't introduce you to him or anyone for that matter for very selfish reasons. You see, Michael is a very handsome twenty-one-year-old man, who also has a considerable amount of wealth. He is David's only son and is extremely intelligent. Unlike most kids, Michael devoured information at a very young age, and as a result, David put him in an expensive school for gifted students. Michael finished his degree in political science at the age of eighteen, and law school this year at twenty-one. He's tall, has broad shoulders, curly black hair, and brown eyes. Oh, and the ladies in the office refer to him as a god," he said laughing. "I was afraid that you might fall in love with him as I am sure he would have fallen in love with you. So, I wanted to marry you first then introduce you."

"So, let me get this straight, you kept me hidden because you thought I would jump his bones? What makes you think I wouldn't even as your wife? I mean if I want to I could, right?" she said, waiting for a reaction.

Eric's face turned pale and he stared at her, not saying anything at all. He was wondering if Jenny had deceived him this whole time. Had she played him?

"Relax," Jenny said as she saw him turning ghost white. "I would never do that to you, and do you know why? Because if I were in a room with the richest and most handsome men from all over the world, I would still only see you. Because I love you, Eric Barrett. You're the only man that has ever touched me, the only man I will lay down with, and the only man I share one soul with. You will never have to worry about that.”

Eric wished he could make love with her right at that moment.

“It’s funny you should say that,” she continued, “because I saw some of the women you dated online and thought I couldn't hold a candle to them, and you're worried I would find someone else attractive enough to leave you? Were both pretty insecure,” Jenny said laughing.

“Not anymore, Jenny. I have you in my life and that’s all I want, and as far as being the only person in the room, it’s the same for me. Without you, I’m nothing, and knowing this, I was willing to end my life if you weren't going to share it with me. So, I think we’re pretty secure in each other.” He gently kissed her.

“I’ve been thinking,” she said.

“This sounds serious,” he responded with a smile.

“Well, it is. I’ve been thinking that we have a pretty large empire to run and right now it’s only you, David, and Michael that have the responsibility of making many of the key decisions. Yes, you have a lot of people that work for you, but no one is involved in the big decisions. So, I was thinking we need to build an army of sorts, to defend our empire,” she said.

“The business is not exactly like your description, but close. However, I am intrigued by who would be involved in this army, as you call it. Your brothers?” Eric asked. “I don't mind employing them in key positions, at least they’re family.”

“That would be nice, but that’s not what I was thinking. I was thinking that we need to start having children,” Jenny said.

“I thought you wanted to teach kindergarten?” Eric responded, seriously wondering what could have changed her mind.

“I did, but this ordeal has shown me just how fragile life can be, and that we think we have all the time in the world, but we don’t. So, I would like to focus on family, our family,” Jenny said with a gentle smile.

“Well, consider me a very eager and willing participant in making your dreams come true,” he said with a smirk on his face. But this was a dream come true for Eric as well. He had wanted a family of his own ever since he lost his parents.

“Do you want to have children, Eric?” Jenny asked. “I mean, your mother only had you, maybe children are not a priority in the Barrett family tradition."

"Yes, I would like to have a family as soon as possible. It's what I've wanted for quite some time but never found the right person, until I found you of course." Eric paused for a moment. "My parents suffered a severe setback after I was born. I was an average child and the birth was not a difficult one, but something happened. You see, Jenny, after my mother gave birth to me, she began hemorrhaging. She immediately had to have surgery and it was during that surgery that the doctors found several abnormalities in her uterus. It was a miracle I was conceived at all. Most women would have miscarried as the body wouldn't allow for a child to reach full term, or even be conceived in the first place. I was an anomaly, or a miracle, depending on how you see it. For my mother, I was her miracle child and she loved and cherished me all her life. Both she and my father doted on me and made sure I wanted for nothing. More importantly, they showered me with love my whole life. That's why losing them, the way I did, was so difficult for me. However, I digress.

My mother was heartbroken, to say the least. You see, my parents had wanted an exceptionally large family. They wanted to fill all ten bedrooms in the house. My mother, like you, wanted to have the family run the entire business. She had hoped to have at least six children to help my father run the Empire, as you call it. But she couldn't have another child no matter how hard they tried. My father couldn't stand to see his wife so broken and wanted to adopt as many children as she desired. But she told him that she had thought long and hard about it and concluded that she did not want to adopt any children. If she did that, she would only be able to help four or five children. She told my father that with David's help and my own, once I grew up, the family business would be fine. She would begin a foundation, to help children that had been abused, discarded, or in any way left to fend for themselves. She would also continue her literacy project and help as many children as she could. In this way, she would be a mother to many successful children that would normally suffer trauma or possibly die.

"My dad asked her what she would need to start this endeavor of hers for he would do everything he could to support her. She said she needed to know what a foundation was and how it could be set up. Needless to say,

Dad laughed so hard, Thomas heard him from downstairs. He arranged several meetings for her and she slowly learned how to work it. It's now one of the most successful foundations in the world dedicated to children. It's currently being run by a friend, who has agreed to look after it until I find someone to take over, then he'll retire. Mom used to say that there was no greater satisfaction than to look at the smiling face of a child that had hope in their eyes." Eric looked at Jenny who was in serious thought.

"Eric, would you mind if I did? I mean, would you mind if I tried to help out in the foundation?" Jenny asked. "Children are my life, that's why I wanted to become a teacher, but maybe I could better use my skills here. Much like your mother, I don't know anything about how a foundation works, but I can learn. It just seems like a lifetime of hard work has been left in the hands of a friend, who may not stay for long," she said.

"Jenny, that's an amazing idea," Eric responded, quite proud that she would want to take on such a lofty goal. "I'll put you in touch with George who can show you the ropes, and when you're ready to fly solo, he can retire. Are you sure you want to do this?" Eric asked.

"I've never been so sure of anything in my life, other than you of course, Eric."

Just then, David arrived with a lot of peanut brittle. Eric laughed affectionately when he saw it.

David looked at Jenny and said, "This is what he snacks on when at work, and since he hasn't been in for a few weeks, the office felt it fitting to send it home with him." They all laughed heartily. "Are you both ready to go? I thought we'd avoid the mess outside by going down the service elevator into the kitchen and exiting from there. James is waiting just outside the kitchen doors with a car."

"Why do we still have to do that?" asked Jenny. "We don't have to hide anymore, do we?"

"Jenny, there is a gala soon, it's a fundraiser for the Foundation," Eric said. "It is there that I will introduce you to the corporate world as my wife. Things will change from then on and you will become the center of attention, but for different reasons. People will want to know what designer you wear, who your stylist is, and if you would be willing to meet for luncheons so they can get to know you. It will be a different kind of attention, nothing like this, not anymore. The eligible bachelor is off the market, so hopefully, the chasing will stop. David and I will prepare you for the events, so you don't have to stress or worry about it. Right now, let's just get home. I want to go home and spend time with my wife."

"Easy, tiger. Don't forget it's me, you, and your nurse. She'll be running the show until you're better," Jenny responded.

"You think so?" Eric asked. He took out his cell, put it on speaker, and called Brian.

"Brian, I don't want a nurse in my house. I want to go home and make love to my wife. Don't send anyone because I will leave Thomas with strict instructions not to let a nurse of any kind in the door," Eric said with a very serious tone in his voice.

"Jesus Eric," Brian responded. "You don't make things easy, do you? Fine, go home and make love to your wife. But if you feel anything that is in the least bit abnormal, I want you to call me and I'll be over."

"Did I ever tell you that I love you, Brian? Well, I do, especially right this minute," Eric said with a laugh.

"Goodbye Eric, I've got people with real illnesses that need my help," responded Brian. "I'll check in on you later. And by the way, I love you too."

"See, Jenny, problem solved! Let's go home," Eric said with a smirk on his face.

11

The drive home was uneventful. Neither Eric nor Jenny realized just how tired they were. Eric held on to Jenny as if she were going to run away, but Jenny didn't mind because she had missed being held tightly by him. His hug now felt so reassuring, comforting, and she had a feeling that everything was going to be okay.

They arrived home where Heather and Thomas were happy to see Eric. Heather gave him a huge hug and commented on how emaciated he was. She could feel every rib bone.

"Emaciated or not, I have never been happier," Eric said. "Mrs. Jenny Barrett has finally come home," Eric announced, looking at her very proudly.

"Eric, would you mind if my name were Mrs. Jenny Ali-Barrett?" Jenny asked. "I'd like to keep my name. Don't get me wrong, I love being a Barrett because that's who you are, and I love everything about you, but I don't want to lose me, Jenny Ali."

"Of course not," Eric replied. "On paper, you shall be Mrs. Jenny Ali-Barrett, all of your correspondence will be signed with your formal name. However, please don't be offended if people refer to you as Mrs. Barrett, as that is what they will call you."

"That's fine, I can live with that," Jenny said smugly.

Heather looked at Eric as a mother looks at her son, with love in her eyes. "You must be hungry. I've prepared a delicious dinner for you both" she said.

Eric wanted to say no but didn't want to hurt Heather's feelings. "I'm famished," he replied. "Where are we dining tonight?"

"The formal dining room of course," Heather replied. "It's a very special occasion. Today you came home!"

"How about I take Jenny upstairs and we'll freshen up for dinner," Eric said. "I don't think she has even seen the bedrooms upstairs."

Eric took Jenny's hand and proceeded to the grand staircase. There were two curved staircases coming down from either side of a balcony at the top, looking somewhat like a beautifully large, elegant horseshoe. The steps were lined with a deep wine-coloured runner and black wrought iron pickets intricately and sublimely decorated, reminiscent of the 1920s.

Jenny looked at Eric and said, "I feel like Cinderella entering the palace for the first time. This is such a beautiful home."

Eric smiled and responded, "It is quite breathtaking. It's been decorated over many generations. The two hundred acres of land the estate rests on were purchased in 1855. The original home was built approximately in 1880. The reason for the delay was to secure the proper supplies for the estate: the stained glass, oak, wrought iron, lighting, and furniture was being purchased from London and Paris. Much of the Louis XVI furnishings were modeled on the same ones put into the Palace of Versailles apartments by Marie Antoinette. It was the elegance of neoclassicism that appealed to my ancestors, the return to the Greek and Roman models. Since then, each generation has put its touch on the Estate, bringing forth its elegance. The solarium for example, where I hope you agree to have our wedding reception, was designed and built in the 1920s. When you see it, you will recognize the art style immediately, and yet it's finished and furnished in the same elegance as the rest of the home. The outdoor pool and the two other homes on the estate were built much later. Today, one of the Victorian homes serves as Heather and Thomas's home, and the other is a guest house. Each has five bedrooms, five bathrooms, and large principal rooms all around. The decor in each home has varied over time and I guess one can say the style is antique, modeled much more on a Queen Anne style. I'll take you through the house after dinner if you'd like."

"I think I'm going to need a map. I'm sure to get lost in here," Jenny responded.

Eric noticed she wasn't quite as chatty and bubbly as usual and asked what was going on, all the while thinking she must be so overwhelmed.

"I feel like a fish out of water," she said. "All this class and elegance makes me feel quite inept, like I don't belong." She had worried look on her face. Eric smiled and reassured her that things would be okay.

"Let me tell you a little story," he said. "My mother felt much the same when she first moved in with one bag of clothing and the coat on her back. She was so afraid to touch anything and so insecure about what she could and could not do. My father watched her for a few days and then asked her why she was tiptoeing around. She told him she was afraid of breaking something and was trying to be careful. My father picked up a vase and threw it to the floor, shattering it into a million pieces. She was both afraid of and shocked by his behaviour. He asked her if she knew the value of that vase. She, of course, responded in the negative and he proceeded to tell her that it was valued at over three hundred thousand dollars. Horrified, she asked him why he would be so reckless with it. He said it was because the vase had a set value, and he could replace it. She, however, was both price-less and irreplaceable. He told her there was no need to tiptoe, she could break what she wanted, intentionally or accidentally, it was her home, and everything could be replaced as needed."

Jenny looked at Eric and smiled. "I think I would have liked your father."

"Yes, Jenny, he would have loved you too. So, take my father's advice, don't be afraid of this enormous home. It's yours, and if you want to redecorate any of it, feel free to do so, alright?" Eric said, looking at her, as he always did, with so much gentleness and love in his beautiful green eyes. Eyes, that Jenny could never refuse.

They finally made it up the stairs and Eric showed her nine lavish bed-rooms, each with ensuite bathrooms so beautiful she was speechless. From the drapery to the furnishings, Jenny had only seen this kind of luxury in movies about the royal family and magazines featuring the mansions of the world. Eric then led her to the master bedroom. There was a beautiful king-sized bed with a white canopy made of sheer organza and lace, a bed truly fit for royalty. Eric reached for a light switch that turned on tiny soft lights on the inside of the canopy. When the room lights had been switched off, the small lights looked like tiny stars.

"It's so beautiful, Eric," Jenny said like a child amazed by a lit-up Christmas tree. "I couldn't have even imagined this in a dream."

Smiling at her, Eric said, "Remember how I told you that each generation added its touch? These tiny stars were added by my mother. She thought it made the room look magical. My father didn't care too much about them, all he cared about was making her nights as magical   as possible."

The room was enormous. Part of the wood floor was covered with large, intricate area rugs. On one side of the room, there were two red velvet winged-back chairs and an artistically ornate table in between them. On the other side was a matching loveseat. The Regency era drapes were a beautiful soft green brocade. The bedroom furniture was both incredible and spectacular, complete with a very large, elaborately decorated, white marble fireplace. The room was to die for. Eric commented that this was where his parents would have breakfast every morning before his dad showered and left for work. He would also enjoy reading the paper and catch up on all the local gossip with my mother. The bathroom was palatial, with beautiful Roman columns surrounding an incredibly large, white marble tub, complete with jets.

"Eric, you could dance in this bathroom," Jenny said.

He laughed and said he was fine with that as long as they were naked. Jenny gave him a get-your-head-out-of-the-gutter look and walked into the walk-in closet.

The closet was huge, with mirrors for dressing and all kinds of drawers for ties, socks, belts, anything imaginable. There were a few drawers left open, filled with the most beautiful jewellery Jenny had ever seen.

"I'm guessing these are all real diamonds, rubies, emeralds, oh my?" she said with a smile.

Eric looked for a specific ring. "There it is," he said. "May I?" Then he proceeded to put a very large, beautiful emerald ring on her finger. It was a princess cut with diamonds around the stone and an intricately designed gold band. It fit perfectly.

He smiled. "Dad was right. You see, since this ring was designed in England, around 1800, it has been the formal engagement ring offered by a Barrett. I would have proposed to you with it, but things were a little crazy. However, Dad said that this ring had a knack for fitting perfectly on the hand of the next bride."

Jenny smiled. "It fits perfectly Eric."

"One more sign that you are my destiny Jenny Ali-Barrett. Would you mind wearing it to dinner tonight?"

"I'd love to, but I think I should wear this stunning ring only on special occasions," she replied.

"Jenny," Eric said, "you will have quite a few occasions to wear this and all of these." He unlocked an entire closet with drawers full of jewellery. Jenny's eyes couldn't believe the amount of Jewellery he showed her.

"Eric this should all be locked in a safe," she said.

"Yes," he nodded. "It is insured in case you were wondering, but this entire section of the closet is a locking safe. I will show you how to lock it later," he replied.

"What's that noise?" Jenny asked.

Eric took her in his arms and said, "That's the dinner bell. It means Heather is ready for dinner. I would like to show you the rest of the house after dinner and then retire, in this room, have breakfast, lunch and dinner in here. I want you all to myself for the next few days at least."

Jenny was still stuck on the bell. "You have a dinner bell? What happens if it breaks, you don't eat?" she said sarcastically.

Eric looked at her and laughed. "No silly, one of the servants would come and let us know dinner is ready."

"We said we would freshen up for dinner, but we look the same. Won't Heather and Thomas notice?" she asked.

"No, I'll simply tell them we got caught up with the house and the many stories that go with it," he responded, as they went down the stairs.

"Eric," Jenny whispered with a look of concern. "Did you lock the safe?"

"Yes, love, nothing to worry about," he responded.

They arrived in the formal dining room and Jenny immediately noticed the French furniture. *Hmm, Louis XVI, same as in the apartments of the Palace of Versailles, furnished by Marie Antoinette herself,* Jenny thought. *Well, maybe we will eat cake tonight in her honour.* She laughed to herself and sat down next to Eric. There was a lot of cutlery on the table, and she felt quite embarrassed.

"Okay," Jenny said. "I'm just going to come out and say it. I do not come from royalty or high society and on my table, there was only one dish, one fork, one spoon, and one knife." She looked at everyone who just stared at her and said nothing. "I have no idea what to do with all of these," Jenny said, embarrassed. Eric smiled, quite lovingly, and Thomas responded.

"It looks confusing, but it isn't," Thomas said very gently. "My ancestors were farmers, and we were quite content with one of each utensil as well, but then things went and got so damn complicated." Thomas got up from his chair and walked over to Jenny. He put his hands on her shoulders from behind the chair. "This is how it's done," he said. "Keep your back straight, start from the outside of the place setting and work your way in with each dish that is brought to the table. Now, can we eat?"

Everyone broke out into laughter. "Let's eat," Eric said. "Would you like a glass of wine, Jenny?"

"Yes, I would love a glass, maybe two," she replied.

Jenny watched as Eric turned to one of the servants standing behind them and asked if they would go to the cellar and get a 1962 bottle of Chardonnay. The servant left quickly and returned about fifteen minutes later with the chilled Chardonnay. He opened it and waited to be told to pour. Eric nodded and the servant poured the wine. Jenny was in awe. It was as if she was seeing Eric for the very first time. He had a very commanding presence, and everyone was at his fingertips. When David said he was an immensely powerful man with quite a lot of influence, she never really understood the full scope of what he was talking about. As she watched everyone doing his bidding, she was beginning to understand exactly what that meant. She now began to understand not only his power, but her own as his wife. He had mentioned the Gala and how he and David would prepare her for it and clearly understood why. She would be inundated with all kinds of questions, and she would have to field them all. She would have to know how to respond. Jenny was now feeling scared and very anxious.

Eric was making light conversation, joking and laughing with Heather and Thomas, but realized that Jenny was in her head about something.

"Honey are you okay? You looked a little worried," he said.

She had hardly eaten at all. "Do we have any vodka?" she asked.

Eric looked at her quite puzzled. "A little strong for dinner, isn't it?"

"Oh Eric," Jenny said feeling both scared and frustrated. "How am I supposed to do this? I can get through dinner thanks to Thomas's demo lesson, but how am I supposed to participate in these high society parties, galas, luncheons? I don't know what to say or how to answer and I don't want to embarrass you," Jenny said with tears in her eyes.

Eric, stood up, took her hand, pulled her up, and held her close to him. "Listen, anywhere you are, so too shall I be. I will never leave you alone, anywhere," he said in the most reassuring tone he could muster.

Jenny looked at her husband anxiously. "How do I field the questions I'll be asked? People are going to want to know all sorts of things, after all, I am Mrs. Barrett," she said.

Heather decided to jump in. "Okay, calm down, Jenny. I know this can be a lot to deal with, and I'm sure you're feeling overwhelmed just from touring this house, or the little you have seen of it. You said yes to becoming Mrs. Barrett because you love Eric more than life itself. In the end, keep in mind that they want to know what you have that they didn't, why Eric chose you and not them. There are a lot of ladies who are envious and jealous of you right now. You took what they have been trying to have for years. You need to stand in your power, Jenny. Eric will be right there with you. You stand tall and show them what you're all about. Your beauty, your intelligence, and above all, your kindness. That is your true power. Most of the people you will meet are sneaky, conniving bitches, for lack of a better word. You are a lady, Mrs. Barrett. You have always been, and Eric knows it. He loves you so much, and no one can change that! Now stop stressing, it's going to be fine. We are all here to help you and we will not feed you to the lions, or lionesses in this case. Now, do you want that vodka or will scotch do? Around here we drink a lot of scotch." Heather ended her speech quite firmly.

Jenny just laughed. "Well then, I guess I'm a scotch drinking woman today," she replied. She walked over to Heather and gave her a warm hug. "Thank you," she said. "When Eric goes to work, maybe you can coach me on what I need to know."

Heather poured the scotch, smiled at Jenny wholeheartedly, and said, "I'd love to, my dear. You know, you and Eric's mother have a lot of similarities. She was kind and giving, just like you, and had to learn a lot, just like you. The difference is she had a little more time to get used to being

Mrs. Barrett. But don't worry, we are all here for you and you will be fine. You are already a lady, and an elegant one at that, Mrs. Barrett." Heather handed her the scotch.

"Well said," Eric replied. "I'll have a scotch as well." He took Jenny in his arms and said, "I'm not so sure you should see the rest of the house today. Maybe it's just too much to deal with. I have to keep reminding myself that this estate can be very daunting."

"No," Jenny replied. "I want to see the rest of it. I have to get used to it, so it starts now. Can I have my drink while we do this?" she asked.

"Absolutely," Eric responded.

Heather called to have the dining room cleaned. "Enjoy your tour, Jenny," she said as both she and Thomas left the room.

Eric led Jenny toward the living room. "This room," Eric began, "is primarily used during dinner parties and it is characteristic of the rest of the estate. I don't remember ever being in this room except for parties. What I wanted to show you is this." Jenny looked to where Eric was pointing and saw a beautiful life-sized portrait of two people she assumed were his parents. She was stunned.

"Are they your parents?" Jenny asked.

"Yes," Eric responded. "I had this painted from one of my favourite photos after they passed away. It took me two years just to get the nerve to have it done." He looked at his parents with both pain and love.

"Your mother is beautiful, I can see why your father fell in love," Jenny said. "You have her red hair, and from what I can see, your father's eyes. Aside from the red hair, you do look very much like Christopher Barrett."

"Yes," Eric said. "Everyone has always said as much." Eric looked up at the portrait and continued. "Well, Mom, Dad, I'd like you to meet my wife, Jenny. She is talented, beautiful, and is ready and willing to provide you with grandchildren if I could only get her to bed." He laughed. "I'm very proud of her Dad, and Mom, she'll be taking on various projects at the Foundation. Jenny shares your love of children and I'm sure you'll be very proud of her future accomplishments. I wish so much you could both be here to welcome her. I know this transition would be so much easier for her if she had you to guide her, but we will all do the best we can. I know you're watching from above, so please look after my Jenny as well." Eric smiled at the portrait and took Jenny's hand as they walked towards the solarium. Jenny stopped and looked at Eric.

"There is still a lot of pain in your heart, I can feel it. The passing of your parents has been very difficult for you," she said.

Eric looked at his bride and smiled. "Yes, Jenny, it has been difficult, but with you now in my life, I don't feel so alone anymore," he said as he gave her a gentle kiss.

He continued to walk toward the solarium. He deliberately did not turn on the lights so she could see the glass ceiling that highlighted the splendor of the night sky, brilliantly shining with stars.

"Oh Eric, this is beautiful," Jenny said in awe. "It looks like something right out of *7e Great Gatsby*! I can see why you would want to have our wedding reception here. It's perfect!"

Eric turned on the lights and Jenny noticed that the large windows in the fourteen-foot-tall room were surrounded by incredibly beautiful white and red flowering plants. There were antique Roman columns, marble floors, and a majestic white marble fireplace. The room was surrounded by stunning furniture.

As Jenny stared, speechless, Eric looked at her and said, "This was my mother's favourite room. She and my father would sit by the fire and look at the stars, often laying on the couch in each other's arms. That's one of my most treasured memories of the two of them. They were so happy and so in love." He could almost picture them there now.

"I can see why," Jenny responded. "A room like this would make anyone fall in love. From what I've learned about your parents from you and David, they shared an unbreakable bond, so much so that they died together."

Eric looked at her rather puzzled. "I'm not sure I know what you mean," he replied.

"Well Eric," Jenny continued, "I know their deaths happened suddenly, tragically, and far too soon, but God saw fit to take them together, to not break that bond. Don't you see? Their love was so strong, they passed on together. Can you imagine how hard it would have been for your mother or father to watch the other pass away? Their bond is unbreakable! The loneliness and heartache would be unbearable. They died together with that unbreakable bond of love, and they have moved on, together, enjoying their love still in the next world." She smiled at her husband.

Eric looked at her and said, "For so many years, I've been so focused on the emptiness they left behind, I never even stopped to ponder something like that. I know the pain I felt when our bond was broken, and I would not wish that on my worst enemy. I guess it was a blessing in disguise. Taken too soon but taken together." He put his arms around Jenny and held her close. "Only you can find the good in tragedy, my love," Eric said as he gently kissed her cheek.

Eric showed her the informal dining room; informal living room, which Jenny renamed the TV room because it had a massive one-hundred-inch television; a games room with pool tables, card tables, dart boards, and bars; both an indoor and an outdoor Olympic-sized pools; and several gyms, saunas, tennis courts, and squash courts. Everything was decorated in opulence and elegance. Eric also showed Jenny his father's favourite place. It was a spectacular gallery. The walls were lined with ornate cherry wood panels displaying the family's exquisite art collection. A wine-coloured carpet and deep forest green brocade wallpaper, which had a velvet relief design, completed the gallery. There were ornate chairs and statues, and exquisite lighting lit the paintings. Jenny was impressed as she stared wide-eyed in utter disbelief.

"Enough touring!" Eric declared. "Let's go to bed, Jenny. We can see other parts of the house tomorrow."

"I don't have anything pretty to wear, Eric. I should have something satiny or silky and pretty. It's my honeymoon," she said as she looked at him with disappointment.

"Jenny, you won't need anything tonight, you wouldn't be wearing it for very long anyway." He laughed as they made their way up the stairs and to the bedroom.

Once in their room, Eric called the kitchen staff from a phone in the bedroom. "Oh Thomas, I'm glad you're still there. Would you kindly have a nice breakfast sent up at approximately 9 a.m. tomorrow?" Eric asked. "Thank you, good night, Thomas."

"I'd like to take a shower if that's okay?" Jenny asked.

"Of course, it's okay. It's your home, Jenny, you don't need to ask me," Eric replied. "However, didn't we shower this morning?"

"Yes. But, Eric, I know this may sound dumb coming out of the mouth of a twenty-three-year-old grown woman, but I've never done this before and I have to say I'm a little nervous, and a lot frightened," she said sheepishly.

He took her in his arms and looked at her with so much love in his eyes. "Jenny, why don't you just leave everything to me, relax and enjoy what's about to happen," he whispered. He removed her clothes, laid her gently on the bed, and slowly began to kiss her. Eric made passionate love to his beautiful wife for the first time.

"Oh my God, Eric," she whispered in his ear. When their souls came together it was as if they had been reunited after an incredibly long absence. Jenny enjoyed the pleasure and ecstasy her soul felt as much as he was enjoying her. They made love all night long until they were exhausted. As Eric moved to lie down, Jenny grabbed him and held him close.

"Where are you going?" she asked.

"I was going to lie down beside you to give you a chance to breathe," he said with a chuckle.

"No, I don't want to breathe. I want you to stay," she said as she clutched him close to her. "Eric, you're like a beautiful warm blanket that binds us together as one, and I don't want to lose that."

Eric looked into his wife's eyes with so much love in his heart. "Jenny, I've been bound to you from the first moment I looked into your eyes. When we were apart, I felt restless, empty, unnerved, unhinged, and try as I might to calm it with scotch, I could not. So, I would call you, sometimes extremely late, just to hear your voice," he responded. "You will never lose your blanket, my love. As long as I have breath in my lungs, this heart beats only for you," he said holding her close.

Jenny smiled at him. "Please make love to me again," she said.

"Jenny, you don't have to ask me. I will love you anywhere, anytime, for however long you want, just reach for me and I will," Eric responded as he took his wife in his arms.

Thomas brought breakfast up the next morning and gently knocked on the door, but there was no answer. He knocked louder, no response. He slowly opened the door, peeked inside, and saw they were both sound asleep in each other's arms. He slowly shut the door and returned the breakfast to the kitchen. When Eric woke up, he decided to enjoy Jenny's beautifully voluptuous breasts as he kissed them gently.

"What a delightful way to wake up! Good morning, my love," Jenny said.

Eric smiled at his lovely wife, "It's 2 p.m., Mrs. Barrett. You must be hungry," Eric replied. "How about I call for a late lunch?"

"I'm not hungry, Eric," Jenny said, and she began kissing him.

Eric smiled. "I love you, Jenny."

"I love you back," she replied. Jenny looked at her husband. "Eric, explain something to me. I don't understand how people do this with so many partners. I could never love anyone else but you and only you can make me feel this way. If it were anyone else, they couldn't do what you do because only you can do this. Does that make sense?"

"Yes, it does, my love," he responded.

"Well then tell me, you shared yourself with many women, how could you do that?"

"I didn't love any of them, Jenny. It was just sex, with no meaning attached."

"If it was meaningless, then why do it at all?" she asked.

Eric looked at her with both kindness and love in his eyes. "Jenny, the love I feel sharing myself with you, as you call it, is unimaginable. This is the kind of love most people search for all their lives and never find. When I make love with you, our bodies and souls become one and the passion is mind-blowing, unimaginable! I never, in my wildest dreams, thought that I would find such a love. So, I just went along with meaningless sex, it matched my entire life—empty friendships, untrustworthy relation- ships. It was my money and power people were seeking, not me. I think in general; people sleep with many partners in the hopes of finding the love we have found in each other."

"Maybe if they loved the person they were sleeping with, they would find true love," Jenny responded.

"I think the love we have, Jenny, is rare and very hard to find, and I only hope that our children, when we have a few, will find the same love," Eric responded with a smile. Jenny pulled her man close, and Eric was all over her.

12

At 8 a.m. the next morning, the phone rang.

"Good morning, Mr. Jones," Thomas answered.

"Good morning, Thomas," responded David. "Have they come up for air at all?"

"No sir," responded Thomas. "They've had one or two breakfasts in the past four days. I don't think they need food."

David laughed. "Well, it's all good then. I was just calling to check up on them," he said.

"Is there anything you would like me to relay to Master Eric, sir?" asked Thomas.

"No," replied David. "Nothing that can't wait. Have a good day, Thomas."

"You as well, sir," Thomas replied before hanging up the phone.

Just then, Heather walked in. "I hope they decide to have some food soon, otherwise we won't be able to find either one of them, they'll be so thin," she laughed as she spoke to Thomas.

"I'll take breakfast up and hope they eat this time," Thomas said with a smirk.

Thomas knocked gently on the door, no answer. He knocked harder, no answer. He opened the door gently, took another peek, and left breakfast on the table after realizing the happy couple was in the shower. He smiled at the sounds he was hearing and left the room.

Eric wrapped Jenny in a plush white robe and kissed her gently.

"Where's your robe?" Jenny asked.

"Hmm, I don't like them much," Eric replied. "I usually just wrap a towel around me and sit down for breakfast."

"Just like pajamas, I guess," she said laughing.

"Exactly," he responded. "I guess I just like being naked for as long as I can."

As she walked toward the table for breakfast and looked around, Jenny couldn't get over the luxury of her surroundings.

"This is gonna take some getting used to," she said. "I feel like we're at a very expensive luxury hotel with room service."

"This is how it will be every morning, my love. Sit right here and join me." The table was set up beautifully and a big breakfast awaited them.

"Jenny," Eric said, "you know when I was in the hospital, I heard you. While I was unconscious, I heard you, and felt your absence when you were not in the room. I couldn't see you, couldn't move, but I felt you. It was you that pulled me out. It was you that gave me the strength to open my eyes. Didn't you ever wonder why I opened my eyes with a smile? It's because I knew you were with me the whole time."

"Really? You heard me?" Jenny said with a smile.

"Yes," Eric replied. "I felt you hold me, hold my hand when you weren't lying with me. Jenny, I felt you in my soul, I felt we were one. That emptiness and ache I felt before, it was gone. I never want to feel that way again, Jenny."

"I never want to feel that kind of pain ever again either," she said and kissed him.

"So, you like the idea of the solarium for the wedding reception?" he asked.

"Yes, I do!" she responded. "It's such a beautiful room. Not to change the subject, Eric, but I wanted to ask why you rushed to get married."

"Aside from claiming you as mine before anyone else even had a chance," Eric said smiling, "I didn't think I was going to make it, Jenny, and as I felt like I was not going to pull through I wanted to leave you everything I had; and as my wife, you would be entitled to all of it. I wanted to make sure you would want for nothing."

Jenny looked at her husband, astonished. "And what would I do with all of this, and not you?" she asked. "How could any of this mean anything without you here?"

"That was the only act of love at my disposal, and I took it," he said. "Until my last dying breath, Jenny, my love for you is all I could think about. This was my way of making sure you knew that I loved you."

"What about everyone else you love? Would you have left them penniless?"

"I know you better than you know yourself it seems. Jenny, I knew you would take care of everyone. In my selfish act to make you mine and make sure you would be forever taken care of; I knew that your kindness and generosity would take care of everyone I loved."

"Well, that's great, but I would be left without my love, with our bond broken, and my heart in tatters. Every waking day would be full of unbearable pain that would most likely lead me to take my own life, just to be with you."

Eric got up from his chair, took Jenny in his arms, and said, "That's why I'm thankful that God heard you pleading not to take me, begging to have just one more chance to make things right between us."

"You heard that?" she whispered with tears in her eyes.

"I wept," he replied. "I don't think you noticed tears coming down the sides of my eyes. I wept because I wanted so much to tell you that everything would be okay, but I couldn't move. I love you so much, Jenny." Tears welled up in his eyes remembering that moment.

"I love you back, Eric," she said as she pulled him towards her. "Make love to me, and don't stop, not for a very long time."

13

"Good morning, Thomas," Eric said cheerfully as he reached for some orange juice.

"Good morning, sir," Thomas responded with a smile.

"I think we should have some breakfast this morning, we skipped dinner last night, and I'm sure Jenny must be hungry."

"Nothing like an appetite after a good night's work, sir," Thomas replied with a smirk.

"I'll bring Jenny some orange juice to start," Eric said, smiling as he left the kitchen.

"Breakfast will be there in fifteen minutes, sir," Thomas replied.

Eric went upstairs and woke Jenny up with a kiss. "How about some orange juice? Breakfast is on its way up. I feel great, Jenny! I have so much energy this morning. How about a swim?"

"That sounds like a great idea, but I don't have a bathing suit, I don't have any of my clothes here, Eric," Jenny responded disheartened.

"Truth is, Jenny, I don't think you'll be needing a bathing suit." He smirked.

"Well, I can't walk around the house naked, Eric," she said a little annoyed.

"How about the nice plushy white robe? You can walk around the house and slip into nothing at a moment's notice."

"I don't mind skinny dipping in the pool with you, my love, but at some point, I will need clothes," Jenny replied. "All I have are my jeans and sweater, which really could use a wash."

"Let's have breakfast, go for a swim, and then get you some clothes. Sound good?"

"Sounds perfect," she said as they made their way downstairs to the pool.

After their swim, Jenny went upstairs to put on her sweater and jeans, thinking they were going to go to her mother's house to pick up her clothes. She went downstairs to meet Eric.

"Ready to go?" she asked.

"Go where?" he replied, a little confused. "Didn't we agree to spend as much time as possible together, without interruptions?"

"Yes," Jenny said, "but you said we would get my clothes, so we should go to my mother's house and pick them up."

"No, love. I said we would get you clothes," Eric said as he gently touched her cheek with his hand. Just then the doorbell rang, and Thomas went to answer it.

"I have a little surprise for you, come with me, Jenny," Eric said smiling.

Thomas took the mystery guest to the informal living room. Jenny and Eric followed.

"Mary Anne, thank you for coming on such short notice, I appreciate it," Eric said as he gave the woman a gentle hug.

"Anything for you, Eric," she replied. "I brought what you asked for in several sizes, since you weren't sure. Knowing your taste, I cannot imagine anything larger than an eight." Mary Anne looked at Jenny. "In this case, clearly a four," she said.

"Mary Anne, I'd like you to meet my wife, Jenny," Eric said, holding his wife close.

"Well, hello, Mrs. Barrett. I had heard the rumors, but didn't think they were true," said Mary Anne. "You've managed to snatch the most sought-after man on the planet. What's your secret?" she asked dryly.

Just then, Heather walked in. "That's between her and Master Eric," she said impatiently. "Don't you have some clothing from which Mrs. Barrett can choose? Some of these items may not even be suitable; my lady's palate is very refined," Heather said, looking at Mary Anne and taking Jenny's hand. "Let's have a look shall we?" Heather asked.

Eric looked at Jenny lovingly. "Would you like me to stay with you, my love?" he asked.

"If you want to," Jenny responded. "But if you want to catch up with David and work, I think I'm in good hands here with Heather."

"Are you sure?" he asked. "I can sit right here, love. Anything you want."

"I'll be fine," she whispered as she gently touched his face while looking into his beautiful eyes. Eric left the room and Mary Anne looked at Jenny incredulously.

"I don't know what you've done to him, but he's clearly in love with you," Mary Anne said, looking at Jenny in awe.

"We're in love with each other. One body, one soul, one life," Jenny responded with a sincere smile.

Mary Anne was just speechless. She looked at Jenny completely astonished, then collected herself. "Yes, well then, let's have a look at what you would prefer from the collections I've brought. Eric asked me to bring Prada, Fendi, Balenciaga, Channel, Armani, Dolce and Gabbana, Versace, and Givenchy. Have you requested any other designers?" she asked.

Not knowing who many of those designers were, Jenny responded no. "Eric knows me very well, he's pretty much covered it," she said with a smile.

Heather smiled and squeezed her hand. "You're doing great," she whispered in Jenny's ear.

About six hours later, Eric was working in the library and Jenny came running in. She ran around the desk and jumped into his lap.

"Whoa, what's this?" Eric asked. She was so playful and immensely happy.

"Eric, I have such nice clothes, shoes, bags, oh my God, things I only dreamed of!" she said excitedly. "They're already hanging in the bedroom closet," she said as she hugged her husband and smiled happily.

"Your bedroom closet. Say it, Jenny, say, 'my bedroom closet,' please."

She whispered playfully in his ear, with excitement all over her face, "My bedroom closet." Then she kissed him while still sitting in his lap.

"I think I'm pretty much finished here for now," he said. "You want to model some of those clothes for me? I'd like to see you in them."

"Let's go! I want to show you," she replied. She pulled him up off the chair and dragged him down the hall and up the stairs. He was barely able to keep up with her.

As she showed him what she had selected, he looked at her longingly and said, "Well Mrs. Barrett, you have excellent taste! Your selections are beautiful and will look stunning on you."

"Very elegantly fashionable," she said, with a funny face. "I got something for you too, well, a few things that I think you'll like," she said. "Wait right here," she said as she went into the bathroom and came out with a very sexy, silky nightgown. The back was quite low, and it had a high slit on the side of her leg, outlined in black lace. Most of the nightgown was red silk with bits of sheer black designs.

Eric smiled. "So, you got something silky and pretty." He looked at her with bedroom eyes.

"Do you like it?" she asked in a very tempting stance.

He was all over her. "I love it," he whispered as he took her in his arms and began kissing her. They missed the late lunch Heather had planned and dinner as well.

"If those two had any intention of putting on some weight, they're going about it the wrong way," Heather said to Thomas. "They hardly eat at all!"

Thomas smiled at his wife and said, "Love is feeding those two." He took Heather in his arms and said, "I remember you didn't mind missing a meal or two when we were first married. You remember?"

"Of course, I do. You were the most handsome man alive, and I had you all to myself," Heather replied. "Now you're the oldest man alive, but I love you, Thomas, I always will, until my dying breath."

"Well, Heather, I don't think we'll be needed here. Why don't we go home, get some sleep?" Thomas asked.

"It's after 9 p.m. I can't imagine Eric would need anything now. Let's go home," Heather replied, smiling and taking her husband's hand.

14

Jenny and Eric had settled quite comfortably into wedding bliss. They had a wonderful breakfast together every morning before Eric left for work. On this particular morning, Eric asked Jenny if she was excited about the gala Friday night.

"I'm both excited and a little frightened," Jenny responded. "This is going to be a very new experience."

Eric smiled as he looked at his wife. "Please don't worry about this, Jenny. I'll be by your side the whole time," he responded. "The gala will be the perfect opportunity for you to meet a few people who you'll be working closely with on various projects at the Foundation. I just want to ensure you'll meet the right people, and not anyone looking to profit for their own personal gain." Then Eric said something that warmed Jenny's heart. "All I want, Jenny, is for you to find your place. By that I mean if the Foundation is what you want, then so be it, but, if you try working on various projects and realize that you would prefer to do something else, that is fine too. I hope you find something you're passionate about and work with it. I would like to see you involved and engaged, not just walking around the estate trying to find your way." Eric looked at her tenderly. "Jenny, I want you to be happy, feel comfortable in your home, forge your purpose and direction. I don't want you to feel like you have to take over the Foundation, that's not what I expect from you. Whatever it is you wish to pursue, I will ensure you have the resources to do it."

Jenny looked at Eric reassuringly. "I want to work with children, and the Foundation seems to be the perfect fit. Once I start working on it, I might take on new projects or move in a new direction, but I will most definitely make it my endeavor," Jenny replied smiling.

Eric was pleased with his wife's decision. As he looked at his phone and realized he had to leave, he took his wife in his arms. "Can I get you anything before I leave? Is there anything you would like me to do before I go?" he asked.

Jenny took his face in her hands, gave him a gentle kiss, and replied, "Just come home soon."

Once Eric left, Jenny realized that Friday was quickly approaching, and she was stressing over the gala; what would she wear? What would she say? How should she carry herself, behave? She would be introduced as Eric's wife and she wanted to be everything Eric would want her to be. Jenny decided to consult with Heather.

She found Heather in the library. Eric had asked Heather to take care of a few things for him, and since Heather's computer was being repaired, she had permission to use one of the laptops in the library. Jenny walked in, relieved she had found her, and said good morning.

"Heather, do you have some time for me today?" Jenny asked.

"Of course, Mrs. Barrett," Heather replied. "I was just finishing up with a few things, but they can wait until this afternoon."

"Oh no, Heather, I don't want to interfere with your work," Jenny said apologetically.

"Nonsense," Heather replied. "I'm sure Master Eric would want me to assist you first and then continue with this work. Now what's troubling you, my dear?"

"The gala is in a few days. I don't know what to wear or how I should do my hair, but most importantly, I don't know who any of the people are and I don't want to embarrass my husband by saying something inappropriate. I was researching the gala online and it's a very elegant function, with a lot of powerful people."

"I see the source of your stress and frustration," replied Heather. "Why don't we start with something enjoyable, like selecting a dress. As far as hair and makeup go, Eric has it covered. He asked me to ensure the stylist would be available for Friday, and that has been arranged. All you need to do to get ready is take a shower and sit in your robe. They will take care of the rest. Now, what to wear? Do you have a style in mind?"

"Heather," Jenny said a little anxiously, "I've seen pictures of Eric and all those girls that attached themselves to his arm online. They're all so beautiful, so cultured in how they respond to things. I'm not like that at all. What you see is what you get." She was feeling very inadequate.

"Jenny, those so-called cultured girls that you saw are just short of being prostitutes," Heather replied firmly. "They look good, and their focus is strictly to try to trap a rich man, by whatever means necessary. They spend their time at the gym with their personal trainers and have people teach them how to respond to situations. Everything is a calculated response. A lot of these high society people have difficulty with real relationships. There are many wives having affairs with their husbands' best friends and vice versa. The politics is the same. No one can be trusted so don't believe anything you hear. Eric will guide you through the process, and I'm sure he will not let you go anywhere without him.

"This gala is a fundraiser for the Foundation, something very dear to his mother's heart, and I'm so pleased you'll be taking it on. It will be a lot of work, but you're perfect for the job. Don't worry too much about things, they will come together. Some good people will reach out to you, and Eric, David, and I can help you sort through the good and bad connections. Once you start getting your feet wet, I'm sure you'll be fine. It's just all new to you, that's all. Now, let's start with what you'll wear, shoes, purse, dress, jewellery and of course, which fur coat. Then, we'll talk about some of the people you will meet."

"I have more than one fur coat?" Jenny asked.

"Oh yes, ma'am," Heather responded smiling. "I'll take you to them after we find your dress. Now, what style were you thinking?" Heather asked.

"Well, all the ladies I saw around Eric on the gala website had long, elegant dresses, mostly black, and very form-fitting," Jenny responded. "I don't think they wore underwear, Heather, because I couldn't see any lines at all. They were all so perfect, their bodies I mean, perfectly slim, long legs, just something right out of a magazine, except they weren't airbrushed."

"I'm sensing that you feel a little insecure, Jenny."

"Not just a little, a lot. It's just that he's so powerful and I'm so plain," Jenny said with tears in her eyes. "I need a fairy godmother to transform me into something I'm not, Heather."

"You know," Heather said. "Susan Barrett had some of your same insecurities, and do you know how she dealt with them? She decided that she would look her best for her husband and for herself, no one else mattered. She would respond to him alone and trusted that he would help her navigate the room. Well, as time went on and Susan became accustomed to the events, she took the lead in every situation. Eric will do the same for you. Now, let's not think of anyone else. Do you want to look nice for Master Eric?" Heather asked.

"Of course, I do! I want to look perfect for him," she replied.

"Then let's just focus on that, shall we," Heather said trying to ease Jenny's anxiety. "I think we'll need to go shopping and I know just the place. We'll have to go downtown, or I can call them to the house. What do you prefer, Jenny?"

"I'd rather have them come here. No one even knows Mrs. Barrett, so maybe it's best we do this quietly for now." Jenny replied. "I'm supposed to be Jenny Barrett, confident, strong, a woman who knows what she wants. I don't want anyone seeing me like this, sad and in tears."

"Don't you worry, Jenny," Heather said. "By the time we finish today, you will be all of those things. Never forget, Jenny, Eric fell in love with you because you are blessed with a kind heart and gentle nature, and you are a very intelligent young lady. More importantly, you are everything those women you saw are not. There is your strength, my dear." Heather wiped the tears from Jenny's face, then rushed to make a few phone calls. While they waited for the fashion consultants to arrive, they had a cup of tea and looked at a few gala videos posted online.

Once the consultants arrived, Heather suggested they go into one of the bedrooms, where Jenny could use the bathroom to try on the clothes. Once upstairs, the fashion consultants advised Jenny which styles would flatter her figure. Jenny could pretty much wear anything, but she wanted to look different, not like everyone else. Her gown was going to be a mas- terpiece. Jenny decided on a black lace bodice with a sweetheart neckline that emphasized her voluptuous breasts that Eric loved so much, and a burgundy, taffeta, high-waisted sweeping skirt that had a sheer black organza overlay. The designer was Giorgio Armani. She put it on and walked out of the bathroom.

"Heather," she said. "What do you think?"

Heather's eyes watered as she said, "Jenny, you look perfect. I'm sure Master Eric will be speechless when he sees you."

The consultants coordinated her shoes and purse and asked about the coat she would be wearing.

Heather responded for her. "She'll be wearing a full-length mink cape." The stylists looked at each other and smiled, and one replied, "That will be stunning, Mrs. Barrett." They hung up the clothes in her bedroom closet and Jenny was glad that part of it was over. She felt beautiful in her outfit and her confidence was beginning to grow. As she looked at her gorgeous outfit and beautiful Christian Louboutin shoes, Heather explained to Jenny that she would just be a moment, she had to check with the kitchen to ensure dinner would be ready for when Eric arrived. She picked up a phone in the bedroom and made all the arrangements.

Jenny watched Heather and then said, "someday you'll have to show me how to use that phone," and they both laughed.

"Let me get last year's gala video," Heather said. "We have a recording so I can tell you about some of the key people you will meet and the women that will be shooting darts at you with their eyes because, as Mary Anne said, you trapped the most sought-after man on the planet. I think the recordings are in the informal living room; let's head down there." Heather took Jenny's hand like a proud mother.

"Okay," Heather began, "Of the ladies, Charlotte will be the one that may want to know the most about you. She was the one that caused all that commotion that resulted in the two of you separating and Master Eric almost dying. She planned to cause enough stress to push you away, and it almost worked. She didn't know that Eric would have done any- thing to get you back. So, that's her there." Heather pointed to a very tall, lanky, English-looking lady.

"Well, Heather, I think I look a lot better than she does, don't you?" Jenny asked.

"She couldn't hold a candle to you, Jenny," Heather replied. "She was unable to keep Eric interested when he was at his most vulnerable. She did try though. I never really liked her much."

Just then, Thomas came into the room. "There you are, what are we watching?" he asked.

"I'm getting a people lesson, Thomas. C'mon, sit beside me," Jenny said as she tapped the seat next to her on the couch. "You must know these people too."

"Unfortunately," Thomas began, "I've had the 'unpriviledge,' if that's even a word, of meeting some of them here in this house, about four years ago, before Christopher and Susan passed. If you had met Eric then, I don't think you would have liked him. He behaved like the hotshot, eli- gible bachelor that he was. He knew he was wanted and behaved that way, very cocky. His parent's death forced him to grow up, take his father's place at the helm, and he started to see the world through a different lens. He worked awfully hard and didn't socialize much. He dedicated himself to his father's empire. You know, the only gathering we have had in this house in four years was the funeral." He looked at the screen and smirked. "Oh, that guy. Heather, you remember him, he was such an ass," Thomas said laughing.

"Okay, Thomas, fill me in, who's the ass?" Jenny asked as the three of them laughed. "Stop it," Jenny said as she was laughing. "I need to know this stuff."

They spent the rest of the afternoon identifying the people they knew, warning Jenny against people who could potentially steer her wrong, and laughing over some of the stories Thomas would tell about some of these characters.

Eric came home and walked into this very relaxed and happy atmosphere.

"What's going on in here?" he asked with a smile. "Have we been hitting the scotch a little early today?"

"No," Jenny responded as she got up to give her husband a warm hug and kiss. "Heather and Thomas were giving me people lessons to prepare me for the gala on Friday."

Eric laughed. "People lessons? What are those?"

"See, look, according to Thomas, he's a real ass." Jenny pointed to Craig Baker.

"Yes, Jenny, Thomas would be correct. Craig is a real horse's ass," Eric responded laughing. "Actually, this is a really good idea. Why don't we just have a few laughs," he said as he pointed out a few people and told some pretty embarrassing stories. He hadn't had this much fun in a while. It seemed like the house had lightened up with Jenny in it. David arrived shortly after, as he and Eric had some work to finish, and got into the fun, laughing hysterically at some of the stories he had completely forgotten.

"David, is Mrs. Jones waiting for you at home?" Jenny asked. "Could we not ask her to come over for dinner tonight? I realize it's short notice, but we're having such a good time."

"I think that's a great idea, Jenny," David responded. "Let me call Marie and ask her to come straight over for dinner. It would be good for the two of you to meet."

"Sounds great. Maybe Michael would like to join us as well?" she asked.

"I'll see if he's available," David responded.

Eric poured himself a drink and pulled his wife close to him. They continued to watch the screen and tell stories that had Jenny in tears from laughter.

Mrs. Jones arrived and was shown into the informal living room.

"What is all this noise about?" Marie asked as she walked in.

"Marie!" David said, as he took her in his arms. "So glad you could join us. I'd like you to meet Jenny, Eric's wife."

"Hello," she said. "I'm so happy to meet you. I've heard such wonderful things about you from David. He did say you were very beautiful, and he wasn't wrong. I'm looking forward to getting to know you a little. Maybe we can meet for lunch, I'd love for you to come to our house." Marie looked around. "What's going on here?"

"Well, Heather and I thought it would be a good idea to introduce me to some of the people I would be meeting at the gala on Friday," replied Jenny. "So, we dug up last year's recording and Thomas began telling me stories about a few questionable characters, as he calls them, and we started to laugh. Eric came home and filled us in on stories we didn't know and once David arrived, well, we're now at the point of being hysterical."

David asked Marie if she remembered Craig. "Oh, that idiot," she said, and they all laughed again.

Michael entered the room and one of the servants announced that dinner was ready and seeing the numbers, the formal dining room had been prepared. Michael looked at Jenny and couldn't stop staring. Eric was watching both Michael and Jenny's reaction, all the while pretending to be lighthearted.

Once in the dining room, Jenny looked over to Michael and asked if something was wrong. "We're family, so I feel pretty comfortable asking you what your deal is."

"I'm sorry, Jenny, I know I'm staring," Michael replied. "You just have the most beautiful eyes I've ever seen."

"Well thank you, Michael," she said. "You'll need to get used to them, as I have a feeling, we will be seeing each other often."

Eric watched intently, the smile on his face gone.

Michael looked at her, and Jenny realized she had not explained herself very well."I mean you're family. I see you like my brother, and I expect to see you around here with your mom and dad," Jenny clarified any confusion.

Michael smiled and said, "Oh, yes, of course, Jenny."

She looked over at Eric who was profoundly serious at this point, and she knew why. Jenny had to find some way to reassure him. "How about some dinner music?" she asked. "David, can you show me where I might find a stereo or something to play some music?"

"It's right here, Jenny," David said.

"Can I connect my phone?" she asked.

"Yes, just connect to Bluetooth and you're good to go."

Jenny played the song she and Eric danced to at their first dinner together. "Truly, Madly, Deeply," by Savage Garden. She walked to Eric, licked her lips, looked at her husband, and asked, "Dance with me?"

Eric got up, smiled at her, and held her close. The way they looked at each other, the love between them undeniably strong, everyone in the room knew they were unconditionally bound to one another. Michael looked on, in utter amazement.

Once they finished their dance, Michael said, "Wow, I hope I find that kind of love someday."

Eric smiled and said, "I hope you do too, Michael. I do." While Eric truly wished Michael would find an awesome love, his comment had purely selfish intentions behind it.

"Okay, can we eat now?" Thomas asked.

"Let's eat," Eric responded with a smile.

Dinner was a lot of fun. Many more stories were shared, and Marie added a few of her own about some of the women. They nearly died laughing. Jenny was glad she met Marie. She was easy to talk to and get along with.

As the evening flew by, David happened to glance at his watch and said, "Oh my, it's 1 a.m.! Although it feels like a Saturday night, it's Wednesday, and we have to be back in the office in seven hours. C'mon Marie." He gave her a warm hug and took her hand. "We should go." He looked over at Eric. "This was fun. It's been a while."

Eric looked at him and replied, "It sure has, and maybe it's time we started to live a little. Can't work all the time."

Eric and Jenny walked them to the door and said good night. Heather and Thomas helped the remaining staff clear the dishes. As they were walking back from the entrance, Jenny stopped by the dining room.

"Oh no! No, Heather, we can do the dishes tomorrow, go to bed, it's been a long day. Everybody, just go to bed," Jenny said. "It's late, we'll do this in the morning." Then she walked over to Heather and hugged her like she was her mother. "Thank you for everything," she said. "I love you, Heather. Good night."

Standing at the entrance of the dining room, Eric asked, "Are we done here? Can we go to bed now?"

"You're starting to sound like Thomas." Jenny laughed. "Race you up the stairs!" she said, and she took off like a bullet with Eric in hot pursuit.

15

<hr>

Soon it was Friday morning, the day of the big gala. While they were having breakfast, Eric told Jenny that a few people would be coming over today, sometime around 2 p.m.

"Yes, a hairstylist and make-up artist from what I understand," Jenny said.

Eric sensed that Jenny was upset. "Are you displeased with the arrangement? I thought it would make things a little less stressful for you. You know, not having to worry about hair and makeup."

"Well, Eric, you forgot the manicure and pedicure," she said very sarcastically. "Look, I know you mean well, but these are things I would like to take care of myself. You're used to having things done for you all the time. I'm not, so just the fact that this is happening is a little over the top for me. But this just reinforces that you don't think I can take care of myself or get myself ready for a party. That I need someone to make me look perfect for your evening."

Eric's phone was beeping with incoming text messages, then it started to ring. He turned it off without answering.

"Jenny, honey, that was not my intention at all and if that's how I made you feel, I am truly sorry," Eric replied. "You're right, I should have made the suggestions and left you the phone numbers. Allowed you to decide whether you wanted to call them. I am sorry. It won't happen again." He was still concerned that he had upset his wife.

She could tell he was sincere, but strangely, she felt a little empowered. She had been so caught up in his life that she had allowed him to run hers, and at that moment, it stopped.

Jenny walked over to Eric and said, "From the sound of your phone, something is going on and you should answer it."

"Nothing is more important to me than you are, the world can wait," he replied. "I want to make sure we've cleared the air here and you're not upset with me, Jenny."

"I'm not upset, Eric," Jenny said. "I just don't want you to worry about everything I need, or make arrangements for where I need to go, how I will spend my day, and so on. I can do these things on my own. Yes, I will have to learn how to navigate this house, how to make arrangements, figure out who to contact, who the drivers are, who the house staff is, learn about the Foundation and its programs, which I have been reading about all week by the way. I guess I'm trying to say that I can handle it." Jenny saw a hurt look on his face. She pulled him towards her, put her arms around him, and said, "I am Mrs. Jenny Barrett, after all. I wield a lot of power, and I need to get comfortable with that power."

Eric looked at his wife and recognized that she was absolutely right. "I'm so used to controlling everything that I didn't realize. But, you're right," Eric replied. "And from this moment on, I will be much more sensitive to how I do things and try to be much less controlling of every situation. Would you like me to cancel the stylists, and makeup artists? I can do that if you would like?"

Jenny kissed him and said, "No, you were being very thoughtful, but thank you for asking. Now you should either answer that phone or get to the office. It sounds like they need you."

"Jenny, we should talk further about this," he said. "Maybe I can help you get set up, connected, and perhaps we can discuss getting you a personal secretary. Since you're taking on projects at the Foundation, you will need someone that can field your calls, set up your appointments, type correspondence, and so on. My mother kept an office upstairs, you can decide whether or not you would like to use it. She kept all of her files and information about the Foundation in that office," he explained, trying to be helpful.

"I know, Eric," Jenny replied. "I've been working out of that office all week, learning about the Foundation to be ready for the Gala." She kissed him gently. "You'd better go, it sounds urgent."

"I love you, Jenny, and I'll be back by early afternoon. We should leave here by five."

"I'll be ready."

"What will you be wearing tonight?"

"I've taken care of that already, my love. I think you'll approve," she responded proudly.

"Well done, Mrs. Barrett. I'll see you shortly." As he left the room, he dialed the office number on his cell.

Jenny decided to finish with breakfast, take a shower, and go straight to her office, as she now called it. She had rearranged the furniture and added a few touches to make it her own. She wanted to continue to learn all she could about the projects, her projects, before the stylists came over.

At five o'clock, Eric was waiting patiently for Jenny downstairs. Jenny had finished getting ready and was deciding on the jewellery she would wear tonight. Of all the jewellery she could choose from, Jenny decided to wear the sapphire diamond collection Eric had bought her in Paris and the ring he put on her finger the very first night she came home. *I think he'll like this,* she thought.

Eric called the phone in their bedroom from the one in the library. "Jenny, honey, are you almost ready? We should be leaving soon."

"I was just about to come down but ran back to get your phone call. I'm on my way," she said calmly. Eric walked over to the grand staircase to look for her. When she appeared at the top of the stairs, Eric was speechless. He could not believe his eyes. Jenny was beautiful, but he had never seen her quite like tonight. She was most definitely standing in her power and stunningly beautiful. "Well, what do you think?" she asked.

"I think you look breathtaking, my love. And I also think I'll have to keep you close. There will be plenty of men that will want to steal you for a dance, but I don't think I'll let them," he said as he smiled. "Shall we?" he asked proudly as he met her halfway up the stairs to take her hand. It was then that he noticed the ring and smiled.

"Of course, Mr. Barrett, I would not want it any other way," she said.

Heather brought the mink cape and Eric placed it on Jenny's shoulders before calling the driver.

"James, we'll take the Rolls-Royce Sweptail tonight and we are waiting for you upfront." Eric looked at Jenny. "I'm going to have to hire bodyguards for you. You are stunning, Jenny." He could not stop staring.

They got into the car and drove to the Fairmont Royal York Hotel. As they arrived, they were taken to a hotel suite. From that suite, Eric could monitor the guests as they arrived, so he could prepare for their entrance. David was quite familiar with the routine and met Eric in the suite with Marie. Upon seeing Jenny, David was taken aback. "Jenny! You look ravishing tonight," he said, struck by her beauty.

"Thank you, David, it is my debut tonight and I want everything to be perfect," she said.

"Well, you're off to a great start, Jenny, you look absolutely beautiful," said Marie.

"How about a drink? Anyone for a scotch?" Eric asked.

"I'll have one Eric," David replied.

"Ladies, anything to drink?" asked Eric.

"I'm fine," said Jenny.

"So am I, thank you, Eric," responded Marie.

Jenny was so nervous, she felt like throwing up. She was trying to calm her nerves and didn't want to appear needy, especially after the conversation they had this morning. She thought about various scenarios and how she could respond. She wanted to appear confident, collected, intelligent, not like a disorganized mess, which is exactly how she felt. Eric could sense that Jenny was tense and anxious.

"Are you sure you couldn't use a drink, love?" he asked again. "You look a little anxious or maybe nervous, I'm not sure which."

Jenny looked at him and said, "Are you sure I look okay, Eric?"

"You look magnificent, Jenny, absolutely perfect. Nothing to be worried about. I know this can be a little overwhelming, especially when you don't know anyone in the room except for the three of us here, but I will be right by your side. This is your introduction to a remarkably interesting world, one vastly different from what you're used to. Just trust your gut instincts, they're usually correct. You may not know why, you may not have the background, but what you feel instinctively will be absolutely correct. Let that be your moral and ethical guide to how you respond to the people you will meet tonight. We'll compare notes later when we're alone," he said as he pulled her close and held her tight.

She whispered in his ear, "Thank you, Eric I needed both the pep talk and hug."

At 6:30, someone came to the door. "Mr. Barrett, we are waiting for you now," the man said.

Eric took Jenny's hand, winked at her, and said, "showtime, my love."

They entered the ballroom and walked right onto the stage. Eric took the microphone and began speaking.

"Hello everyone, it is a pleasure and an honor to be here with you tonight. I am delighted to see so many wonderful friends. I'd like to thank you all for your generous contributions and hope you have a wonderful evening. I'm told the entertainment is impeccable and the dinner planned for this evening, exquisite. As you are all aware, the Foundation is very dear to my heart, as it was dear to my mother. She began this foundation almost forty years ago now and since then, it has flourished and helped many children around the world. I have something else that is also very dear to my heart right here. I would like to introduce my wife, Jenny Barrett. Jenny will be taking over the affairs of the Foundation, and therefore many of you will be dealing with her directly. Be careful, she is as shrewd as she is beautiful," he said proudly.

Jenny moved up and took the microphone from Eric, who looked at her with surprise and a smile.

"Good evening, everyone." Her soft, melodic voice was enhanced by the microphone. "I am also very honored to be here with you and my husband this evening. From what I have been able to glean, the Foundation assists children worldwide. I, like my late mother-in-law, have a profound love for children, and while I did not get the opportunity to meet Susan Barrett, I know she was working on several projects that never came to fruition. I am looking forward to realizing those very projects and some, if not all, of her dreams. In her honor, I would like to build them bigger and bolder than she had ever imagined, and your contributions tonight ensure that we can achieve the dreams of so many children that depend on us.

Thank you and have a wonderful evening." She looked at Eric and gave him the microphone.

"For those of you who don't know, my wife has an uncanny ability to leave me speechless. I understand that dinner will be served shortly. Enjoy your evening." With that, they walked off the stage. Eric took Jenny in his arms, kissed her passionately, and said, "You were brilliant, Jenny. I have never been prouder to be your husband than when I stood by your side on that stage just now. You can handle this, and quite successfully! C'mon, it's time to meet and schmooze. Remember, trust your gut instincts and you'll be right."

Their passionate kiss did not go unnoticed by the many cameras angled in their direction. Eric and Jenny were a power couple, holding hands, walking, and talking confidently. Jenny trusted her instincts and was supported by her husband at every turn. People fell in love with Jenny. Her kindness and gentleness were immediately evident in how she handled herself and responded to other people. She was quite refreshing in a room full of sharks. Many commented on her beauty, others offered to meet concerning the Foundation. Some offered to meet in extremely questionable locations. Jenny responded that she was in the process of hiring a personal secretary who would reach out to their respective offices.

Eric realized that Jenny possessed natural skills and abilities she didn't realize she had. She was a very astute judge of character and quickly learned whom she could trust and whom she could count on to work closely with in her new endeavors. Eric saw his Jenny in an entirely new light. She was a force to be reckoned with, powerful in her softness, incredibly force- ful in her gentleness. She had an ability to reap large contributions with her kindness.

Dinner was over and the dance floor was now open. Eric had requested a song to open the floor and dedicated it to Jenny. Savage Garden's *Truly, Madly, Deeply*. As they danced and looked into each other's eyes, it was quite clear there was both an incredible love and an unspoken bond that united them. If any woman was wondering whether they still had a chance with Eric, those hopes were quickly dashed. After that dance, Charlotte left the room and did not return.

It had been an extraordinarily long night and they were both very tired.

Rather than going home, Eric thought that perhaps they should retire in the penthouse.

Once in the car, Jenny asked Eric, "You have a penthouse?"

"*We* have a penthouse, Jenny. And yes, it's in the building where the office is located." Jenny had never been to the office and learned from Eric that the office was on the third floor. "Remember I told you about it. When I work late it's easier to go to the top floor than to drive all the way home. I often spoke to you from there when I called you at night," he said.

"You said it was a condo," she exclaimed.

"Well it is, it's just on the top floor," he said laughing. "And by the way, we own the building too," he added with a smile.

They arrived and took the elevator thirty floors up to the penthouse. Jenny was impressed that the elevator opened right into the suite. "How do you lock the doors?" she asked. "You can't just shut down the elevator."

"I can lock the doors with this button and the elevator will still function, but won't open into the suite," he explained. "There's a switch here right by the elevator doors and another on a keypad attached to the phone in the bedroom," he explained.

"Convenient," she said.

"Have a look," he said as he pointed to the living room area. Jenny noticed that the ceiling in the living room was made of glass. It looked like the solarium at home, and the stars were flickering very brightly tonight.

"Eric, this is beautiful, just like your solarium at home," she said.

"*Our* solarium, Jenny," he replied.

"Can we sleep on the couch under the stars tonight?"

"Actually, the couch opens to a very comfortable bed, so the answer to your question is absolutely."

"Hmm, I don't have anything to wear to bed. Had I known, I would have packed a bag," she said with a smile.

"You won't need anything tonight, love," he whispered into her ear as he unzipped her skirt. Eric turned off the lights and lay with Jenny under the stars, the insatiable passion between the two was ignited; a fire that would burn all night.

16

The next morning was spectacularly sunny. While they finished with breakfast, Eric asked Jenny how she would like to spend the day. It was Saturday and a day off for Eric. Jenny said she would like to go horseback riding. She would love to go back to the farm. Eric thought that would be an excellent idea. They would need some riding clothes, nothing fancy, jeans, a sweater, and boots, and while he had clothes to wear in the bedroom closet, Jenny would need her clothes. He was just about to arrange with Heather to have her clothes brought to the penthouse but stopped.

"Jenny, you'll need clothes to wear. How about I give you Heather's cell number and you can decide what you would like to have sent over for riding," he said.

She smiled. "Thank you for not calling Heather directly. How about we just go shopping for a pair of jeans and a sweater? You know, like everyone else in the world?"

He looked at her very intently and then said, "Come with me, Jenny." They went into the master bedroom where Eric had an array of moni- tors and one exceptionally large television. He turned on the TV and the monitors. The TV was airing the CBC news network, and the monitors displayed CNN, BBC, RAI, Sky News, Euro News, France 24, and several other networks Jenny didn't recognize. On the left side of the TV, several monitors displayed updated information on any topic Eric entered. This morning, he entered the keywords Eric, Barrett, married, Jenny, and pressed enter. Jenny saw her face all over the screens with various captions underneath; primarily indicating that the world's most eligible bachelor was off the market in different languages. As she watched the live news feeds, the world seemed to be commenting on their nuptials and sending well wishes. She was absolutely stunned.

"Wow," she said, "everyone in the world knows who I am."

Eric looked at her with the usual love and gentleness in his eyes. "Honey, that's why we can't shop for jeans like everyone else does. The world just became a lot smaller for you. Where once you were invisible, now you are noticed everywhere you go. Crowds will always be around you, people will recognize you and want to know as much about you as possible. You will have to learn how to deal with that, and my advice is to respond to questions as vaguely as possible, revealing nothing at all about yourself."

Jenny realized the enormity of what he was saying to her, and it both saddened and frightened her. Her life would never be the same again.

She pondered that thought and said, "I think I'll take Heather's cell number now, if you don't mind, to let her know what I'll need to have sent over."

"Smart move, Mrs. Barrett." He gave her his cell phone.

"Just the number will be fine, Eric. I don't want to pry into your personal information."

"Jenny, there is nothing in there that you do not already know. I just thought you might want to scroll through and send yourself any other contacts you think might be useful," he replied.

"Good idea! Hadn't thought of that," she said sheepishly.

He was just about to turn off the media centre when Jenny said, "Please leave it on for a bit. I want to know what people are saying about us."

He looked at her and said, "Well, they're calling us a power couple, with a lot of energy and big plans to change the world. A little exaggerated, but nice."

"No, it's not exaggerated," Jenny said looking at her husband humbly. "We will change the world, my love. We will do great things together."

Eric took her in his arms and kissed her gently. "With you by my side, there is nothing I cannot accomplish." Then he smiled as he looked into her beautiful eyes and said, "*We* cannot accomplish."

While Eric went to get changed, Jenny called Heather and then scrolled through his contacts. At that moment, she realized the incredible opportunity God had given her to help as many vulnerable people as possible.

17

They arrived at the farm and Jenny was overjoyed. It was a place much like their home, where no one could pry into their lives, where they could just be happily married newlyweds in love.

"Are you sure you want to do this today?" Eric asked. "It's really cold outside. It's almost February."

"You mean it might be cold for the horses? I don't want to cause them any discomfort, they are beautiful animals," Jenny replied.

"No, honey," Eric said smiling. "The horses will be fine, I was talking about you! That's what I love about you, that selfless concern for others is always front and center in your mind. In this case, horses," he laughed.

Jenny began to feel dizzy and almost fell into Eric's arms. He caught her and gave her a worried look. "Are you alright?"

"I'm not sure, I just felt lightheaded for a moment," Jenny responded. "I'm sure it's nothing. Let's ride!" she said excitedly.

"No, not until I'm sure you're okay. Maybe you should have something more to eat," he said as he made his way to the kitchen.

"Eric, I don't need any more food," Jenny responded gently. "I'm okay, stop worrying, I'm fine. What will you do if I get a cold, fly me to the hospital?" she said laughing.

"No, I would fly Brian, to the farm," he responded seriously. "No way I would have you in a regular hospital. They're full of germs and diseases."

Jenny just smiled and shook her head. "Let's ride," she said, almost in a whisper as she held Eric close. Eric left instructions with the kitchen for dinner, and they made their way to the stables.

They spent most of the afternoon riding and laughing, just being themselves without anyone around. It felt like the first time he had taken her there when she didn't know who he was. They were just two people enjoying a wonderful afternoon together. As the temperature dipped, they made their way back. They took the horses into the heated barn where they were tended to by the farm staff on hand.

"Thank you," Jenny said to the horse handler. "The horses were well behaved and are probably very cold. Make sure they get some good food and a warm blanket." She gently patted her horse.

"We'll take good care of them, Mrs. Barrett," the horse handler responded with a smile.

As they walked toward the farmhouse, Jenny quickly grabbed Eric's hand to steady herself. He hugged her with a very worried look on his face.

"Lightheaded again?" he asked.

"I don't know what's going on, maybe I'm just more tired than I realize," Jenny said. "It was a terribly busy and stressful day yesterday," she continued. "And we didn't get much sleep last night, I might add."

They made their way into the farmhouse where Jenny sat down on the couch.

"I think you should get some rest, and I'll light a fire to keep you warm so you can sleep comfortably," Eric said as he looked anxiously at his wife. "I'll be right beside you, holding you as you sleep," he said reassuringly.

"How about right here on the couch," she responded. "Like when we were in Blue Mountain, before everything went crazy."

"That sounds perfectly splendid."

"Thanks for being so good to me, Eric," Jenny said as she caressed his face.

"Don't ever thank me for loving you, Jenny. You've filled my life with so much joy, that at times I think my heart will burst." He kissed her gently and made sure she was comfortable on the couch. Then he began building a fire. As he looked over at Jenny, who had already fallen asleep, he began to worry. He decided to call Brian and ask a few questions. *It may just be that Jenny is right and she's just tired,* he thought. *She's not used to the life I live, but a little reassurance from Brian would be comforting.* He dialed Brian's number.

"Hello Eric, is everything okay?" asked Brian.

"Yes, Brian. I'm sorry to bother you. Do you have a few minutes right now?"

"I wouldn't have answered the phone if I didn't, Eric," Brian responded. "What's on your mind?"

"It's Jenny. We decided to come out to the farm to go horseback riding and once we arrived, she was lightheaded and almost fell over. I thought we should wait, but she said she was fine. We rode all afternoon but as we came in, she reached and grabbed my hand to steady herself, once again feeling lightheaded. She seems to think she's just tired from the weekend events, you know the stress and anxiety she was under concerning the gala. Should I be worried, Brian?"

"Eric, to answer that question I will have to ask you a few personal questions. Are you okay with that?"

"Of course. Ask away."

"Has Jenny's appetite increased lately?" Brian asked.

"Now that you mention it, yes, she always seems to be hungry or nibbling on something."

"Okay, is she on birth control?" Brian asked.

"You think my Jenny's pregnant?" Eric smiled from ear to ear.

Brian took a deep breath. "I can't be sure without a proper test, but I can say for sure that if she's not on any kind of birth control, those are symptoms of pregnancy. But, Eric, it could be many other things too, so don't get your hopes up. I know how much you want a family, and I wouldn't want you to be disappointed when that may not be the case."

"Would you be able to conduct this test as soon as possible?"

"Go to the local pharmacy and get a pregnancy test and find out for yourself," he said. "More often than not, they're pretty accurate. The doctor just simply confirms the diagnosis."

"I might just do that then," Eric said, unable to contain his excitement. "Thank you, Brian, and I'm sorry for troubling you with this. I'm just worried about her."

"It's no trouble at all. Keep in mind it may be something else as well, and if that test comes back negative, I will need to see Jenny. Let me know either way. I'll talk to you later," Brian said as he ended the call.

Eric hung up the phone, a little more worried now. What if the test was negative? What could this be? Would he lose the only thing that made his life worth living? He went from casually worried to completely anxious just thinking about it. He laid down beside her and held her close to him. Jenny awoke.

"How do you feel?" Eric asked smiling.

"I feel great, so well rested and warm. How about you?"

"Good. Are you hungry, Jenny?" he asked with a quirky smile on his face.

"I'm starving. Is dinner ready?"

"Yes, I think it is. Let me check with the kitchen." Eric left the room but returned moments later, confirming that dinner was ready.

"How about we eat then because I'm really hungry. Must be this country air," Jenny said.

"Yes, something like that," he said smiling.

Eric carefully watched Jenny as she ate and noticed she ate more than usual.

"Jenny are you finished with dinner?" he asked.

"Yes, I feel full now," she said with a smile of complete contentedness.

"Can I ask you a few questions?"

"Sure, what's up?"

"Jenny, are you on any kind of birth control?"

"No," Jenny responded. "I didn't get a chance to discuss anything with my doctor. Everything happened so fast, but it's on my to-do list. I think I should start taking something as I want to get the projects for the Foundation going and I can't do that with a baby around. The gala inspired me to start working on the projects and I'm excited to get started. I know we talked about having a family, but I want to wait a year or two and work on this. Are you okay with that, Eric?"

"Sure, I'm fine with that, but I think it may be too late," he said with a funny expression on his face. "You see, I called Brian while you were asleep as I was concerned about the light-headedness happening so frequently and Brian asked me if you were on any kind of birth control."

"He thinks I'm pregnant," she responded.

"He said that the constant hunger and dizziness are symptoms of pregnancy, but that he couldn't be sure without a test. Jenny, if you are pregnant and you don't want this baby right now, we can do something about it, but we would have to act soon. Would you mind if I got a test from the pharmacy to find out?"

"Yes, of course, that's a good idea," she said.

Eric arranged to get a test and then took her in his arms. "It's going to be okay sweetheart, don't worry about it."

Jenny looked into his eyes and could see he was worried. She asked him why.

"I'm concerned that if the test comes back negative, we will have to investigate, and it's the fear of the unknown that worries me. I can deal with anything, except uncertainty," he said anxiously.

An hour later, Jenny took the test. It was positive; Jenny was pregnant. She showed Eric the result and he was relieved.

"Okay," he said. "At least I know you're okay. Now, you need to decide what you want to do, Jenny."

"What do you mean?" she replied bewildered.

"Well, before we took the test, you said you wanted to wait to have children so you could work at the Foundation. If that's what you truly want to do, we will need to arrange for an abortion," he said trying not to sound sad as he said it.

"Eric Michael Barrett!" Jenny was shouting at him. "I can't believe those words came out of your mouth. Do you really think I would kill a child that was made with so much love? This baby was conceived the first night you took me home, the first night I experienced how much you loved me. How can you say that?"

Eric reached for her, took her in his arms, and with tears in his eyes said, "Oh, Jenny, you have no idea how glad I am to hear you say that. I've wanted a family for so long but was prepared to wait. I wanted you to want it too."

"I can be a mother and work at the foundation," she said to him. "Women do it every day without the resources I have available to me. I know this is important to you, and it's what I want too. I just didn't think it would happen so quickly. Most couples try for at least a few months before getting pregnant. I thought I'd have a little more time to take the proper precautions."

"So, you don't regret it?"

"No Eric, I don't!" she responded. "Our love is so strong we created life," she whispered as she kissed him.

Eric was so happy he didn't know what to do with himself. He wanted to tell the world but thought he should wait to confirm the results with Brian. In the meantime, he pampered his Jenny hand and foot. They spent the day on the farm and went home Sunday night.

As soon as she got home, Jenny went to her office. She worked without realizing the late hour. Eric walked into the office. "I like what you've done with this office, it looks great," he said smiling. "But do you realize it's 1 a.m. and you should be in bed by now," he added very seriously.

"I didn't realize it was so late, Eric," she responded. "I just got so into what I'm doing and, well, I realize now that I don't have time to waste. I have a lot to accomplish before the baby arrives."

"Let's go, Mommy, there's a little boy or girl in there that just wants to sleep," he said as he put his hand on her belly and smiled.

"You're right, my love. Let's go to bed," Jenny said as she took her husband's hand.

The next morning, as they shared breakfast, Eric said, "Jenny, I have arranged only one thing for you today and I hope you don't get upset with me. Brian will come by to get a blood sample from you. Just to confirm the pregnancy and test for anything else, okay? I'm just looking out for you honey, looking out for both of you."

Jenny smiled at him and said it was fine. She kissed her husband as he left for the office. "I'll be home as soon as possible," he said as he walked out the door at six o'clock. By 6:30, Brian was at the door.

"I know it's a little early," Brian said to Heather, "but I thought I would drop by on my way to the hospital." Heather looked at Brian with utter confusion. Seeing her reaction, Brian realized she didn't know. "I just need to see Jenny for a few minutes," he said.

"Is there something wrong with Mrs. Barrett?" Heather asked concerned.

"No, I just need to see her about one of her projects," Brian said, wishing Eric had warned him that no one had been told. Heather was relieved and let Jenny know that Brian was here. She ushered him into the library. Jenny arrived, hugged him, and apologized for her husband, who had most likely applied pressure on Brian to come as quickly as possible.

"Eric is just like that, Jenny. He just needs to be sure before he announces this to the world, and make no mistake, he will in grand fashion, as he does anything that he cares about." He took a blood sample and said he would call her as soon as he had the results.

"Brian, just call Eric," Jenny responded. "He's on pins and needles right now and I know that you're a busy man. Eric will let me know, of that I'm certain." She walked him to the door then headed up to her office.

At around 11 a.m., Jenny's phone rang.

"Hello, Eric," she said smiling, knowing Eric had some good news to share.

"Hello, Mommy, it's confirmed," Eric said. "We're having a baby and you'll be relieved to know that there were no other anomalies in the blood test. Honey, our baby is four weeks old. In eight more months, I'll be able to hold him or her in my arms and I can't wait. Please let Heather and Thomas know. I'll be making an announcement and I want them to know before they hear it from the media. Perhaps you should call your parents as well."

"I will. I love you," she said.

Jenny hung up the phone and went to look for Heather. On her way down the stairs, she began feeling sick. She raced to the kitchen and made it to the sink just in time to throw up. Heather and Thomas just stood there.

Jenny laughed and said, "Well, that was quite an entrance. Good morning to you both. I just wanted to tell you before you heard it from the media. I'm—"

Heather jumped up and hugged her. "You're pregnant Jenny!"

"Yes, Heather. We will have a little Barrett running around soon," Jenny said smiling.

"Eric must be beside himself," Heather said. "Oh, how proud his father would have been! He often talked about how much he looked forward to the day he'd become a grandfather."

Jenny looked at Heather, who had tears in her eyes, and said, "Well, we should tell them appropriately. Maybe take a trip to the family cemetery.

In the meantime, I should call my mother."

"Not so fast," said Thomas. "Let me hold you. Well done! Since you've arrived, the house has been full of happiness and laughter. It feels like home again." Thomas hugged Jenny.

"Thank you, Thomas," Jenny said as she kissed him on the cheek.

Jenny's mother was thrilled. "Oh honey, I'm so happy for you. Whatever you need sweetheart, I'll be there. I know Eric will take care of everything, but sometimes, you might just want some motherly support," she said.

"Mom, we need to have dinner here soon. It's just been so crazy, and things are happening so quickly, I barely have time to catch my breath before something else happens," Jenny replied.

"Jenny, just take care of yourself now. Ramadan is around the corner and although you're not fasting, we can get together for Iftar at our house. I'll pray to God to look after you and the baby," said Jenny's mother. "Jenny, please thank Eric again for the very generous gifts. We still can't believe he did all those wonderful things for us." As Jenny inquired what these gifts were, she was both impressed and appreciative of the incredible husband God had blessed her with.

"Thank you, Mom. I love you. Give Dad a kiss for me, and we'll talk soon." Jenny hung up the phone and realized just how blessed she was to be surrounded by so many wonderful people.

Eric arrived home earlier than expected and Jenny asked if they could talk for a few minutes.

"Eric," Jenny said, "I think we should go to the family cemetery and visit with your parents. We should tell them about the baby."

Eric smiled and said, "I already did. I passed by on my way home. I haven't been able to concentrate on anything at all today. I'm so excited! I asked my parents to look after you and our baby from above."

"Why did you go alone? I wanted to be there with you?"

Eric took a deep breath. "Because I haven't been there in four years. I talk to my father while standing in front of the portrait in the living room because from there it's not so finite. I feel like they're still with me. I have not been able to go to the gravesite since they've passed on; the thought was just too painful for me. Well, today, I had some joyful news to share with them and that made my first visit bearable. I saw them and initially, it was quite an emotional moment, but I collected myself and shared the news with them. It was strange, I felt an uncanny peace as if I were being surrounded by love. It's the first time I've felt their presence since they passed. I stood there and was not alone. Did you tell your folks?"

"Yes, they're happy for us. I told mom that we should have them over soon, we've just been so busy. Mom told me that you gave them some very nice gifts. You paid my parent's mortgage, put two hundred thousand dollars into my brother's account to pay for his education debt and his Ph.D., and also gave my other brother keys to a new condo in downtown Toronto and had him hired as a manager at BMO. Why did you do that?" Jenny asked.

"They're my family too, Jenny, and I hope I was able to show them I love them by making at least one or two dreams come true," Eric responded. "I explained to them that I have been very blessed in my life and wanted to help them in whatever way I could without making them feel indebted to me in any way. What I did for them may feel like a lot, but it's not for me."

"I am very grateful," Jenny replied. "You have changed their lives in ways they only dreamed of before you came along. I didn't expect this at all. You just caught me by surprise. How did you get all their personal information? Their bank accounts, mortgage information?"

"You forget who your husband is sometimes. I have access to everything, legal and illegal. Are you not happy with my decisions? I thought you would be pleased."

"I was just taken by surprise," Jenny said. "I explained to my mother that I had no idea you had done any of those things. She mentioned that having you over at the house was nice and that you were so loving and caring towards them. She told me that they refused the wonderful gifts because they just couldn't accept something so lavish and that you explained to them that you loved them very much and all you wanted to do was help make their lives a little easier. They were very grateful, as am I." Jenny took her husband in her arms. "Let me show you just how grateful I am for that, Mr. Barrett," Jenny said with a naughty smile.

Eric smiled and led the way.

18

Breakfast was brought in at 6 a.m. as it was every morning, but Eric was not dressed to go to work. He was still in bed and the phone was not ringing nonstop.

"Eric, do you not feel well this morning?" asked Jenny.

"I feel fine, Jenny. Why do you ask?"

"Well, normally you're out of the shower and we're having breakfast at this time. You're still in bed"

"I took a few days off to spend with you. I was thinking we didn't have much of a honeymoon, so I thought we could fly to, well, anywhere you want to go. We have homes in most places in Europe, and luxury hotels in key places worldwide. I thought you could just enjoy yourself a bit. Things have been stressful for you, and I notice you're a bit tired. A nice holiday might be just what you need right now," Eric responded in a particularly good mood.

"That's sweet, but it's not a good time to be taking a jet anywhere," Jenny responded. "You're right, I do feel tired but that's because I'm in the first trimester of my pregnancy and it's perfectly normal to feel tired. I wouldn't want to jeopardize the pregnancy now. I'm not sure a trip is appropriate. Maybe after the baby is born, we could take a trip then."

"Okay. Is there something troubling you, Jenny?" Eric asked as he sat up in bed. "I'm not sure if it's the pregnancy or something else."

"Eric, I don't know if I can do this. The only place I feel safe is at home.

It's become a beautiful prison. I can't go out because there are always people prying and taking photos. I can't just go out! I have to make sure I look perfect, behave perfectly, answer appropriately. Eric, I am not perfect and the stress of having to live like this is killing me. How will my baby survive in this environment? It's so toxic!" she said with tears streaming down her face.

"Jenny, come here," Eric said gently as he took her in his arms. "Listen, you don't have to try so hard to be perfect. Just be yourself and you will be perfect. That's why I was so drawn to you because you're so honest, generous, kind. Don't pretend to be something you're not. I don't want you to change anything about yourself, and neither should you. The way you look and how you respond are perfect because they are you, and I love you. Don't feel pressured to be any other way. Yes, we have a certain decorum when we attend engagements, but any other time, feel free to be yourself. If you want to go out wearing jeans and a sweater, do so. It's fine and if people take pictures, they will only do so to show the world just how beautiful you are no matter what you wear. You will never say anything inappropriate because you speak from your heart, truthfully and honestly. Don't put any pressure on yourself to be anything else, but yourself. I fell in love with you because you were exactly what I was looking for and I didn't find you amongst all these people that you now see and frequent often. Don't you see Jenny, you are perfect just the way you are."

"But will they accept me the way I am?" she asked.

"They're already in love with you because of the way you are," Eric responded. "You have no idea how many compliments I get daily about my wife. How wonderful she is, how generous and beautiful she is, how intelligent she is, how hardworking she is, how dedicated to helping the vulnerable she is. Oh, Jenny, I could go on all day."

Jenny straightened herself in bed. "They say that about me?"

"You don't realize the skills and power you have, my love, but suffice it to say I turn down a lot of engagements on your behalf. People wanting you at their luncheons, presentations, university boards, groups, functions, and so much more. I turn them down not because you're not able, but because I think you have a lot on your plate already and you've been so tired lately. Yes, Jenny, they love you."

Jenny looked at her husband with kindness in her eyes. "Eric, would you kindly do me a favour? Would you let me decide to turn them down? I know you mean well, but maybe I should be meeting these people and going to these functions and sitting on these boards. I want to be in control of these aspects of my life. Maybe I wouldn't feel like I do if I were more involved in my own life." She was trying not to hurt his feelings as she knew he meant well.

"Fair enough. I know we've talked about this before. I'm too controlling and find it very difficult to stop, especially when it comes to you. But you do understand, Jenny, it's because I love you so much and want to protect you as best as I can. However, you're right, I'll just transfer the calls to your secretary, but promise me one thing. That you will never change who you are. You are an incredible force just the way you are. People are already trying to imitate your style and mannerisms, that's how powerful you are, Jenny."

Jenny smiled. "Believe it or not, it kind of makes me feel better to know that people like me and accept me for who I am. I don't feel like such a loser. I'm glad you stayed home today, and we could just talk."

"Do we have to just talk? Can we spend the day in bed, just loving each other? That's my favourite part of being in this room. I get to hold you and love you and share everything in my heart with you. I'm just a little worried about you. I want you to get more rest, honey, please."

"Well, it sounds like I won't be getting much rest today, but I'm not complaining either," she said with a naughty smile on her face.

19

Feeling much more empowered, Jenny spent the next day working in her office. She arranged to have a private secretary and began setting up appointments to speak with key people at the Foundation. She had reviewed several projects already in the works and had identified creative ways to strengthen what they were doing. The project Jenny was interested in starting would require a lot of her time and energy.

Jenny wanted to build a facility that would house pregnant teenage girls who had no support or had been disowned by their families because of the pregnancy. The goal was to provide the girls with proper nutrition, exercise, socialization, recreation, and a bedroom, so they could bring their children into the world without fear. The new centre would be housed with educational facilities, where the girls would train for meaningful jobs while waiting to give birth. Social workers would be present to assist with housing and other needs. In essence, everything they would need to be single mothers with a well-paying job. The girls also had the option to give the babies up for adoption if they didn't feel they could look after them. The centre would have several families that would have been screened and thoroughly investigated to ensure the children would be placed in loving homes. However, unlike other agencies, the birth mother and adoptive mother would co-parent. The baby would know that they were so loved that their two mothers worked together to provide a home full of a rich culture of love, where they worked together for the benefit of the child they shared. In many cases, this would materialize in visitation rights for the birth mother to spend time with her baby and the adoptive mother. The adage "it takes a village to raise a child" in practical application. Jenny knew this was just the beginning. She had to meet with several people to collect the information she needed and had to pitch her idea to the board of directors.

Eric came home and went straight upstairs where he knew she was working.

"Jenny, have you taken a break at all today?" he asked. "I know how important your work is to you, but you need to rest as well."

Jenny jumped out of her seat and put her arms around him. "Eric, I'm so excited about this project! I really must get at least the 'bones' of it underway before I have the baby," she said. "I cannot waste any time right now."

Eric looked at his wife lovingly. "Jenny, I can certainly appreciate how excited you are about this project but working ten- to twelve-hour days isn't healthy for you or our baby. Can we at least agree to a regular nine to five day? Preferably more like ten to two." He suddenly had a realization and looked at Jenny very intently. "This is the real reason you didn't want to travel, isn't it? Okay, I understand," he said a little annoyed, "but you need to take care of the both of you right now."

"Okay," she said realizing that he was somewhat angry. "I will reduce the hours as I do feel tired. I have several meetings set up for next week, which means spending time at the Foundation."

Eric gave Jenny a worried look. "Alright. We'll stay at the penthouse next week. You'll be closer to work and so will I. This will give you the option of coming home and resting between meetings. I think that's a fair compromise, don't you?"

"Sounds perfect," Jenny said with a gentle smile. "My doting husband always comes up with a plan to keep me close. I love that about you, Eric."

"Well," Eric replied, "my job has just gotten harder as there are two of you to think about now." He took her in his arms. "Why don't you take a break and tell me all about this project you're working on over a nice cup of decaf tea. We can sit in the solarium, and you can put your feet up and I'll give you an unforgettable foot massage." He took her hand and led her down the stairs. On their way, Eric asked Heather to prepare a nice cup of tea and bring his wife a healthy snack.

Once seated comfortably in the solarium, Eric said, "Now, how about you tell me about this project of yours."

As Jenny began to talk about her ideas, Eric was astounded by her constant desire to improve the lives of people she had never met. He was so fascinated with her generosity and kindness. Eric made a lot of money by being the ruthless businessman he was, and in his world, there was no place for kindness and generosity. Eric secured multimillion-dollar deals, was responsible for several corporate takeovers, and flourished in a world of sharks. Jenny was his redemption from that world, and he loved her more than life itself. He was intrigued by her ideas and said that if for whatever reason, the board did not agree with her plan, he would fund her entire project. He would build the centre to her specifications and encourage corporate sponsors to donate to ensure the centre would have more than enough money to keep going. Either way, he would get it built and supported. He asked that she keep him in the loop as he could bend a few arms if necessary. Jenny hugged him and thanked him.

He looked into her eyes and said, "Jenny, I'll give you anything you want, but please make sure you take care of yourself and our baby. Without the two of you, I am nothing."

"Of course, my love. I would never put the life of my child in any danger, you know that. How about we start by having dinner, we're famished right now," Jenny said, playfully pointing to her growing belly.

20

Eric's birthday, April 10th, was fast approaching and Jenny wanted to make it special, meaningful. She had been trying to figure out what she could get a man who had everything. She was almost four months pregnant and had an appointment to see Brian at the hospital that day. It was just a regular, routine visit. As Eric was leaving the office to join Jenny at the hospital, he was stopped by David.

"Where are you going, Eric?" David asked. "We have a crucial meeting in half an hour." David looked at him with astonishment.

"Yes, that's today," Eric said. "David, you and Michael can handle this right? I'm heading to the hospital to meet Jenny for an appointment. I may be about an hour or so."

"Eric, I'm afraid that's not possible," replied David. "Our client specifically asked for you to be there otherwise this meeting is canceled and the deal lost."

"Fuck! Alright," he said, feeling both angry and disappointed. "I'll call Jenny, let her know I won't be attending and then we'll meet in my office to review details and ensure we've covered all the particulars before they arrive."

Eric called Jenny and explained his dilemma. He apologized for not being able to be there but said he didn't have a choice. He would try to cut the meeting short but wasn't banking on that happening. Jenny told him not to worry.

"It's just a routine checkup. You won't miss anything," Jenny said, trying to calm him down as she sensed his anger. "It's not like you'll miss seeing the baby in an ultrasound." Eric was placated and met with David. He would follow up with Brian as soon as possible.

Jenny met Brian in his private office, a small clinic that he kept within walking distance from the hospital. Brian was a little concerned as Jenny had just completed her first trimester and was somewhat larger than she should be.

"Brian, is something wrong with our baby?" Jenny asked with a very worried look on her face.

"Let's not jump to conclusions, Jenny," Brian responded. "I have a few suspicions but need to do an ultrasound to be sure. Since you're here now, we can do that. I have the facilities here in the clinic."

The colour drained from Jenny's face. "Eric will be heartbroken," she said. "He wanted to come but had an important meeting and I assured him it was a routine visit. I specifically told him not to worry because it's not like he would miss seeing the baby in an ultrasound." She looked at Brian anxiously.

"We can wait until you can arrange it with Eric if you want," Brian responded, trying to relax his now very anxious patient.

"No," Jenny replied. "I won't have any peace unless I know the baby is okay. Is it dangerous to have two ultrasounds?" she asked.

"No, we can do a second one, but I recommend we wait a month or so in between," he said. "The baby will be about five months and will be visible for Eric to see him or her." Brian smiled reassuringly.

"Okay, Brian, let's do this one today and keep it just between us. I don't want Eric to feel bad about it," Jenny said, looking at Brian apprehensively. As Brian started the scan, he had a silly smirk on his face. His suspicions had been confirmed.

"Jenny," Brian said, "you're having twins."

Jenny was ecstatic. "Oh Brian, Eric will be so happy. Can you tell if they are boys? You see, my grandmother had twin boys."

"Fortunately for you, they are positioned in such a way that we can see pretty clearly, and yes, they're boys," he responded.

"Brian, would you kindly provide me with a printout of our boys?" she asked.

"I can do one better; I can give you a CD so you can show Eric. He can see his boys as if he had been here today with you. I'm sure he'll be over the moon when he finds out," Brian said, feeling excited and happy for Eric.

Jenny had a brilliant thought. "Brian," she said, "can I have both please, and would you not say anything about this to Eric? Just for a few weeks. I've been trying to figure out what to get him for his birthday and I think this is the best gift I can give a guy who has everything."

Brian became profoundly serious as he pondered her request. "I will do my best, but I won't lie to Eric. He's like my son and I won't break that trust."

"No," Jenny replied, "I don't expect you to, maybe just reassure him that the visit went well and was unremarkable, is that okay? You and I both know he will call you."

"I will do my best not to spill the beans, Jenny, but it's not going to be easy to fool a shark," he replied.

"Thank you, Brian." Jenny gave him a warm hug and left the office. She took the CD and the ultrasound photo of her boys and called James to pick her up to take her home. She left a message with Eric that she would see him at home for dinner.

Eric's meeting ended at eight o'clock. He was exhausted. David poured a round of scotch to celebrate. It had been a grueling meeting, but Eric always came up on top. He was both shrewd and sharp, skills his father had honed and began teaching him before he had even entered law school. He had worked alongside his father for several years, while in law school and afterward. Eric had absorbed those lessons like a sponge, and in meetings like this one, those skills were quite evident.

"You were brilliant tonight, Eric," David said. "I don't know if it was the anger of not being able to be with Jenny today, but you were sharp!" he continued. "Do you realize you secured a four hundred million-dollar deal tonight? I have to be honest with you, I didn't think we would get that much out of this deal. I was convinced we could get a couple hundred, but four hundred!" David was in disbelief.

"I'm exhausted," Eric replied. "How about we go home, it's been a long day." As Michael and David said good night and left the office, Eric checked his messages. He heard Jenny say she would meet him at home for dinner. He was weary and just wanted to drop. He called Jenny. "Hello, my sexy husband. Where are you? I'm in the mood for some passionate love tonight," she said playfully.

Eric laughed. "I just finished the meeting and feel worn out. It was one of the most grueling meetings I have had to date. I did, however, secure four hundred million dollars tonight," he said proudly.

"Wow, Eric," Jenny responded. "That's cause to celebrate, maybe not tonight though, you do sound very tired. Why don't you go to the penthouse, have something to eat, take a shower, put on your PJs, and by that time, I'll be there."

"I don't wear PJs," he laughed.

"I know. I'm on my way."

Eric locked up, went upstairs, and picked at the dinner that had been carefully planned for him. He sat down for fifteen minutes, just enjoying the peace and drinking his scotch. He picked up his tired body and jumped in the shower. By the time he finished and walked out of the bathroom, Jenny was waiting for him in bed, smiling.

"Aren't you a sight for sore eyes?" he said as he whipped off his towel and climbed into bed. He kissed her and said, "You know, it's getting harder and harder to hold you close to me. You're really growing fast."

"Must be those powerful Barrett genes," she said laughing. He rubbed her belly and asked about her visit with Brian.

"It was good," she said. "Just the usual, everything is developing as it should. He said I should take a little more time to rest."

"For once, Brian and I agree on something," he responded laughing.

"Eric, why don't you just hold me and get some sleep," she said.

"Why did you come over here, Jenny? I would have come home."

"Because you sounded really tired on the phone," she replied, "and the most sensible thing to do was to stay at the penthouse for the night, but I wasn't going to sleep without your arms around me."

He held her close and said, "I love you, Jenny." Then he passed out from exhaustion.

The next morning, Eric was in the office by 8 a.m., well-rested and quite pleased with himself. He had left Jenny asleep and had left Maria strict instructions to ensure Jenny had a good breakfast. He left a note on his pillow.

Please call me when you're awake. I love you.
-Eric.

"First order of business, call Brian," Eric said to himself as he dialed Brian's number.

"Hello Eric," answered Brian.

"Good morning, Brian. Anything I should know or do at this stage of the pregnancy?" he asked.

"I have nothing more to add to what Jenny already told you. Everything is fine and progressing well. Just continue as you have been, things look good," Brian answered, trying to cut the conversation short before Eric started asking more questions.

"When can we do a sonogram" Eric asked. "I'd like to see my son or daughter, maybe find out what we're having so we can plan for him or her," he said.

Brian hated to be put in this predicament. "I mentioned to Jenny that we should plan to have one done in the next little while," Brian answered vaguely.

"From what I read we should be having one quite soon. Why are you pushing it back?"

Brian was about to make up medical information for the first time in his life. "Well, if you want to know the sex of the baby it's best to wait the two months. Why don't you discuss it with Jenny and let me know? I need to go now." Brian hung up the phone before Eric had a chance to say anything.

Eric wasn't sure about what he had just heard, but he sensed that Brian wasn't worried about Jenny and that put him at ease, for now.

21

April 10th had arrived. Jenny had arranged for a beautiful dinner for the two of them in the solarium. The room was decked out with candles everywhere. It was a magical sight. The candles, the flowering plants in the room, stars above, and a small table, just for the two of them.

Eric came home that day and screamed, "Where is my wife? Jenny, I'm home!"

Jenny walked out to the grand staircase to meet him. She was beautifully dressed; her hair was up with curls loosely coming down around her face.

Eric looked at her and said, "Wow! Are we going someplace I don't know about?"

Jenny smiled and said yes, we are, then took his hand and led him to the solarium. Eric could not believe his eyes. He smiled at the candles and soft lighting. In the centre of the room, white sheers cascaded from the ceiling and draped a small table.

"Do you like it?" she asked.

"It looks magical, Jenny. What's the occasion?" he asked with a smirk on his face.

"Why don't we sit down, dinner is ready," she said excitedly. She had made sure three of his favourite dishes had been cooked to perfection.

"I would share a glass of wine with you, but you know I can't," she said pointing to her belly. "Don't want them drunk before they come out." She was dying to tell him the news and could barely wait for him to finish eating.

"Are you done with the meal?" she asked.

"Very much, I'm stuffed. Look, my belly almost looks like yours," he laughed.

"I have a gift for you, Eric," she said as she presented him with a small box.

Eric looked at her, laughed, and said, "With all the money we have, you bought me a cd?"

"Just open it," she said, rolling her eyes and smiling.

The smile left his face when he saw the picture of the ultrasound. "What's this, Jenny? I spoke to Brian, and he told me we had to wait a few more months at least. Why did you do this without me?" he asked angrily.

"First of all, it was the day you had your big meeting and—"

He interrupted her. "That was two weeks ago! Why didn't you tell me?"

"If you would give me a chance, I'm trying to explain," she said softly. "That day, Brian was concerned because I seemed to be quite large for being just over three months along."

"Is there something wrong with the baby, Jenny?" he asked as his heart beat increased.

"That's why I did it. To make sure everything was okay. I didn't tell you because I thought I would surprise you with the news. Brian is the only one that knows, and I swore him to secrecy for two weeks. He didn't want to at first and then said that if you pushed for answers, he would not lie to you. I agreed. Look carefully at the ultrasound, Eric," she said. "See here?"

"Jenny, are we having twins?" Eric asked as he looked at the photo in amazement.

She nodded. "Twin boys, my love. That's your birthday gift. There's a CD underneath that we can watch together. You can see them move and hear their heartbeats." As she spoke, tears of joy ran down Eric's face.

"My heart is so full, Jenny, I don't know how to thank you," he said. "The joy I feel right now is immeasurable. You have brought so much happiness to my life. All the money in the world could not have bought what you've given to me in four months of marriage; the happiest days of my life. How can I ever thank you! What can I give to you that would have you experience the happiness I feel at this moment?"

Jenny put her arms around him and whispered softly as she kissed him, "A little girl."

He held her tight and said, "After we have the boys, I'll do my best to make that dream come true. We may have to try a few times until we get it right." As he held her close, Heather came in, wondering if she could have the table cleared. Eric looked up at her with tears still in his eyes and said, "Heather, have the candles put out and the table cleared. You and Thomas, meet us in the TV room."

"Of course, is everything okay? Jenny?" Heather asked concerned.

"Meet us in the TV room. Eric has something he would like to show you," she replied.

Eric took Jenny's hand and walked toward the room. He placed the CD in the player and waited for Heather and Thomas. Once they arrived, he hit play.

"I'd like you to meet my boys," he said, tears streaming down his face. "Heather, I can't describe to you in words how happy I am right this minute."

Heather hugged him warmly. "Twins!" she exclaimed.

They could hear tiny heartbeats and saw the boys moving around.

"There's so much to do, Jenny," Eric said. "We have to get two of every-thing, come up with names, and I'd like to hire a personal trainer for you. I've been reading that it's healthy for the baby, babies, and mother to have an exercise program."

"I'd love that. Now is the time that the weight gain happens, and I'd like to put on only baby weight," she replied.

He looked at her anxiously. "Please don't worry about that now. Just take care of yourself and the boys. The upcoming months will be very trying for you," he responded, looking concerned.

"Eric, I'm not made of glass. I'm working on my project as you know, and I will continue to get as much done as possible," Jenny replied.

"Okay, Jenny," he said. "But all meetings happen here. Ask your secre-tary to arrange meetings at the house. I don't want you driving all over the city, it's dangerous."

"Alright," she said reassuringly. "I can do that."

Heather thought it best to leave the two of them to enjoy their blessings. She took Thomas's hand and said, "Well, we'll be off to bed. Good night."

Eric gave them both a warm hug. "You both have been my surrogate parents when my parents were taken from me. You've been with me since I was ten years old, and I'm so glad I could share this moment with you. Good night."

Eric pressed play another four times before they went to bed. Once upstairs, he picked up his cell phone and called Brian.

"Eric, this had better be good because it's 2 a.m.," Brian said.

"I'm having twin boys!" Eric responded.

"Yes, you are," Brian said, "and I'm glad I don't have to keep that secret anymore. I hated not telling you, but Jenny wanted to give you a special birthday gift."

"Thank you, Brian," Eric said. "This was one of the best days of my life. My wife keeps giving me so much joy. Thanks for not spoiling it for her."

"Good night, Eric, I'm happy for you both."

But Eric couldn't sleep. He rubbed Jenny's belly and talked to his boys until dawn when he finally dozed off.

The following morning, Eric called David and told him he would not be in. David was shocked. Eric did not take days off unless he was dead or dying. He asked him if everything was okay, to which Eric replied he had never been better. He told David about his birthday present and how incredibly thankful he felt for being given such blessings. He wanted everyone to know and started with David. His intention for the day was to inform the major news networks, he owned, and have the announce- ment go viral. Normally, he would shelter himself, friends, and those he considered family from any intrusion into their private lives. Not today! He wanted to shout it from every mountain top, so loud his parents would hear. He was the proud father of twin boys and in approximately five months, they would be introduced to the world. In a matter of two minutes, the world was talking about Eric Barrett's announcement. He was inundated with congratulatory phone calls and text messages.

Once he had responded to most of them, Eric poured himself a scotch and walked over to the living room. He looked at the portrait of his parents and asked them to look after his boys, their grandchildren, as he felt in his heart they had looked after Jenny.

"Well, Christopher," Eric said as he looked at the portrait of his parents, "it's the beginning of an incredible era for the Barrett family, and while I wish with all my heart that you were both here, I know you'll be there in spirit when my boys are born. I love you both and miss you very much, more so on days like these." As he turned to leave the room, he saw Jenny standing in the doorway. She looked at him intently, walked over, and put her arms around her husband.

"So, you've let a few people know about our boys," she said sarcastically. "Are you sure you didn't miss anyone?"

"Pretty darn sure I covered everyone," he said with a smirk on his face. "Jenny these next five months will feel like an eternity. I can't wait to see them, hold them, love them."

"Yeah, feed them, change their stinky diapers, have them throw up all over you," she said laughing.

"I can't wait for all of it, Jenny. This house will be transformed in the way my parents had always dreamed of. Full of happy children, running around," he said.

"Mmmhmm, and exhausted parents running in behind." She smiled at him.

Not surprisingly, in the next few months, cards and gifts for the boys arrived steadily to Eric's office, while closer personal friends had them sent to the house. Jenny didn't know what to do with the many gifts that arrived daily from all over the world. She decided to put many of them in storage, which is where Eric also sent the ones that were arriving in the office. He instructed his secretary to ensure a thank you message was sent in return. Needless to say, more than a few storage units had become necessary. Jenny thought that once her centre opened, the gifts would be useful there.

22

One afternoon, a visitor showed up to the house quite unannounced. Jenny could hear Thomas's loud voice trying to get rid of a very insistent person at the door. The voice was that of a woman. Jenny walked towards the door and asked Thomas what was going on. It was there that she saw Charlotte.

"It's fine, Thomas," Jenny said in her soft, melodic tone. "Would you like to join me in the library, Charlotte?"

Charlotte followed Jenny into the library and stated that she was not staying long. She explained to Jenny that this was far from over. Jenny could play pretty little wifey and provide Eric with heirs, but sooner or later, that wouldn't be enough for Eric. She knew him better than he knew himself. She told Jenny that she didn't have the stuff or the know-how to keep a man like Eric.

"I just came to warn you," Charlotte continued. "I will have him back in my arms, especially when you don't look very appealing after childbirth. And where do you think he will go? I'll be there to remind him of what he's missing, and I can assure you, he won't be coming back." She turned to leave, but looked back at Jenny and said, "Good day, Jenny, is it?"

"Mrs. Eric Michael Barrett to you," Jenny responded coldly. Charlotte left and Thomas was quite happy to slam the door after her.

Heather rushed into the room after Charlotte left. "How did that bitch get past security and to the front door?" she asked Thomas.

"She must have had an old code to open the gates. I'm going to change that right now," Thomas said as he left to change the code.

"Heather, I'm not feeling well right now. I'm in a lot of pain. Please call Brian," Jenny said.

Heather made the call and passed the phone to Jenny. Brian asked Jenny what she was feeling and asked if there was any spotting. Jenny informed him that she didn't think there was any spotting, but that she was in a lot of pain. Brian asked that she pass the phone to Heather as he had strict instructions right now. Jenny passed the phone to Heather and held her belly with both hands. She was crying, hoping that her boys would be okay.

"Heather, I think Jenny might be in early labour," Brian said. "I'm concerned, it's far too soon. The twins aren't due for a few months. We must take the proper precautions right now. Please get the helicopter ready and have her transported immediately to the hospital and let Eric know. He will freak out on all of us if he's not informed. I'll be waiting for her here. Hurry, Heather, it's important she get here as soon as possible."

Heather did exactly as she was told. She explained the situation to Jenny and helped her get to a limousine parked outside the front door. James would drive them to the helipad. As Thomas contacted the pilot and readied the helicopter, Heather reported to Eric that Charlotte had come by the house and while she had not overheard their conversation, Jenny was visibly upset and went into labour shortly after Charlotte left. Eric was furious and asked how she got there, to which Heather explained that Thomas thought Charlotte must have had an old gate code.

Eric responded angrily. "I'll meet you at the hospital. Where are you now?"

"We're almost at the helipad," Heather replied. "James is driving as quickly as possible," she added with a note of concern in her voice.

"Keep her comfortable, Heather," Eric said. "Can I speak to Jenny? Can she talk?"

"Hello, Eric. I'm in a lot of pain, and I'm so worried about the boys," she said crying hysterically.

"Jenny," Eric replied in the calmest tone he could muster, "the boys are Barretts and they're tough. Don't you worry. I need you to stay calm, breathe, it will all be okay. I'm on my way to the hospital and I'll meet you there."

Jenny replied with a weak, "I love you, Eric," before Heather took the phone back.

"Eric, we need to board the helicopter, see you at the hospital." Heather hung up the phone.

Eric was livid. He called Charlotte, who conveniently did not pick up the phone. He rushed into David's office, told him what happened and that he was going directly to the hospital. He stared at David with a look in his eyes that David knew all too well. It was the same look Eric had when he was going in for the kill.

"I want you to use every means we have at our disposal to make sure that bitch is destitute: no home, no career, no money, and no means of acquiring any. I want her to crawl back to me. I'm going to take care of her once and for all," Eric said to David.

"I'm on it, Eric. Don't worry about this, get to the hospital right now," David responded.

Brian had directed Eric to go to the birthing unit once he arrived. He began walking through every room screaming Jenny and Brian's names loudly. At one point, security was called, and as they reached to apprehend him, Eric yelled at the guard, "Touch me and I will destroy you. Jenny!"

Hearing the commotion, Brian ran down the hall and asked security to let him go.

"This way, Eric," he said, and took him into the operating room, where Jenny lay on a stretcher. Eric reached for her and took her hand with a comforting smile on his face.

"Jenny, I'm here now, and whatever happens here today, we will deal with it together. I love you, only you, you're my life, do you understand?" he said to her lovingly.

Jenny took his hand and held it tight. Her labour pains were becom- ing much sharper and the next eight hours would prove to be the most difficult and painful experience of her life. Brian wanted to give her an epidural, but Jenny wouldn't have it. She said it would be easier for her, but not for her boys. It was a gruelingly painful experience for Jenny, the labour pains were quick and sharp, but she was not dilating enough. Brian was considering a C-section, but Jenny refused.

"Give it time, Brian, please wait as long as we can," Jenny said.

"It may not be wise to wait much longer, Jenny," Brian replied.

"Are the boys in any danger if we wait?" she asked.

"Not at the moment," Brian said, "but it's you I'm worried about."

"I want to wait for as long as we can," Jenny said. Eric was extremely tense and worried. "Jenny," he said. "I think Brian is right, this plan of yours may have horrible repercussions, and I think we should listen to Brian."

"Hold my hand, Eric. All I need is your support. Just trust me on this, okay?" Jenny replied in excruciating pain. Brian came back into the room with another doctor.

"Jenny, this is Doctor Cass, one of the most respected gynecologists in the hospital. I thought we should get another opinion about your situ- ation. I can deliver a baby, but when there are complications, I think we should follow Dr. Cass's advice. I'm a cardiologist after all," he said.

"Hello, Dr. Cass," Jenny said, almost in a whisper.

"Alright, Jenny, let's see what is going on," Dr. Cass replied. Once he had assessed the situation, he looked at both Eric and Jenny, a little con- cerned as he was aware that Jenny did not want a C-Section. He carefully thought about a few strategies.

"Okay, Jenny, you have dilated, slightly, but not nearly enough, and the boys are applying pressure, that's why you're in so much pain," he said.

"Should we be considering a C-section?" asked Eric as Jenny shot him an incredibly angry look.

"I can apply something we call PG gel to the cervix," he explained. "This gel contains prostaglandin, a hormone that helps the cervix soften and helps dilation. If this fails, then a C-section will have to be performed. It's not safe for you or your twins. The boys will be extremely stressed."

Eric gave Jenny a serious look. "Honey, I think we should listen to the advice of two high-profile specialists and schedule a C-section. It's dan- gerous for you and the boys at this point, and Jenny, I will not lose you, or the boys," Eric said, his tone very serious and forceful.

Jenny looked at him intently, the look she got when she was serious. "Eric, you are not making this decision! Now, we are going to have these boys, they're going to be healthy, and I will give birth to them naturally,"

Jenny said, practically yelling at him with tears in her eyes. "Hold my hand, never let go, and help me through this."

Then Jenny turned to Dr. Cass. "Apply the gel and do what you have to do to help me have my boys naturally," she said, her face expressing the immense pain she was feeling. With that determination and Dr. Cass's assistance, Jenny gave birth to two five-pound baby boys. They were quite large considering they were so premature. Immediately after giving birth, Jenny's body began to shake fiercely. Eric's face was pale as he was terrified.

"What's wrong with my wife?" he asked the doctor in a panic.

Dr. Cass replied, "She'll be fine. The shaking is a reaction to the immediate hormonal shifts that happen right after delivery."

As the nurses covered her with heated blankets, Jenny smiled at Eric and closed her eyes, exhausted. Eric held his wife as tightly as he could and whispered in her ear, "Well done, my love, well done."

Once Jenny was out of the recovery room, she was transported with her boys to a room in Brian's clinic. Eric was somewhat confused as Brian didn't have rooms in the clinic for patient use, so he asked Brian why they switched. Brian made it clear that Jenny was like the daughter he never had, and he was sure there were all kinds of reporters and photographers camped outside right now wanting information about her and her boys. This was his way of ensuring some peace for Jenny. She had been through a lot. No one would know where to look for her. Eric hugged Brian with tears of gratitude in his eyes. Now safely and peacefully in a private room, Eric held his boys close and thanked God they were healthy. Jenny awoke to see Eric talking to the boys, introducing himself as their father and informing them that although he couldn't feed them since he didn't have breast milk, he would make sure they were fed, in every way, until his dying breath.

"Maybe we can start right now," Jenny said smiling at her husband. "How about you pass one of my sons over to me?" she asked. Eric got up from his chair and kissed her gently

"Mrs. Barrett, you are amazing! The experience you've just gone through. To say it was an ordeal is an understatement. I'm so impressed with your courage and strength, Jenny. I felt helpless, all I could do was stand there powerless to help you in any way. I am so proud to be your husband," he said with pride in his eyes. He passed over one of the boys for Jenny to feed and then they switched. They were fed, changed, burped, and put to sleep.

Although he was sure his wife would want to talk about Charlotte, Eric had no intention of asking what had transpired between the two of them. He knew Charlotte well and knew that if anything, she would try to undermine Jenny, attack her in the worst way possible. Everything he had tried to prevent from the first day he met her had happened. Now, Eric was determined to reassure his wife of his love and make sure this would never happen again. He lay beside her, held her close to him, and kissed her gently. He saw a hurt look on her face.

"Whatever you heard, whatever she said to you, is untrue. I love you Jenny Barrett and there is no one else in my heart, other than the boys." He looked at her tenderly.

"Who told you what she said to me?" Jenny asked. "There was no one in the room."

"I know Charlotte, how she does things, and I'm pretty sure of what she might have said," Eric replied. "I don't want you to worry about her. I'll take care of Charlotte. I almost lost my wife and my boys because of that bitch, and I will take care of her once and for all. All I want you to do is focus on you, me, and our sons. That's all that matters. Now, Jenny, you've been through a lot. I'm not going to leave your side until you're discharged, and we are all safely home. Why don't you just rest, okay. I'll look after the boys if they need anything. The only thing I can't do is feed them."

Jenny looked directly into his beautiful green eyes and said, "Eric, normally I would tell you to just leave it alone, she's just jealous. This time, Eric, go for it. Take care of that bitch!" she said angrily.

He pulled her close to him, smiled, and said, "Don't you worry, I'm already on it."

While Eric made phone calls to the office and worked during feedings, Jenny filled out the birth certificates for the boys. After watching the birth, Eric decided that Jenny had, without question, earned the right to name her sons. The first baby she named Zain Alexander Barrett, the second, born two minutes later, she named Christopher Matthew Barrett. She signed the forms and asked Eric to put his signature in the father's section as she carefully watched him for his reaction. Eric read the first form.

"Let's see," he said. "Zain Alexander Barrett, now that's a strong and powerful name. I like it! I think he has my red hair. I hope the freckles don't come with it." He then turned his attention to the second form and was speechless. Tears streamed down his cheeks.

"I know how much you loved your father and so I think it's fitting that we give our son his grandfather's name. I only ask that you treat the boys equally, showing no favouritism," she said sternly.

"I'd never do that, Jenny," Eric replied. "They're my blood and I will love them equally, always." He smiled proudly at his sons.

"Zain does have your hair, and my eyes, a killer combination," Jenny said with a proud smile. "Christopher has my hair, and your eyes," she continued as she looked at Eric.

"He has my father's eyes. With the darker hair, he'll grow up to look more like his grandfather than I do," Eric replied, trying to control the emotions that were getting the better of him. He quickly collected himself. "However, no matter who they look like, I hope they will take part in running our empire. I could use all the help I can get. Right boys, how about you give daddy a hand?" He smiled proudly as he held them both in his arms. His phone rang, so he passed the boys over to Jenny and was out the door, discussing business.

While in the clinic, Jenny meticulously cared for her boys. Brian had asked that no one visit the centre. He knew there would be all kinds of reporters and photographers camped in his clinic; he wouldn't have any of it. Eric and Jenny agreed to Brian's stipulations and welcomed the time to just enjoy their family. A few days later, Brian entered the room and said he was pleased with the boys' progress. They were eating well and had not lost any weight.

"Typically, newborns tend to lose a little weight a few days after they're born, but not these two," Brian said. He had not seen any traces of jaundice and was willing to let them go home, where he thought they would probably be much more comfortable. Eric immediately made arrangements to take his family home, where, unbeknownst to Jenny, her family, and a small group of friends, about a hundred people, were waiting to meet their beautiful boys.

Once in the door, Jenny was absolutely stunned. The house was decorated in beautiful hues of blue, with many smiling faces ready to greet them. Jenny looked at her husband and laughed.

"I love you, Eric," she said smiling.

"I hope you're not upset with me. I'm so proud of them, I want everyone to know."

Jenny's dad was in tears when he heard that she had named her son after his father. Jenny hugged him and said he was a strong man of great character and she hoped Zain would be just like him. It was a long but pleasurable evening. Jenny enjoyed showing off her beautiful boys and listening to the multitude of baby stories from so many of the ladies she now considered her close friends. Many offered to come and help her, while others stressed that she should make sure she continues to build in "me" time and hoped she would continue their weekly meetings at the spa and lunch engagements. Jenny felt blessed to be surrounded by so many wonderful people who truly cared about her and her family. As the evening wore on, Jenny began feeling tired. She excused herself and told everyone that while she wanted to stay, her boys needed to be fed, washed, and put to bed. Eric excused himself, told his guests he would be back shortly, and immediately followed his wife.

Once in the nursery, Eric kissed the boys good night and then turned his attention to his wife.

"Jenny, I'll do the entertaining, why don't you rest with the boys," he said.

"That's a great idea," she responded. "You don't mind?"

"No," he said. "I know your parents were just leaving and I'll see them off. Most people remaining are my close business associates. We only talk shop because we don't know how to do anything else. Just rest," he said as he quietly left the room.

Jenny dedicated the next month to her boys, ensuring they were gaining weight and developing well. Thankfully, the boys were very well behaved, and with both Heather and Jenny's mother around, as hovering mother hens, Jenny returned to work on her project. They loved being around the boys and it gave Jenny some time to focus. She felt she was so behind. The unexpected birth of her boys had delayed her plans significantly. She connected with her secretary to find out that nothing had been at a standstill. Mr. Barrett had given strict instructions to continue working on the centre as per Jenny's instructions, and should the architects, designers, or anyone for that matter, have any questions or concerns about the plans for the centre, he was available to meet with them. In fact, Eric had met, on several occasions, after work to ensure the project was on schedule. *Is there anything he won't do for me?* she thought with a smile. She decided to call him at work, something she tried not to do unless necessary. She got his voicemail. She waited but Eric did not return her call, which was unusual. She called the secretary who informed her that Mr. Barrett was in a meeting and could not be disturbed at the moment. What Jenny didn't know was that the meeting was with Charlotte.

23

Charlotte had come into the office demanding to speak with Eric. Initially, David asked her to leave, but Charlotte was hysterical. Eric heard the commotion and walked out to see what was going on. He thought he heard a familiar voice and smirked. He saw Charlotte and asked that both she and David come into his office. He gave specific instructions to his secretary to hold all his calls. Once in the office, Charlotte didn't mince words. She was irate and hysterical.

"You've made sure I had no other choice but to come here," she said lividly as she looked at Eric. "I can't work, I was told to leave my house, and I have no way of obtaining funds to look after myself."

Eric looked at her in disgust. "David is here as my witness that there is no wrongdoing going on in this office," he said. Then, he lunged at her, put his hands around her neck, and pushed her up against the wall. "I nearly lost my wife and my boys because of you. Did you think I wouldn't destroy you? Don't you ever come near my family again, is that clear?" he said in the coldest and angriest tone he had ever used.

"Or else what?" Charlotte responded, barely able to speak.

"Use your imagination, Charlotte. You know who I am and what I'm capable of."

"Yes, and I know you love me, you've always loved me, Eric," she said.

"You're delusional, I never loved you, Charlotte," he said as he looked directly into her eyes and kept his grasp firmly around her neck. "I left you so many times because I knew I could never be with you."

"Really, and do you think Jenny can make you happy?" she asked. "She churned out a couple of kids knowing that's what you want, but she doesn't have the stuff to make you happy. She's, some simple girl you found at a coffee shop, for heaven's sake. Now who's delusional?"

Eric tightened his grip around her neck and said, "Listen carefully, Charlotte, and I'll put it in simple sentences so there is no misunderstanding. Jenny makes me happy. Jenny is my wife and the love of my life. I will use all my power and every resource I have at my disposal to protect her and make sure she has everything she desires. She just has to think it, and it's hers. Now, I'm going to do you a favour, for old times sake," he said sarcastically. "I'm going to buy you a one-way ticket to Heathrow airport. Don't come back." He released the grip he had on her neck.

"And what will I do in London?" she asked. "I won't be able to work, you've destroyed my career. There isn't anyone that will give me a job. You made sure of that. I have nowhere to go and no way of supporting myself. My accounts have been frozen, and loans recalled. How will I survive?"

"You've been looking in the wrong industries for employment," he said, very pleased with his response. "I'm certain you can wait tables to make some money until my wife decides to forgive you," he responded with a vicious smile. "David, get this bitch a one-way ticket to London and get her out of my sight."

David was just about to usher her out the door when Charlotte angrily turned to Eric. "And how do I get to the airport?" she asked angrily. "I have no means of getting there."

Eric took twenty dollars out of his pocket and put it in her hand. "Take the bus, Charlotte," he said. "It won't be enough for a cab." He smiled knowing that she was accustomed to taking only limousines. "Now get out." He turned his back towards her and went back to his desk.

David and Nancy arranged for a one-way ticket and provided Charlotte with a printout. David then showed her the elevator. He walked back into Eric's office.

"I'm really glad we're friends, Eric, because I sure wouldn't want to be your enemy," David said laughing.

Eric looked at David and responded quite seriously, "I don't know what you're talking about, I was lenient."

Jenny decided to wait until Eric was home to speak to him about the project. How far had he taken this in the four weeks she spent with the twins? What were the next steps? Jenny spoke with her secretary, who could only tell her that everything had been forwarded to Eric's office and was being handled there. Jenny tended to her boys, who were becoming more and more adorable with each passing day. She loved being a mother and she loved spending time with her boys, but she was also determined to ensure this project would see completion. As she finished feeding the boys and put them down for a nap, Jenny got an unexpected phone call. When she picked up the receiver, she realized it wasn't a phone call but rather a text message sent to their landline. An automated voice read the message.

"You won, bitch." There was no further communication. She thought it was a mistake and didn't think any more of it. At dinner, Jenny mentioned it to Eric, who smirked.

"That was from Charlotte," he said, and proceeded to tell her what happened in the office.

Jenny looked at him with a huge, satisfied smile on her face. "When should I forgive her?" she asked.

"If it were up to me, after what she put my family through, I would say never," he responded. "That's why I'm leaving this entirely in your forgiving hands, but make no mistake, she has been set straight. I'd let her wait tables for the rest of her life." He paused. "I'm just going to check on the boys. I've missed them all day." Jenny followed him, and they spent the night in the nursery, cuddling their kids and each other. These were the moments Eric cherished. He had decided before the boys were born that he would spend as much time as possible with them. Jenny realized how important this time was to Eric and decided to wait to discuss the project.

Early in the morning, during breakfast, Jenny brought the project up. She had a lot of questions for Eric and wanted to know where things stood. She wanted to get back to working on it but now felt that it was out of her hands and in the hands of someone else at Eric's office.

Eric realized she was somewhat upset and explained to her that it was simply temporary. He wanted to ensure that her project remained on schedule. He knew how important it was to her and wanted to help her reach her goals.

She asked him if the meeting with the Board of Directors at the Foundation had taken place. Eric didn't think so, but he would arrange for Darren, who had been put in charge of the project temporarily, to meet with Jenny at the house.

"Are you okay with that?" Eric asked. "Darren can provide you with an update of where the project is at, what has been done to date, and you can take over from there."

"Yes," she said enthusiastically. "I'm okay with that."

"How about we go back to bed, where you can shower me with love and abuse my body all morning long?" he said with a smirk on his face. "I don't have any meetings scheduled until late afternoon. The boys will sleep for a few hours at least, right?"

She pushed him back onto the bed and fell into his arms. They lay together for as long as the boys would let them, enjoying each other completely.

Jenny gently reminded her husband that she had twin boys who needed her a little more than her big boy did right now. Eric laughed out loud and said he should shower anyway, get ready for work. Just as he was leaving, he asked Jenny when she wanted to see Darren.

"Today," she responded. "The boys will be down in the afternoon at around two. If he could come around then, that would be perfect," she said.

"Of course, he can," Eric replied. "He'll come over at whatever time I tell him, so expect him at 2 p.m."

Darren arrived on time and Jenny worked with him for about four hours. She was up to speed and told him she wouldn't need his services anymore. She thanked him for all his hard work and hoped he realized that this was something very dear to her heart and something that she had to manage on her own. She would involve him if he still wanted to work with her, but she would be managing the project from now on.

"If it's okay with Mr. Barrett, I would love to help you with this project, Mrs. Barrett. It's so vital to so many women and children, I would like to be a part of it," Darren responded.

Jenny smiled. "Leave it to me, Darren. I'll explain your new role to Eric. I don't think it will be a problem to move into this department," she said.

"Thank you, Mrs. Barrett," Darren replied. "However, if Mr. Barrett decides that I should return to my previous employment, I will do so, of course."

"I think I have a little pull and can get him to agree." She laughed then ushered him to the door, telling him not to worry.

24

Within five months, Jenny met with the Board of Directors, architects, technicians, designers, and construction personnel, and was finally ready.

The ground-breaking ceremony had been scheduled, and today was the day. Jenny felt nervous but confident as she had been working extremely hard with so many people. It had to go well; she had personally taken care of every detail herself. Jenny had learned a few skills from her husband, the workaholic. Many influential and powerful people involved in the project would all be in attendance tonight. As they drove to the Fairmont Royal York Hotel for the presentation Jenny was quiet and nervous. Eric reached over and took both her hands in his, "it's going to be fine. Just be the wonderful person you are, and you will excel. I've seen your work and it is nothing short of amazing. You have nothing to worry about." Once they arrived Eric, Heather, Thomas, Jenny's parents, and the boys sat front and centre to offer their support. Jenny gave a short speech about why this centre was so important, and how it was dear to her mother-in-law's heart.

"First, I'd like to thank all of you for being here today. I think Susan Barrett would have been genuinely proud of what we have accomplished here together, with your generous contributions. I'd like to present a 3D virtual tour, designed by our clever tech team that will give you an idea of what the facility will look like and some of the services it will provide. So, without further delay, allow me to present to you The Susan Barrett Centre for Pregnant Teenage Girls." Once the virtual tour was over, Jenny thanked everyone who had made this project possible.

"From the architects to the designers, technicians, social workers, project management team and so many others who have collaborated with me to create this facility, I thank you all for your tireless hours of hard work. It's because of you and the generous donations of the amazing people in attendance here this evening that so many young girls and children will be saved. There is a scaled model of the facility and the services it would provide at the back. Thank you, so many teenage girls and unborn children thank you, and I look forward to thanking each of you personally as you enjoy the delicious dinner prepared for this evening." Jenny put down the microphone and walked towards her family. Eric had no idea she had named the centre after his mother. He held his boys close to him and, holding back tears of joy and pride, he whispered, "Gentlemen, your mother is pretty amazing," and kissed them both.

Holding his wife with pride as they mingled with the donors, Eric saw just how much Jenny had grown in such a short time. She had become a confident, knowledgeable businesswoman, who was well respected and admired by the very same people she had approached to secure the funding. Jenny was an incredible force and had been recognized as such by a very discerning group of people who were highly respected members of society. They held Jenny in very high regard, not because she was Mrs. Barrett, but because she was a powerful, unstoppable force.

With the project now underway, Jenny would continue to manage each stage of construction. She had already involved the Foundation's HR department with finding and screening educators, social workers, caseworkers, secretaries, department managers, cooks, all other personnel necessary to open the Centre in approximately ten months from now.

25

The boys' first birthday arrived quickly, and Eric made sure this day was memorable. The party, Eric decided, would be held on the farm. He wanted to arrive an hour early to ensure everything had been taken care of, and once they arrived, Jenny could not believe her eyes.

"Quintessential Eric," she whispered to herself as she smiled. Eric had hired a highly recommended party planner, after interviewing at least twenty, to ensure the boys had everything: cartoon characters, games, ponies, clowns, the latest Marvel characters, all of it. He had invited the children of his closest friends, which amounted to a party of one hundred or so children along with their parents. Needless to say, it was quite a show, and Eric basked in his children's happiness. Eric took his boys by the hands and walked them to the stables where he had bought ponies for them. He took his time with each of his sons, holding them carefully as they rode their ponies for the very first time.

Eric had made sure the boys had every advantage. His sons had already started their education. Both boys demonstrated "gifted characteristics" and Eric ensured they were challenged to excel. At a year old, they both had what was considered an extensive vocabulary for children who normally just babbled at this age. Zain and Christopher were able to express themselves, albeit not in full sentences, but close. They outshone other kids their age, which was noticeably evident at the party. Eric was the proud father of what he called his dynamic duo who would take the business world by storm someday. He was only too ready to show his boys the ropes, much like his father had shown him.

They arrived home, exhausted from an awfully long and eventful day. Jenny carried Christopher in her arms asleep, while Eric carried Zain. They went upstairs to put the kids to bed. Eric shut the door gently and walked towards their bedroom.

"They're sound asleep," he said, both exhausted and happy to finally be alone with his wife.

"Most likely exhausted from all the riding," responded Jenny as she was herself getting ready for bed.

"The happiness and joy in their eyes today just filled my heart, Jenny. I hope they'll be this happy every day of their lives."

"Did you see Zain's face when the Marvel characters showed up? They put on an amazing show, all the kids were riveted and mesmerized."

"Yes," Eric responded, "I had a lot of people ask me for their contact information."

"Well, I for one did not expect anything short of a spectacular day, filled with all things exciting for one-year-old boys," Jenny said laughing. "And true to form, you delivered magnificently."

Eric looked at Jenny proudly. He put his arms around his wife and said, "Our boys are a year old, my love. I think it's time we started working on their little sister, don't you?"

Jenny smiled. "Eric, don't you want to wait until our boys are a little older?"

"By the time our baby is conceived and born, our boys will be two," Eric replied. "I don't want a big age gap between them. I also want a big family, Jenny. The boys have given me so much joy, I want more children."

"Everything with the Centre is under control and on schedule," she replied. "I'll call Brian tomorrow and make an appointment to have the IUD removed. Can you guarantee me a little girl?" she asked playfully.

"I will do my best, Jenny Barrett. I'll give it everything I've got."

26

The next few months were quite busy for Jenny. The Centre would open in three months, and she was working around the clock to ensure it would be fully operational. The local shelters had already identified quite a few girls that would benefit from their services, as had the Children's Aid Society and many similar agencies. Jenny was stressed and tired. Her only comfort was her husband and her boys.

Eric had taken it upon himself to look after the boys' education since they were six months old, and they were now involved in a myriad of programs in their own home. This allowed Jenny to work on her project and spend time with her precious boys.

They shared their usual morning breakfast, which now also included two beautiful boys. They shared so many wonderful mornings, which made it exceedingly difficult for Eric to leave every morning. He hated having to travel for work and when he did, he made sure to call at seven o'clock every night to read the boys a story and kiss them goodnight through a video conferencing tool specifically designed for the boys. Any scheduled meeting would have to work around the boys' time zone.

On this particular morning, just after breakfast, Eric had taken the boys down to the tutors before going to work. The boys were progressing quite well, and he was immensely proud of them. He gave them both a hug, kiss, and a high five. He called for Jenny as he was leaving, and Heather responded with an "in here Eric." He went into the kitchen and found

Jenny throwing up in the sink.

"Are you okay?" he asked.

"Yes, I came down to get some apple juice and didn't quite make it," she said.

Eric smiled. "Jenny?"

"I know," she replied. "I'll call Brian after my meeting today."

"What time is your meeting, sweetheart?" he asked with a huge grin on his face.

"It's at 10 a.m. and should be a few hours. I'll call him then and set up an appointment," she said smiling at him.

Eric wasn't comfortable with that at all. He held his wife close to him, looked at her, and saw his little girl in her eyes, at least he hoped it was a girl. He kissed her and said he would call her later. Once in the car, he called Brian.

"Hello, Eric, is everything alright with Jenny and the boys?" Brian asked.

"Yes, Brian. How come you never ask if I'm the one that's sick?"

"Because, if you were, it would be Jenny I would be talking to and not you. So, what's up?"

"I think Jenny's pregnant," Eric responded. "She has a meeting from ten to twelve today. It's about eight now and I realize you're probably on your way to the clinic. Do you think you could drop by, take a blood sample?" Eric knew Brian wouldn't refuse. Brian loved Jenny as if she were his daughter.

"Fortunately for you, I was just leaving the house. Tell Jenny I'll be there in about half an hour. I'm meeting someone near King City, so this works out beautifully," Brian replied. "Once I get back and have the results, I'll call you, Eric."

"Thanks, Brian," Eric responded. "I think it's time we build another wing to that clinic of yours. Give it some thought and call my office so we can begin making plans." Eric said.

Brian was delighted. "Eric, I'm not doing this to get a new wing, you know that, right?"

"Yes, Brian," Eric responded, "but it's the least I can do for the person who has not only looked after my family but is a member of it."

"Alright, then. We could certainly use an expansion at the clinic to look after some needs currently not being met at all. We just don't have the means or the space. I'll call you in a few hours," Brian said before hanging up the phone.

Eric then called Jenny and told her that Brian was stopping by. Jenny was not surprised. She, Heather, and Thomas were standing in the kitchen taking bets about what time Brian would be stopping by that day. The closest was Heather, who guessed 9:00 a.m.

At 12:01 exactly, Eric called Jenny. "Is your meeting over?" he asked.

"Yes, actually it ended ten minutes ago," she said.

"Well, I have news for you, Mrs. Barrett. Eight months from now we'll be welcoming a new addition to the Barrett clan. We, my love, are four weeks pregnant," Eric said with excitement in his voice.

"You know, Eric, it will be something to open the clinic pregnant. I couldn't have arranged this if I tried. It's another blessing, another miracle God has given us and the timing, impeccable," she replied, feeling blessed and pleased with everything in her life.

The next few months passed swiftly, and Jenny was preparing for her ultrasound visit with Brian. Eric would, of course, meet them at the clinic. Jenny had given both Eric and Brian strict instructions not to divulge any information about the sex of the baby. All she wanted to know was that the baby was developing well and was healthy. She wanted to be surprised this time. She didn't want everything preplanned. This time she wanted to plan with the baby, knowing exactly what would be perfect for him or her because they were going to do it together.

At the end of the session, Brian reassured Jenny that everything was fine, and the baby was progressing well. He gave her a copy of the ultrasound that was rather unclear, but she accepted it anyway. Eric saw Jenny to the limousine and told her that he would be home as early as possible. Perhaps she should just go home and get some rest. Jenny went home to spend time with her boys and work on her project.

Eric rushed back up to see Brian. He had a particularly important meeting to get back for but risked being a few minutes late. Brian was not surprised to see him, in fact, he was waiting for him to return.

"So, everything is okay, Brian?" he asked. Brian nodded with an enormous smile on his face.

"Can you tell me if the baby is a girl?"

"Eric, I can tell you that they are both girls," Brian responded.

"Is it possible to have another set of twins?" Eric asked smiling.

"My first response to that question would be no. Lightning never strikes twice in the same place, but for you, I'd have to say that it's a miracle, Eric." Brian gave him a big hug.

Eric had tears in his eyes and got down on his knees and prayed for the very first time out loud. "Thank you, God! She wanted a little girl and because she is such an amazing person, kind and generous with everyone she meets, YOU saw fit to double her reward. Thank you for blessing us." He rose from kneeling on the floor and looked over at Brian with joy and excitement in his eyes.

"Jenny will be so surprised when she finds out," Eric said. "It will be so hard to keep this news from her. However, that's how she wants it and that's how it will be."

"Eric, please make sure she doesn't push herself too far," Brian said. "She works almost as hard as you do."

"I'll try, she can be pretty stubborn sometimes."

"A trait you both share I'm afraid. I gave her an ultrasound picture that didn't show anything at all. Here's a clear one that shows the twins and the CD. I'm sure she'll want to have it later. Call me if you need anything."

Eric was half an hour late to his meeting, but he was so happy he didn't care. As soon as he entered the office, David grabbed his arm and asked him if he knew what he was doing. David explained that the clients waiting in his office and were none too happy right now. Eric smiled from ear to ear.

"David, please don't tell Jenny because she didn't want to know. Keep it to yourself until they're born. I'm having twin girls!" Eric said unable to contain his joy.

David looked at him in disbelief, gave him a big bear hug, and expressed his happiness. Thinking on his feet, David smiled and said, "Maybe we can use this information to quell their anger."

27

The day was beautiful. The sun was shining, and everyone felt its energy. Today, the Centre would be open for business. Jenny was exceptionally large and heavy for six months pregnant. She was also surprised to find that Armani, her favourite designer, had a maternity division. She was able to look both classy and large. She came downstairs to find her husband putting tiny cuff links on the twins. Jenny shook her head, laughing.

"Do you think little boys, not even two years old, need cuff links?" she asked.

"They do if they're wearing miniature tuxedos, which I had tailored for the occasion. I think the Barrett men look quite dapper, don't you?" Eric said with a smile a mile wide. Eric finished putting on the cuffs and smiled at them. "High five boys," he said, and the twins each slapped one of his hands.

"We should get going, Mommy, or you'll be late for your big day," Eric said.

"How do I look?" she asked.

"Honestly, like a huge stuffed turkey," he laughed. Eric walked towards Jenny and gave her a warm hug. He looked at her tenderly and said, "But the most beautiful, cutest turkey I have ever seen."

"Do you want to take mommy's hand, Zain?" Jenny asked. Zain gave her his hand and then pulled it away.

With a smirk on his face he said, "Daddy's." Eric, Christopher, and

Zain all burst into laughter.

"Go ahead, take Daddy's hand," Jenny said. "I should have called you little Eric," she said. Eric had already called for the limousine, which was waiting for them upfront. The car ride was pleasant and uneventful. They arrived and their car doors were immediately opened by people waiting to assist them.

Cameras were everywhere and shutters could be heard clicking away every second. Surprisingly, the boys were unaffected. They were used to being the centre of attention and they both had huge smiles on their faces as their parents took their hands. Christopher took his mother's hand, while Zain grabbed his father's, but not before giving everyone a wave hello, which was very well received with a collective "Ahhhhhh, how cute." Eric looked over at Jenny and just shook his head.

"What a ham," he said to her laughing.

Once inside, the couple made their rounds with the kids, and finally, Eric settled them in their seats in the front row. They quietly waited for the show to begin.

Jenny waddled onto the stage and welcomed everyone in her unmistakable assertive but soft voice.

"Welcome, everyone!" Jenny began. "The day has finally arrived, and it would not have been made possible without your generous donations. Thank you! I'd like to welcome Mr. Brown, our mayor, and the many members of both the provincial and federal governments for their generous support. It's with the combined efforts of our corporate sponsors and public supporters that we can improve the lives of so many. The Susan Barrett Centre for Pregnant Teenage Girls is a clear indicator of exactly that.

"As I stand here before you, I have my beautiful boys sitting front and centre, a year and a half now, and I am six months pregnant. My children were born very privileged. They were not born in an alley, their mother was not disowned and thrown into a street or worse yet, born with several defects because of abuse, drugs, or alcohol. Yet for many young teenage girls, these are very real circumstances.

"Susan Barrett, my mother-in-law, I believe would have been immensely proud today. You see, as I was reading and learning about the foundation, I came across a note, written in her handwriting. Where are the tech people, can we put that up please?" Jenny highlighted a small section. "You see, right here. 'Help for pregnant teenage girls.' Susan Barrett had penned a dream that she could not realize as her life had been cut short far too early. Today, together, we have realized not only her dream, but the dreams of so many young mothers, and so many children. Susan said there was nothing more rewarding than to see the hope in children's eyes. Today, we've given these soon-to-be-born children that hope. More importantly, we provided support so they may flourish and perhaps lead in powerful endeavors of their own in the future. So, to that end, I declare the Susan Barrett Centre for Pregnant Teenage Girls open. Please feel free to enjoy the refreshments provided. In a few moments, we will partake in a walk-through of the facility, and key personnel will be here to answer any questions you may have. I will pass the microphone to Doris, one of the many wonderful organizers of today's tour. Thank you, with all my heart, thank you! There are numerous individuals and organizations to thank for your tremendously generous donations, which I have personally overseen with a special gift that will be sent to your respective offices. Doris will now take it from here and I will join you on our tour."

With that, Jenny made her way off the stage and walked towards Eric. He was beaming with pride. He hugged her and said, "My mother, had she been here, would have been so proud of you. As am I, my love." They spent the next several hours touring the facility and mingling and talking with their guests and supporters. The boys had been taken to one of the many playrooms and were supervised by Jenny's mother and Heather. They had arrived at 3 p.m., it was now 8 p.m. and Jenny was exhausted. As they were on their way home, Jenny looked over at Eric.

"That went well, don't you think?" she asked.

Eric responded with tenderness in his eyes. "It was flawlessly organized and made quite an impression on several influential people. Jenny, what you did today was amazing, and the numerous girls that will benefit from this facility will be astounding. Not to mention the adoption centre. It took a lot of work, but you did it."

"I'm so glad we're going home. I don't know which of us is more tired," she said as she watched the boys sound asleep in the car.

28

Jenny was seven months pregnant and was extremely heavy. Brian was concerned that she may develop toxemia, which he had warned Eric about. So, Eric kept a close watch on her symptoms. There was no point in bringing Jenny to the clinic when Eric could arrange to have any treatment done in the privacy of their own home. So far, there hadn't been a need.

Jenny told Heather she was feeling a little tired and was going to lie down for a while. Eric wasn't home yet, which was unusual as he never missed putting the boys to bed, which told Jenny that whatever he was doing, it was important. Even when Eric had to travel, he always made sure that he was never gone longer than a week. If Eric was not home, Jenny knew something serious had happened.

Eric arrived home at about 10 p.m. that night. He was weary and forlorn. He had spent the evening at the hospital. One of his closest employees, Harold Cutler, only forty-two years old, had been in an accident and didn't make it through the surgery. His wife and children were devastated. Eric had spent the evening with David at the hospital and then back at the office arranging a trust fund for his three children. His wife would be very well taken care of through her insurance policy. Eric was so shaken, realizing firsthand that life was very fragile. *Any one of us could lose everything that makes life meaningful in the blink of an eye,* he thought. He went straight to the bedroom where he told Jenny why he was so late and why he didn't call to tell her. It was just a very trying night.

"Jenny," Eric said as he looked at his wife, anxiously, "I love you and our boys so much, and while I can protect you, all of you, from just about anything, there is always a chance that we can lose everything we love in a heartbeat."

Jenny put her arms around her husband and said, "Eric, we have no control over how and when we die. All I know is that God has a time for each of us. In this case, He sent you to provide for Harold's children. I could not be any prouder of you than I am right this minute." She reached to hold her husband closer, but her belly wouldn't allow it.

Eric rubbed her belly and smiled; "this is a pretty big balloon you have here my love."

"Brian keeps reassuring me there is nothing to be concerned about, but I am," Jenny responded. "I wasn't even this big with the twins, but I trust his professional opinion and that's the only thing that gives me peace."

"Just a few more weeks now. Hang in there," Eric replied as he kissed her gently.

* * *

Thomas had not been feeling well for quite some time, but rather than seeing a doctor or even telling Heather about it, he kept it to himself. Jenny was looking over documents for the Centre in the library when she saw Thomas holding his stomach. She quickly got up and went towards him to ensure he was okay. He explained that he had been getting these pains for a while, but he didn't want to worry anyone, especially Heather. Jenny insisted that she at least call Brian and ask him a few questions. If Brian didn't think there was anything to worry about, it would be their little secret.

Jenny shut the door and called Brian. She put him on speaker so that Thomas could hear and respond to Brian. From the responses that Thomas was giving him, Brian was concerned. Thomas was now close to seventy years old. He had been with the family for quite some time and for Eric, Thomas was like a father. He and Heather were there to help him through the worst times of his life. Brian insisted that Thomas come immediately to the clinic. He would be there to meet him. Jenny looked at Thomas and demanded that Heather be informed. If Brian was worried, there was something to worry about. Against his wishes, Jenny called Heather and informed her of what was going on. Heather held her husband tightly in her arms as tears rolled down her face.

"Go with Thomas to Brian's clinic," Jenny said to Heather. "I'll be alright here. I have a lot of help and I'll call Eric to let him know what's going on. Hopefully, we will get good news once Brian runs a few tests."

Jenny had Heather and Thomas driven to the clinic and then called Eric. She explained to him what had transpired, and that Thomas had been driven to the hospital where Brian would take care of him upon arrival. Eric's heart sank when he heard the news.

"Jenny, call your mother and have her picked up to stay with you. I'll head over to the clinic," he said. "Please, Jenny, I don't want you and the boys alone, not at this stage in your pregnancy."

"Eric, we have a house full of servants," Jenny replied. "We're hardly alone, but I will call my mother if it puts your mind at ease."

Eric walked into David's office and, once he told him about Thomas, they both left for the clinic. On the way over, Eric called Jenny's mother who informed him that she already knew from Jenny and was on her way over to the house with Jenny's dad.

As soon as Thomas arrived, Brian lost no time at all and ran several tests. He tried to reassure Heather and Thomas that it could be anything and that most likely they could get whatever was ailing Thomas under control.

When he read the results, Brian broke into tears. It took something enormously powerful to break Brian. He and Thomas had shared a lot over the years. He had fond memories of himself, Christopher, Thomas, and David arguing over bridge games and going hunting. Memories just flooded his heart. He had to take ten minutes to try and collect himself before he could face Heather.

Brian decided to send Eric a text message to meet him in his office immediately. Eric excused himself and took David with him, citing a message he had received with regards to work that had to be handled immediately. They left the waiting area and went to Brian's office. When they opened the door and saw him in tears, they prepared for the bad news.

"How bad is it, Brian?" David asked.

"It's bad, David," Brian responded in tears. "And I'm not sure how to break it to Heather. I just don't know how."

"Brian is Thomas dying?" asked Eric with trepidation.

Brian nodded and said, "He has stage four pancreatic cancer. He must have been fighting it for quite some time, but never said a word. If it hadn't been for Jenny, who noticed his pain and called me, we would never have known at all."

Eric and David both had tears rolling down their faces. "Tell me we can still do something; tell me we can slow this down. Whatever you need, I'll pay for it," Eric said.

Brian responded, shaking his head, "I'm afraid it's too late now, Eric. There is nothing we can do."

"How much time does he have?" Eric asked almost afraid to hear the response.

"At best four months, at worst a week."

Eric took a deep breath. "David, can you call Mark and let him know. Heather's going to need her son now more than ever. Brian, we have to tell Heather. We've shared some good times and Heather is part of this family, our family. We'll support her and Thomas through this. We all love him very much, so let's make these next four months memorable for him." Eric was unable to stop the tears as he spoke. David left to call Mark, and Brian and Eric prepared to explain the findings of the tests to Heather and Thomas.

Heather was utterly devastated. Thomas took the news surprisingly well. He was pleased that God had given him a rich and full life, with so many blessings and wonderful people.

"We're all going to die one day or another," Thomas said as he held Heather close. "God just thought he would let me know, so I have a few months to straighten out any wrongdoings, you know, get forgiveness. Then I'll be able to meet my maker in heaven, with a clean conscience." Heather held her husband close and cried on his shoulder.

"C'mon sweetheart," Thomas said, "we both knew this day would come. Let's make the best of the time we have. Let's not spend it in sadness and tears. I want to enjoy you and every waking moment I have with you, Heather. And besides, we don't want Jenny sad right now, she's just about to pop." He looked toward Eric with a smile. "Please don't mention any of this to Jenny. She will take it badly and I don't want anything happening to her; she's in a delicate condition right now." Eric could not control himself any longer, he reached for Thomas and sobbed in his arms.

Mark and his family arrived and were immediately supported by David, Marie, and Michael, who had arrived once they heard the news. Together, they decided the next steps, and Brian was instructed to provide everything and anything Thomas would need at home. Eric also asked Brian to secure any available treatment that might slow the cancer down. Whatever was available, even experimental treatments, he would take care of it.

Thomas and his family went straight home. David and Eric went back to the office. While David poured a double scotch for the both of them, Eric called Arthur and Elaine of his housekeeping staff. He explained to them that Thomas was not well, and that Heather would now need to spend time with her husband. He told them that as of this minute, they were responsible for the management of the house. He explained that although they might see Heather around the house, she was not to be bothered in any way. If they had questions, he would answer them, and he left his office number with Arthur.

Eric hung up with Arthur and looked towards David. "Yesterday Harold and today, Thomas. David, I don't think my heart can take this pain," he said. "How do I tell Jenny? What do I tell her right now? News like this could send her directly into labour and she's only seven months, carrying twins." Eric looked at David in despair.

"Eric, I think you should tell Jenny the truth," David said. "It may hurt, and it may be devastating, but Jenny should have a chance to say goodbye. She will never forgive you if she finds out you knew and denied her the opportunity to spend time with Thomas."

"You're right," Eric replied. "I'm just going to try to tell her as gently as I can. Listen, why don't you, Marie, and Michael come over tonight and we'll have a bridge game, like old times. Mark will be there, and he plays. We'll have a good family night."

"Sounds like a good plan," David responded. "I still have a lot of work to finish, and I will try to get something done before I go today." Eric nodded and said he would try to do the same although it would be difficult with the pain, he felt in his heart right now.

Eric finished working and was on his way home. He thought about how he would tell Jenny. When he arrived, he found Jenny and Heather had just finished bathing the boys, much later than usual, and Thomas was reading the boys a story.

"What's going on here?" Eric asked smiling. "Sounds like we're having way too much fun." The boys jumped out of bed and ran over to Eric. He picked them both up and took them back to bed. "Looks like Uncle Thomas was reading a nice story. I'm going to let him finish and then come and tuck you in, okay boys?" Eric left the room devastated.

Heather gave him a warm hug. "I'll get the boys to bed. You should get some dinner," she said. Eric told Heather that David, Marie, and Michael would be over later. He thought it might be a good idea to have a bridge game and a few laughs with Thomas.

He proceeded to go down the stairs where he saw Jenny, looking at him very intently.

"Is someone going to tell me what's going on?" She asked.

"Yes," Eric replied and led her into the library. He sat her down on the couch and began telling her that Brian ran some tests on Thomas while he was at the clinic to find out what the problem in his stomach might be. The results were not encouraging, and he re-did the tests, three times. Jenny already had tears in her eyes.

She looked up at Eric and said, "He's dying, isn't he?" Eric could hardly bring himself to say it. Tears ran down his face as he nodded his head. Jenny held her husband close, and they cried together.

"Jenny, Thomas didn't want me to tell you. He was afraid it might be too much for you to handle right now," Eric explained. "David and I felt you should know because you might want to spend time with him, say goodbye."

"How long does he have?" Jenny asked.

"At best three to four months," he replied. "Jenny, Thomas wants to spend the time enjoying the life he has left. He told Heather he didn't want to spend time crying, he wanted to spend it living, enjoying her and his family as much as possible. David will be coming over later with Marie and Michael. We thought we could spend the night playing bridge and enjoying some family time." Eric looked at Jenny and could see the pain in her eyes.

Jenny wiped the tears from her face. "That's a great idea. If this is how Thomas wants things, then that is what we will do! I'm going to go and bake some chocolate chip cookies, he loves my cookies, and then I'm going to hug him so tight." She burst into tears.

Eric held her close as they cried in each other's arms. Heather knocked on the door, took one look at Jenny, and cried. Jenny took Heather in her arms, wiped the tears from her eyes, and said, "Heather, let's go make some of those chocolate chip cookies Thomas likes so much." She took Heather by the hand, and they went into the kitchen.

Thomas wandered into the kitchen looking for Heather and once he saw Jenny, he knew she had been told of his situation.

"What are you doing in the kitchen?" Thomas asked.

"I'm making some cookies," Jenny said. "David, Marie, and Michael are coming over to beat you at a good game of bridge, I'm told, so I thought the cookies would take away the sting of a loss."

Thomas took her in his arms. "I love you, Jenny Barrett. I loved you the first day we met. Remember, I gave you an etiquette lesson?" he said.

Jenny looked at him with tears in her eyes. "You've helped me through so many things, and I will miss you very much, Thomas."

"Jenny, it's not forever," Thomas said. "I'm just going first, and I'll be there with Christopher and Susan, while we wait for the rest of you to join us when God says it's time." Thomas smiled. "Then we'll have a great big party where cutlery won't matter," he said laughing. Jenny held him tight as David walked into the kitchen.

"C'mon old man, we've got a score to settle. Are you prepared to lose tonight?" David said with a smile on his face.

"I'm prepared to school you tonight, my friend," Thomas replied as they left for the games room.

The night was full of laughter and good family fun. Thomas was genuinely happy and for part of the night, everyone seemed to forget the terminal situation. Once everyone left and said their goodbyes, Heather looked to her husband.

"It's time for us to go too, Thomas," she said.

Thomas reached for Jenny, kissed her, and whispered in her ear, "Remember what I told you in the kitchen, it's not forever. I love you,

Jenny Barrett. You brought so much love and joy to all of us. You're the daughter I never had Jenny, and I'm so glad God brought you to us here."

Jenny reached for Thomas and held him as close as she could. "I love you too," she said, "so much, Thomas." She held him close as she sobbed in his arms.

"Stop now, Jenny," Thomas said. "I'm still with you child. Let's spend time laughing, not crying. Life is for living." He kissed her gently on her forehead. "It's time we all got some sleep." He took Heather's hand and led her out the door.

Once at home, they laid in each other's arms. Thomas held his wife closely, kissed her, told her how much he loved her, how much joy she and Mark had brought to his life, and how blessed he felt for the time God had given them together. They talked and laughed together until they both fell asleep. Those were the last words Thomas would ever voice.

Funeral arrangements were made, and Thomas was laid to rest. Heather resumed her duties in the house. She told Eric she needed the distraction. Mark offered to have his mother move in with him, but Heather wouldn't have it. She belonged with Eric, and she would stay there, as had her husband, until her dying day. The next few months were quiet. Everyone felt Thomas's loss. Heather took it upon herself to ensure that Arthur and Elaine were well equipped to run the house. She spent her time showing them how, when, and where things were done. By the time Jenny was ready to have her babies, they were ready to run the Estate quite efficiently.

29

Eric awoke, his bed soaking wet and his wife sitting on the edge of it.

"Jenny, did your water break?"

"You're very astute and your powers of observation unparalleled," she responded sarcastically.

Realizing she was in a lot of pain, he said, "I'll call Brian and tell him we're on our way. How can I help, Jenny? What can I do?"

"Just make the phone call and then help me get dressed, please, Eric. I'm sorry I was so short with you, I'm just in a lot of pain," she replied.

Eric arranged for the helicopter to transport them to the city. Then called Brian, Heather, and Jenny's mother to tell them they were on their way to the hospital. Heather stayed behind to look after the boys and gave Eric strict instructions to keep her posted. They arrived at the hospital within fifteen minutes and Brian was waiting to receive Jenny. Once on a stretcher, she was immediately taken to the birthing unit as Brian went to make a few arrangements.

Once Brian walked into the room he found Eric holding her hand. "I have something to tell you, Jenny," Brian said. "Eric already knows. You didn't want to know anything, so we didn't tell you. But I'm going to have to spoil the surprise because I'm going to need you to work with me here. You're having twins again. And this time they're girls." He smiled. "You remember the first time, it's a little grueling, but we survived. Hopefully it won't be the same experience."

Jenny squeezed Eric's hand hard and smiled from ear to ear.

"You did promise me you would do your best to give me a little girl and in true Barrett fashion, you went over the top," Jenny said with tears of joy in her eyes. She nodded to Brian, took a deep breath, and said, "Okay, let's do this!"

"Do you want an epidural, Jenny? It will make things a lot easier for you?" Brian asked.

"No, I don't, Brian, and you know why," she responded.

To say the next twelve hours were arduous would be an understatement. Eric wished he could do something to stop the pain Jenny was experiencing but felt helpless. All he could do was hold her hand and provide some comforting words of support. He was astonished by Jenny's unfathomable strength and determination. As he watched his wife endure labour, he thought to himself, *men have no idea what strength is, until they watch a woman go through labour in excruciating pain. A man would never put himself through this kind of pain twice, and yet women selflessly and incredibly continue to birth life.*

The girls were finally delivered; two beautiful, healthy girls, each weighing about six pounds. Eric was delirious with joy, which was to be short-lived.

Brian informed Eric that something was very wrong. Jenny was hemorrhaging. He would have to leave the room while Jenny was prepped for surgery. Eric had no intention of going anywhere. He and Brian started to yell at each other, but Eric was not leaving the room. He held Jenny's hand, which was now limp as she was under anesthetic. Brian contacted Dr. Cass, who entered the room to consult with him. They had to work around Eric who continued to hold Jenny's hand.

An hour later, the quickly assembled team of specialists had stopped the hemorrhaging. Brian reassured Eric that Jenny would be fine. She lost a lot of blood and would be weak for a few days. She needed to rest, and probably would not talk much as she would not have the strength once she awoke. If Eric wanted to help Jenny, he should leave her to get some rest. Brian advised Eric not to have any more children. He explained that they were able to stop the hemorrhaging this time, but there were no guarantees they could do it again. They already had four children. Eric explained to

Brian that he would leave that decision to Jenny. Furious, Brian reminded Eric that Jenny would do anything to please him and if she thought that he wanted another baby, she would put her life at risk to give it to him.

Eric smiled, and said, "Yes, Brian, that's very true, but Jenny would never do anything to harm her children; she wouldn't leave them motherless."

Eric sat up all night, feeding and changing his girls. He had given consent to have Jenny's breasts pumped so the girls could be fed the colostrum he knew they needed. Jenny of course had taught him all of this when the boys were born. She told him the colostrum was vital for building their immune system, providing immunity, growth, and tissue repair factors. How he remembered this after everything that had happened in the last forty-eight hours was beyond him. All he knew was Jenny wouldn't want her girls on formula. He put the girls to sleep and hummed a little lullaby, which they seemed to love. Then he took off his shoes and socks and laid down beside Jenny. She was weak and still very pale. She often opened her eyes and gave him a feeble smile. He held her tight, as he had every night since they were married.

He told her stories about how the boys were doing. He told her how impressed he was with their progress. The boys had an uncanny ability in math, which he thought would serve them well in business. Their progress was off every and any normal chart. At two years old, Christopher and Zain Barrett were taking riding lessons and French lessons. Eric was proud of their progress in swimming, their skating lessons were coming along well, and in all their other activities they demonstrated significant accomplishment. He talked incessantly, all night long, hoping Jenny could hear him.

Eric had never been religious but found himself praying night after night, for his boys, girls, and most of all their mother. He wanted to take her home to her boys, who longed so much to see their mother and new baby sisters. The girls didn't know it yet, but they had a mother like no other. A woman that is capable of so much selfless love. He thanked God for all the blessings he had given him. His mother, father, and Thomas who were no longer with him but would forever live in his heart and home. He thanked God for the blessings of his children and the love of a woman he felt he did not deserve. She was truly an angel and his only worry right now was that God missed her so much, He might take her back. So, Eric begged every night through his tears, that he leave her with him, just a little longer, just so his children could benefit from the love he knew all too well.

"Just a little longer," he whispered. Just then, Jenny touched his face and dried the tears from his eyes. She held him as tightly as she could, gently kissed him, and closed her eyes.

A few hours later, the girls started crying. Eric jumped from the bed and went to fetch the breast milk. Jenny opened her eyes and sat up in the bed. She felt a little dizzy, but she got up and walked over to see her girls for the very first time. She sat down in the chair next to them and gently touched their faces.

"Oh my," Jenny said as she smiled. "The two of you will break a lot of hearts. The most beautiful girls in the world were given to me. How blessed am I?" she said with a smile. "Mommy wants to hold you so much, but I'm afraid I can't do that without a little help right now." Eric walked in barefoot with two small bottles in his hands, which he dropped when he saw Jenny sitting beside her girls.

"Jenny," was all Eric was able to say.

She looked at him and smiled. "Well, you've made a bit of a mess!"

He rushed over, took her in his arms, and kissed her passionately. "I've missed you so much, we all have," he said. Jenny took his head into her hands and kissed his lips gently.

She looked directly into his eyes and said, "I need to feed my girls. Will you help me?"

"What do you want me to do, Jenny?" Eric asked. Jenny instructed him to help her get back into bed and then stuff pillows around her so that the baby couldn't fall as she held her.

"Now pass me one of my daughters, the hungrier one of course," she said and watched his response.

"I'm not sure I can tell who's hungrier, Jenny," Eric responded, a little confused.

Jenny just laughed at him and said, "I'm sure they're both hungry, Eric." The girls were fed, changed, and put to sleep. Eric laid down next to his wife and held her close to him.

"I thought I lost you, Jenny. You were so pale, so weak, and I was beside myself. I had no idea what I would do. How would I face my family? How could I tell my boys that their father had failed to bring their mommy home? That he had failed to protect the only thing in his life that made it worth living. I prayed, Jenny. I prayed so hard that God would give my family a chance to experience the love I have felt each day since you first spilled cold water all over me. It was almost as if God woke me up that day, from four years of the most painful days of my life, and yet that pain was nothing compared to what I felt thinking I was losing you. I'm so glad He gave you back to me," he said with tears in his eyes.

Jenny just shook her head. "I could not live my life without you, Eric, and I pray that someday when our time comes, He will take us together. Even during these difficult last few days, I felt you holding my hand, holding me tight every night and I knew it would be okay. We would be okay," she said. He kissed her passionately, just as Brian walked into the room.

"Okay, it's that kind of behaviour that brought you here in the first place," Brian said. "Will you two never learn?" He laughed. "It's good to see you up and well, Jenny. You," he said looking at Eric, "look like hell. Why don't you go home, take a shower, change, and get some rest? Jenny is fine."

"I'll go home when I can take my family with me," he replied.

"Just like your father, stubborn as hell. Well, Jenny, I'm sending some food for you both I guess and once you're able to stand and walk, I'll send you home."

"I was up and, in the chair, Brian. I just felt a little lightheaded, but I'm fine," she said.

Brian smiled and took her hand. "That's great news, Jenny. I'm sure before you know it, you'll be home with your beautiful girls, and that dreadful-looking mess," he said looking at Eric and laughing. "I'll go and make arrangements for a nice meal," Brian added as he left the room.

"Have you given the girls names?" Jenny asked Eric.

"No, they're still Barrett one and Barrett two," Eric replied. "I thought we could do that together."

"I'd like their names to have meaning," she said. "Christopher was named after your father and Zain after my grandfather. They were both incredible men of character, and I hope our boys will be the same. I remember my dad was in tears when he heard I had named one of my boys, Zain. So, I've been thinking about this long and hard. I'd like to name my first daughter, Elena Catherine, my mother's name. Your thoughts?"

"Your mother has been a guiding force, an objective confidant, and a loving friend to you your whole life. I could not be happier, Jenny." He decided to get the birth certificate forms and start filling them out. "Okay," he said, "form one, Elena Catherine Barrett. It has a nice ring to it he said." He completed the form then reached for the other one. "Next," he said.

"I'd like to give the second one Thomas's name but of course I can't name her Thomas," Jenny said, "so I was thinking Masey. M-A-S-E-Y. The last three letters of Thomas. What do you think?"

"I think that's beautiful, Jenny. I know how much you loved Thomas. I did too. But you'll have to add an 'i' in there, you know, kind of like Daisy but with an M," he replied. "Otherwise, people will call her Mass-ee."

"You're right," she said. "I hope Thomas won't mind. Her middle name would be Heather. Maisy Heather Barrett."

"I'm sure Thomas is rolling in his grave with joy," Eric replied smiling. "I love the way you fused their souls in our daughter's name. I'm sure she will have an amazing heart. You, Heather, and Thomas have incredible hearts," he said tenderly. Eric began writing form number two. "Maisy Heather Barrett. It sounds beautiful, full of love and empathy."

"Which one was born first?" Jenny asked.

"That would be Elena," Eric replied. "She has my red hair and your beautiful eyes. Maisy has your hair and my eyes. They're both stunning and I'll be up many nights worrying about them out on dates."

A few days passed and Brian was pleased with Jenny's recovery as well as the girls' development. He completed their discharge papers as he felt they would be much more comfortable and happier at home. Jenny had given Eric strict instructions not to have a welcome home party. She wanted to just go home, spend time with her boys, and enjoy her girls. Eric said only Jenny's family would be home when they arrived.

"Nothing would keep your mother away from seeing her new grandchildren," Eric said smiling. When they arrived, Heather and Jenny's mother rushed to take the girls and cuddle them. Once Jenny revealed their names, both Heather and Jenny's mother cried from joy and gratitude.

"Maisy," Heather said. "Thomas would have loved that." She took the little girl in her arms and kissed her relentlessly, as if she had somehow, in a very strange way, just got Thomas back. The happiness in Heather's heart was indescribable.

30

Time seemed to fly in the Barrett household. Heather had been dead for some time now. She had spent most of her time with Maisy and enjoyed ten full years of happiness with her until Thomas took her home. He needed her and missed her far too much. Heather loved all the children, and she never showed any favouritism, but there was something about Maisy. From the first day she came home, Heather felt a strong connection to the little one and had a soft spot for her. Maisy somehow instinctively understood that and had suffered greatly from her loss. It was Elena who helped her through it, not leaving her sister's side for one minute, not at school, at their activities, or at home. Eric had always said that Elena had inherited her mother's selfless ability to love. In reality, it was Maisy that had her mother's character. The girls were united not just as sisters, but in spirit. They were both highly creative thinkers, evident in their studies and their ability to take apart a problem, see each component, and resolve the issue. A gift, Eric believed, they inherited from their mother, but Jenny saw a lot of Eric in her girls.

Many changes had occurred in this time. Christopher and Zain were now fourteen years old, and their characters could not be any more different. Christopher was reserved and staunch, much like the grandfather he was named after. Zain was a little Eric. He had a great sense of humour, a big heart, and the ability to make anyone feel comfortable and at home. Christopher had his mother's hair and his father's green eyes, where Zain had his father's red hair and his mother's blue eyes. Both boys were handsome and intelligent. Eric had enrolled them in the same school for gifted boys that Michael had attended where they flourished. Michael was now thirty-three and had been married for three years. He had a beautiful little girl named Sarah. David, who was now sixty-four, continued to work with Eric. David was prepared to work until his dying day. He didn't see the sense of sitting at home. Retirement for him was like being put out to pasture and waiting to die. He would rather work. Of course, David had the luxury of taking days off, touring the world, and coming back to work.

The empire had grown significantly, and Eric had expanded beyond his dreams. He now had offices in London, Paris, Milan, Germany, New York, Moscow, Doha, and, of course, home base in Canada. He was extremely busy. His office tower at Yonge and Eglinton was insufficient for his expanding business. Barrett Industries had expanded to include two additional thirty-storey buildings on Bay Street with the Barrett Industries logo at the top of the buildings. Of course, there was still a Penthouse. The previous penthouse Eric gave to one of Harold's children as a wedding present. Jenny continued to work at the centre, which had expanded to include many more services that Susan Barrett had only dreamed of. Jenny was now the Chief Executive Officer of both the Foundation and the Susan Barrett Centre. Many changes had taken place in the last ten years, but one thing never changed; the love Eric and Jenny had for one another. Each night, Eric held Jenny tightly and fell asleep in her arms. Their love was the stuff dreams are made of and the envy of so many worldwide.

31

David called Eric early one Saturday morning, completely distraught. Michael's wife and daughter were on their way home from having spent the weekend in Disneyland, but never made it home. Their jet experienced some technical difficulties and crashed, killing everyone on board. Michael was on his way to collect his family's remains. Eric was in shock.

"How can I help, David?" Eric asked.

"There isn't anything anyone can do, Eric," David replied. "I just need someone to hold me up and tell me we'll get through this somehow. Marie is completely devastated at the loss. My daughter-in-law is gone and so is my only granddaughter." David sobbed into the phone.

"I'll be right over," Eric said.

Jenny had overheard the entire conversation and was in tears. She knew Ellen, Michael's wife, well, and their little girl, Sarah, although younger, played with her girls.

"My God," Jenny said. "Eric, Michael must be devasted, ravaged by pain and anguish right now, and he's out there alone. We need to find out where he's gone and meet him. He'll need his big brother right now. I'll help Marie and David in any way I can." Jenny had tears in her eyes and a look of deep concern.

Eric looked at her in amazement. "How do you do it, Jenny? How do you feel everyone's pain and know exactly what to do? Or say? No one thought of going to meet Michael. Everyone thought he needed to feel his pain as a man and feel it alone, but not you. I love you so much. Let's get over to David's where I'll find out where Michael is and arrange to meet him. I think you're right; he will need support to bring his family, or what he finds of them, home. I doubt Michael will be able to think at all in the excruciating pain he must be feeling right now."

Eric left Jenny to give Arthur instructions. He informed Arthur that he would be away for a few days. Then Eric sat with his children and gently told them what had happened. They were to get dressed, as quickly as possible, as they would all be going to Uncle David's to help him through this painfully difficult time.

"Life teaches us many lessons," Eric explained to his children, "and dealing with loss is the worst lesson of all. The only way to help Uncle David, Auntie Marie, and Uncle Michael get through it is by giving all the love and support we can provide. Love is the only thing that heals a broken heart, love, and time. That's why I need you four to come along. We need to give them all the love we have right now. The kids quickly went to get ready, except Maisy, who walked up to her father and hugged him.

"You're right," she said to him. "If it had not been for all of you, and especially Elena, I don't think I could have handled Heather's death."

Eric held her close, kissed her gently on the forehead, then held her face in his hands as he said, "Maisy, my beautiful Maisy, then you know exactly what we have to do." He encouraged her to go and get ready as quickly as possible, and then left the room to make a few phone calls.

Upon their arrival, Eric left the children with Jenny so they could comfort Marie and Ellen's parents, who had arrived as well. Eric took David aside and poured them both a scotch.

"I know this is devastating. Remember when we lost my mother and father, then Thomas and Heather, each time we thought we wouldn't be able to go on, but we did. We did it for the sake of our families. I know this is a catastrophic blow that no one could have anticipated, but you have a family that needs you now, more than ever. Your wife is inconsolable, as are Ellen's parents. Not to mention Michael, who has gone to find and bring home the remains of his family alone. David, you need to do for them what you did for me. You need to be that rock they can rely on, the decision-maker when no one is even able to think, and the father that

Michael will need to help him through this. Michael is shattered right now, and he may take to alcohol, drugs, anything to numb the pain that he feels now and for some time to come. You must make sure he pulls through this. Like you pulled me through the most destructive times of my life." Eric looked compassionately at David. "David, I'd like to go and meet up with Michael. I've always considered him my younger brother and I'd like to be there for him now. Where did he go?"

David gave Eric all the information he would need to find Michael as well as Michael's cell phone number. "He will respond to this number. Only I, his mother, and his wife use it to get in touch with him," David said shattered. "How will I do this Eric? How can I support my son when I cannot deal with it myself?"

"Just like you did when Christopher died," Eric responded sombrely. "You were closer than brothers and you managed to help me. I'm sure you fell apart during that time, but for me, you were the only person I could rely on, and that has never changed. Now, I have a jet on standby. I'll get Michael, you take care of Marie. Jenny and the kids are here, offering what they know how to give; their love."

The two men walked towards the family in the living room. David took one look at Marie, let out a deep breath, and rushed to hold her.

"We'll get through this, my love. Together we'll get through this," he said as Marie held her husband and cried.

Maisy put her arms around the two of them and said, "I'll help too," which brought a smile to both their faces.

It took quite some time for Michael to adapt to his new reality, and much of what Eric feared had come true. Michael had been rushed to the hospital with alcohol poisoning several times and David had him admitted to rehab twice for alcohol addiction. Those had been the worst four years of David's life, but he had managed to work through it, with the support of his wife. They continued to provide unconditional love for their only son, and Eric did not leave Michael's side. He would do everything to ensure his little brother came through this. Eric often picked him up from the streets, bruised and beaten, completely drunk and a lot of the time left for dead. He would go to Michael's house, get him out of bed, force him into the shower and help him get dressed for work. It didn't matter if he did nothing in the office, he was there, with his family, where he belonged. It was in his final time in rehab that Michael decided to accept counseling as well as medication to help him focus his attention on something other than his pain. Eight months later, a much older, worn, thirty-seven-year- old man appeared at the door of Eric's office.

"Michael, it's so good to see you!" Eric said as he jumped up from his desk and gave him a warm hug.

Michael smiled. "Thank you, Eric. Thank you for everything you have done for me and my parents. It has been an exceedingly difficult time for all of us. I was wondering if you still had a place for me here. I'll work my way back up and don't expect any favours," he said. "You've done quite enough, and I am indebted you." Michael looked at Eric, his eyes tired and still filled with a lot of pain.

"What are you talking about little brother?" Eric said smiling. "There's an office with your name on it that hasn't been used in a while. I'm in desperate need of a sharp mind to help me, and I know there isn't one sharper than yours. We deal with the worst of society, snakes and sharks, in this business and as far as I remember, you are an incredible deal maker." Eric walked Michael over to his office, helped him set up, and connected him to several projects that were both high stakes and high profile. "I think you'll start here my friend. I'll check in on you later," Eric said.

David walked into the office; he had aged significantly through this horrible ordeal. He walked past Michael's office daily to get to his own. Today, David noticed the door was open.

"Michael?" he said almost in a whisper.

"Good morning, Dad! How are you?" he asked, smiling at his father. David dropped his coffee in disbelief, tears ran down his face as he responded to his son.

"I've been waiting a long time to see this door open, Michael, I'm so glad you're back," David replied.

Eric had been watching and casually walked up to David. "I believe you dropped your coffee and while I keep extra shirts in the office, I can't do anything about your pants," he said laughing. "Our boy is back, just like old times, and he has been given a pretty tough portfolio. Maybe you can spend part of your day walking him through it. I have a meeting to attend."

Eric patted David on the back and left.

This was the beginning of what would be an incredibly happy change in the Jones household. They had just been given a second chance with the son they loved so much. The stress had been particularly difficult on Marie. She suffered greatly these last four years and had developed some particularly ghastly health issues that Michael was completely unaware of. Eric decided to have the Jones's over for dinner in honour of Michael's return to work. David was only too happy to accept.

Dinner was set up in the formal dining room. The table was much fuller now. Eric headed the table with Jenny at his side. Christopher and Zain were sixteen now and coming into their characters. Elena and Maisy were fourteen and quite beautiful. The Barrett children were very well-read, able to participate in any conversation and hold an argument. Sitting around the table at dinner was a lot of fun. Eric enjoyed sparring with his children and was utterly pleased with how well their skills were progressing.

The Jones family arrived, and everyone was seated at the table. Michael sat down next to Elena and had Maisy directly in front of him. He smiled and said, "Eric, you've surrounded me with such beauty, I don't think I'll be able to eat at all!"

"Yes, they're as beautiful as they are intelligent," Eric responded proudly. "I'm sure you'll enjoy some great conversation with my treasures."

The evening was full of joy and laughter, a much-needed change for David. The sparring began and Michael jumped into the battle. They enjoyed an evening of great conversation, from political science to religion, philosophy, and all kinds of literary genres. David looked at his watch and was surprised to see that it was 2 a.m. and no one seemed tired at all. The energy at the table was electrifying. He called a timeout and announced that it was 2 a.m., and while they were young and full of energy, this old man needed to go home.

Jenny and Marie had spent the evening in the library where they enjoyed a glass of wine and discussed Marie's next steps. Would she be having surgery or was there something else that could be done? Marie had a tumor in her left lung, horrifically close to her heart. She had the best medical attention that money could buy, David made sure of that. If surgery was her only option, Jenny suggested Michael stay with them so that the family could support him through this difficult time. They had several rooms and a guest house.

"Life has been very difficult for Michael already, I'm not going to have him face this alone," Jenny said to Marie. Marie thanked Jenny profusely and held her tight in tears.

"What would I do without you, Jenny?" she said. "You and Eric have been my solace, my support, and my haven, through the worst times of our lives."

"Listen, Marie, if the tables had been turned, I know you would be there for us, all of us," Jenny said. "Don't give this a second thought. I love you, Marie, and Michael, he's always been Eric's little brother." Michael walked into the room to let his mother know they were leaving and saw her crying. Jenny saw him standing at the door and quickly responded before he had the chance to ask.

"We've had a little too much wine and started reminiscing of old times with Thomas and Heather. It's quite enough now, don't you think so, Marie?"

"Yes," responded Marie. "I think it's time we go home after an amazing evening. Thank you, Jenny."

"Don't thank me, Marie. You're family," Jenny said, giving Marie a warm hug.

32

David knew it was time to bring Michael up to speed on his mother's health situation. He also knew that Michael had suffered quite a lot. He didn't want Michael to blame himself for his mother's condition. After giving the situation a lot of thought, it was clear to him that he was so completely distraught over Marie's condition, he could not tell Michael with the sensitivity it required. He took the opportunity to speak with Eric to help him get some clarity on how to proceed with Michael. As David spoke, Eric realized the pain he was in, and that the situation was delicate; especially since Michael was just getting his life together. Eric asked David if he wanted him to speak with Michael.

"I think Michael might be upset if he doesn't it hear from his father," he replied. "After all, it's a critical family matter. However, I just don't feel like I can deliver this difficult news to Michael delicately." David looked at Eric with concern. "Michael has been through so much, I'm not sure he can handle it right now. Hell, I can't handle it right now."

"David," Eric responded, "Marie will come through this surgery just fine. You have secured the finest medical team in the world to ensure that it goes well, and it will. Of course, there is always the small chance it doesn't, and life doesn't give us any guarantees. What we do know is that you have done everything humanly possible to ensure a positive outcome. Use that knowledge to cancel out the insecurities. We do it here every day, all the time. We get the outcomes we desire because we plan well, secure the knowledge we need, and assemble the best team available. You have done all of those things, David, so expect a favourable outcome," Eric said encouragingly. "Now, as far as Michael, leave him to me. We have been through a lot together and we have a good relationship. Let me take care of this."

"I have been so fortunate in my life," David said. "I've had Christopher, your father, who was not a friend, but a brother to me. When he left us, he took so much of me with him. In time, I began to see him in you, as you matured. I've been blessed with you, Eric. You've been there to help me through the darkest times of my life, and this is one more of those times. Yes, Eric, I would be grateful if you spoke with Michael. I can't even think of Marie's situation without tears in my eyes."

Eric walked around his desk and gave David a huge hug. "You've been my father when I didn't have one. You are a significant part of my life, and I will always love and respect you. We are wonderfully comfortable, both of us, we don't need things, but we need each other. I will always be here for you and your family," Eric said as held him close as he would his father.

The next day, Eric asked Michael into his office to discuss Marie's situation with him. Eric explained that his mother was not well and stressed that it was not his fault. He explained that his mother had a tumor in her left lung that was remarkably close to her heart. The tumor was not cancerous, that much they knew, but it had to be removed. She was scheduled for surgery next Wednesday.

"Michael, these are things that happen, often with age, and if you think it is the result of any stress you may have caused, it isn't. I don't want you blaming yourself for something you did not do," Eric said to Michael gently. "David is having a really difficult time with this, but make no mistake, he has assembled the finest medical team in the world for Marie. She will come out of this just fine. Jenny and I know how difficult this will be for you and while David stays at the hospital with Marie, we would like you to stay with us until Marie comes home." Michael had tears streaming down his face.

"Will this never end, Eric?" he said. "Will God take from me all that I love?" Michael asked in tears.

"Michael, I was thirty-one when God took everything from me. I thought my life was over and honestly, I delved into every kind of debauchery there was for about a year. Then, I collected myself and started to run the empire my father left me. I did this with the help of your father. You still have them both. Marie will be okay, I'm certain," Eric said encouragingly. "We'll support her through the surgery and afterward. Enjoy them while you have them." Eric tried to keep the focus of the conversation positive.

Michael looked at Eric and said, "You're right. I am truly fortunate to have them in my life. Thank you for the offer, Eric, but I think I should be with them during this time." Michael gave Eric a warm hug.

"As you wish, Michael," Eric responded. "Come by the house anyway even if you don't want to spend the night. Have dinner with us. You know, I met Jenny at thirty-five when I thought my life was over and had buried it in work. She saved me. You may still have a saviour yet."

That night, Eric went home and while sitting with Jenny in the solarium, sharing a scotch, he told her about Michael's decision, held her in his arms, and told her how much he loved her.

"Jenny, you and I have been through a lot together. We have built a huge empire, expanded on so many fronts, and you, my right hand. My beautiful, classy wife, the CEO of the Foundation she knew nothing about. We have grown in so many ways. We have been blessed with four incredible children, who I enjoy and am thankful for, my love. So thankful. I have been blessed with the gift of you!

"When I come home each night, I look forward to holding you close to me, making love with you, and reconnecting my soul to yours; that connection that I think about and miss all day. I often wonder what people do when they don't have what I have, how awful their lives must be. Then I remember my life before you walked into it. Jenny, it was no life at all. I had everything anyone could want and had absolutely nothing. I was a powerful man but didn't understand true power until I met you. You showered me with everything I could never buy. With all the money I had, I could never buy the joy and love you've given to me. The feeling I felt when I found out I was to be a father, the feeling I felt when you named one of our boys Christopher, the feeling I felt when you named the Centre after my mother, the girls, oh God, Jenny, it would take me a lifetime to itemize everything, and none of it cost a cent. It was all given to me with selfless love. I don't know why God has favoured me so much, but I know that although I am one of the most powerful men on Earth, I am nothing without you, Jenny Ali-Barrett." He took her in his arms and kissed her passionately, under the stars. They went to bed and enjoyed each other until they fell asleep.

In the morning, Eric was in the kitchen getting some orange juice when Zain walked in. "Morning, Dad. You had quite a night," he said with a smirk on his face.

Eric looked at his son. "What do you mean?"

Zain gave his dad a look and said, "I think we both know what I mean, Dad. Good for you, both of you. Sex is an important part of a good relationship and at your age, you should be proud of yourself."

Eric laughed, looked at his son, and said, "Zain, it was a hot, passionate, rapturous, euphoric night. One that you only dream of, my son." He left the room, smirking on his way up the stairs. *Our boys are growing fast,* Eric thought.

33

Eric Michael Barrett was sixty-three today. There had been so many changes in his life, some extremely painful. When David passed away, it was as if he had lost his father for a second time. He was able to console Michael, but it was Jenny who consoled Eric. She always helped him through the most difficult times of his life. Marie couldn't live without her husband and died not two months after. Brian said she died of a broken heart. With her passing, Michael was utterly alone. He had never remarried, buried himself in his work, and looked after his parents. Now, Michael was surrounded by vast wealth and an empty life. Eric felt sorry for him and had him over to the house often. Eric knew too well the feeling of emptiness and utter loneliness.

Eric had raised a few sharks of his own. Christopher and Zain, now twenty-eight, and Elena and Maisy, twenty-six, all worked with their father. Christopher and Zain looked after the holdings in Russia, China, and the Middle East, while Michael, Maisy, and Elena, looked after the holdings in Europe, the United States, and Canada. He had built, without exception, the empire his father had dreamed of with the Barrett family at the helm. The Barrett boys had developed a reputation for being ruthless in business, one that they were immensely proud of, as was their father. But tonight, it was all about family.

Zain came into the dining room and looked around. "Ooh, very special," he said to his mother as he touched the table settings.

Jenny laughed. "It's a special night, Zain, and I want it to be perfect."

"Speaking of perfect," Zain said, "Do you mind if I have someone join us tonight?

Jenny smiled at him. "Someone special?" she asked.

Zain took a deep breath and with a huge smile on his face said, "Very special. I think she's the one, Mom, and I want her to meet everyone tonight."

"Of course, dear. Will she be joining us for dinner? I'll have another place setting added to the table."

"No, Mom," Zain replied. "I think that would be a bit too much for her to handle the first time around. She'll need a little time to absorb all of this."

"Okay, when do you think she'll come? I'll have to leave word at the front gate. They've been instructed to let in only family tonight, no interruptions."

"After her shift at the hospital, so about eight o'clock. I've sent a car to pick her up," he replied, and left before his mother could ask any other questions.

Eric came home early. Feeling blissful and blessed, he screamed for his wife as he walked in the door. Horrified, Jenny came running, not knowing what was going on. Eric grabbed his wife and kissed her.

"Well, happy birthday," she said, "but this part of the party wasn't supposed to start until much later."

"Jenny Barrett, I love you. I love you. At fifty-one, you're still hot and sexy," he said as he began kissing her neck.

Jenny laughed. "Have you been drinking?" she asked him.

"Nope, just high on life," he said smiling.

"Well, I have some news. Zain is bringing someone home to meet the family tonight."

"This ought to be fun," he said with a smile from ear to ear.

"Be nice," she replied. "He's anxious. This girl means a lot to him. He said she may be the one."

"Okay, I'll be nice, a little." he smirked.

As each one of his children arrived for dinner, they filed into the dining room.

"Happy birthday, Dad," Elena said as she gave him her gift. "Please open it later, I don't want to hear any ribbing from my brothers." She rolled her eyes as she leaned over to kiss her dad.

"I've noticed you've been spending some time with a young man, anything we should know?" Eric asked Elena.

"I don't know what you're talking about," she said as she blushed.

Eric smiled at her. "Elena, Cole is a good man, has a good head on his shoulders, and I'd be proud to call him my son-in-law, just in case you were wondering."

"So, it's okay that I invited him to come tonight?" she asked. "I just thought he might see the family; in action, I mean. He may decide to run after tonight, especially if Christopher and Zain get started on him."

Eric laughed. "I wouldn't worry about that. I think Zain may be a little tamer than usual tonight. But just so you know, Cole has told me he's quite serious," Eric said as he smiled at his daughter.

Elena smiled, "He did?"

Eric nodded. "Mmhmm."

"I should get changed for dinner." Elena smiled as she left the room just as Jenny came in with Eric's favourite scotch.

"Well, my dear, it seems like we have more than one guest tonight. Elena asked Cole to come over for dinner and she's stressed her brothers won't give him a chance," he said smiling as Jenny sat in his lap.

Jenny looked at Eric. "Oh, I've met Cole. He can hold his own."

Christopher and Zain arrived. Both boys had such a presence it was impossible not to know they were in the house.

"Hey, old man, happy birthday," Zain said as he grabbed his father and gave him a bear hug. Both boys were over six feet tall and very handsome.

Eric smiled. "Thank you. I understand we will be meeting someone tonight?"

Christopher looked at Zain. "Are you kidding me? The nurse?"

Zain gave his brother a mean look and said, "Yes, the nurse, and you behave tonight. Embarrass me and I will pulverize you. You know I'm good for it."

"Wow," Eric responded, "this sounds serious, I'm looking forward to tonight."

"Dad, go easy," said Zain. "At least the first time she meets you guys, can you just try not to embarrass me?"

"That's a tall order, Zain, but we'll temper ourselves, right Christopher?" Eric responded.

"Sure, Dad. Whatever you say," replied Christopher with a smirk on his face.

Maisy was late getting to the house, but eventually, they all sat down for dinner.

"Hey, Dad, happy birthday," Maisy said as she gave him a warm hug.

"How is my beautiful daughter?" Eric asked.

"I'm good, Dad," Maisy replied softly with a smile.

"You look tired Maisy; do you need some help?" Eric asked. "I've noticed that you work some long hours, sweetheart."

"No, Dad, I'm good," Maisy responded. "I don't think we need any additional staff to help us if that's what you're thinking."

"Okay," Eric replied. "But you will let me know if things become too stressful, right?"

"Of course, I will, Dad," Maisy said, looking at him with unease.

Eric noticed that Michael hadn't arrived yet, and asked Jenny if he was coming.

"I asked him, and he said he would drop by later. Had a lot to do at the office, apparently," Jenny replied.

Eric looked directly at Maisy. "Honey, are you certain you don't need more personnel?"

"No, Dad. Everything is under control," Maisy responded as she looked over at Elena.

Zain was never quiet, but right now he was extremely nervous, and everyone could tell, even Cole.

"C'mon, Zain, what woman wouldn't want to be part of the Barrett family. Aren't you stressing out just a bit too much?" Cole asked.

"All the money in the world won't keep this girl from walking. You got the stuff to hold on to her big brother? Do you?" Christopher said, teasing his brother with a smirk on his face.

"Shut the fuck up," Zain responded. "Don't talk about Maryam like she's some slut, she's not!" Zain said to Christopher angrily.

"Easy tiger," Eric said. "She means a lot to you."

"Yes, she does, Dad, and I hate feeling this vulnerable. Zain Alexander Barrett, always in control, women at the snap of his fingers, and right now, I don't know my head from my asshole. I just want this to work. I love her so much and when you meet her, you will too."

Seeing his brother distraught, Christopher apologized. "Okay, little brother, we'll be nice tonight."

Cole walked over to Zain and said, "If it's any consolation, I know exactly how you feel. I love Elena a lot, and I know I don't deserve her, she's amazing! I often doubt whether I have enough for her to stay, or whether someone else will take her away from me. I get it."

Elena took Cole's hand and smiled. "There's no one else in my heart, Cole."

Zain looked over at the two of them. "Yeah, why can't Maryam just say something like that every once in a while?" He said nervously.

Just then, the doorbell rang. Christopher smiled. "Tun tun tun! The moment of truth." Zain shot his brother a wicked look and left the dining room.

Zain felt both anxious and nervous and rushed to open the door. Maryam was standing there smiling.

"I didn't know what to bring so I picked up some pastries," she said. "Driving in, I kind of feel stupid. You probably have the best pastries in town right here." As she walked in the door, she had a deer-in-head- lights look.

"Oh my God, Zain. I knew you were rich, but not this rich," she said feeling extremely uncomfortable.

Zain took her in his arms and held her tight for a few minutes as he looked into her eyes. Then whispered, "How about I take your coat?"

"I'm sorry I didn't get a chance to change. I'm still in my work clothes," she said apologetically. He kissed her gently and said it was fine. The dining room was dead quiet as everyone was attentively listening, unfortunately, unable to hear a word.

Maryam took off her shoes and Zain looked at her. "You don't have to do that," he said.

She responded with, "Yes, I do. I don't want to make a mess of these beautiful floors." As she walked into the dining room with Zain, her jaw dropped. She had never seen such opulence in her life.

Seeing that she was thunderstruck, Zain took her hand and said, "Well, let me introduce you to everyone here. This is my father, Eric, my mother, Jenny. Christopher you've met, unfortunately. These are my beautiful sisters, Elena and Maisy. This handsome guy here is Cole, Elena's boyfriend."

Jenny got up and gave Maryam a big hug. "Welcome, Maryam. It's so nice you could come tonight," she said with a warm smile.

"I'm sorry about my clothes. I didn't get time to change after my shift. Zain had a car waiting for me and I didn't want to be late," Maryam said apologetically.

"It's no problem," said Jenny. "We're just happy you could join us to celebrate Eric's birthday tonight."

Maryam looked over at Zain. "It's your dad's birthday and you didn't tell me?" she asked mortified. Maryam looked at Eric. "I'm sorry, I don't have a gift for you. I thought I was coming in to meet everyone over a cup of coffee," she said looking disappointed.

"Having you here to spend a nice evening with us is my gift, Maryam. Why don't you sit down? Tell us a little bit about yourself."

"Okay, well, I'm a pediatric nurse at Toronto General where I am over-worked and underpaid but love my job. I enjoy working with children very much. I'm an only child and live in a ridiculously small apartment in the city, close to work. I'm not sure what else you want to know," she said rather shyly.

"How did you meet?" Christopher asked. "Zain wouldn't go near a hospital if his life depended on it."

"It's a funny story," she replied. "Do you want to tell it, honey?" Maryam asked Zain.

"Yes, honey, why don't you tell us," Eric said with a smirk on his face. Zain gave his dad a dirty look and began telling the story.

"I was at the hospital for a meeting. We, Chris and I, were looking into providing funds for a wing to be expanded, most likely in the MARS building, which is attached to Toronto General. Christopher and I had talked about it and felt it would be a good tax shelter for us, you know, donations, charity, that sort of thing. The meeting was supposed to be in one of their board rooms but because of scheduling errors and, well, just incompetence in my opinion, we met in the pediatric wing. I finished the meeting and just as I was leaving, a nurse looked over at me and said, 'You're Zain Barrett.' I stopped to tell her that I was, and figured I could get her number, when I saw Maryam barrelling through the hallway. I stopped her dead in her tracks and said, 'whoa, where are you going in such a hurry?' She said she was late for her shift and if she didn't get there soon, she could lose her job. So, she told me to kindly get out of her way. She had the most beautiful hazel eyes I had ever seen. I asked if I could walk her to the nurse's station, where the manager recognized me and immediately started fussing about. I asked if she was late for her shift. 'Not if you say she's not Mr. Barrett,' he said. Well, I told him that I didn't think she was late and that I thought she was early and should start in about an hour, no pay deduction of course." Zain laughed. "'Of course, Mr. Barrett, of course,' he said trying to please me. That's when Maryam looked at me and asked who I was. I sheepishly asked if I could buy her a coffee and I would tell her all about it. That's how we met."

"With all the money you have, you bought her a coffee. Shame on you Zain Barrett," Eric said with a smirk on his face.

Maryam rushed to his defense. "Oh no sir, I was more than happy with the coffee!"

Zain put his arms around her and held her close. "He's just playing with you. This family is a little sick like that, you'll get used to it."

Maryam looked at Zain. "You mean you want me to come back here?" she asked with a smile on her face.

"Yes, Maryam, I want you here as many nights as I can have you," Zain said anxiously.

"What do you mean by nights, Zain? Just because you're insanely rich doesn't mean—" Zain stopped her in mid-sentence. "I just meant dinner," he said smiling.

Maryam looked into Zain's eyes, with both love and relief. "Okay," she said as he took his hand.

Eric smiled at her. "Maryam, you're welcome here any time, whether Zain is home or not. I think you'll fit in just fine."

She looked at Eric and said, "Oh, I don't know sir, we're not cut from the same cloth if you know what I mean."

Jenny smiled at her. "Maryam, I felt very much the same when I walked in here for the first time. I thought to myself there is no way I can participate in this world; I know nothing about it. What I can tell you with absolute certainty is that you have Zain, and he will be all you'll ever need, trust me. He really loves you and will be by your side always."

Maryam smiled, feeling comforted by Jenny's words and soft voice. "Thank you," she said shyly.

"You will have to learn to drink scotch, though," Jenny said laughing. "Let the initiation into our family begin!" Jenny reached for the scotch and poured a glass for Maryam and one for herself. "Bottoms up, Maryam!" They both drank while everyone around laughed.

Eric pulled his son aside. "Don't ever let her go, Zain. She has a good heart, and she's lovely."

"Yeah, that's what I think too," Zain replied, smiling at his father.

Michael never came, which Eric found rather strange. He decided to address it with him at work.

34

Maisy had no idea how to tell her father that she and Michael had been seeing each other for the past year. He was twice her age, but she loved him. Michael never thought he would ever find love, especially the kind of love he had found in Maisy. They decided to keep their relationship private, at least for now. This left Maisy feeling incredibly stressed most of the time. How do you hide a relationship from your father when you work with both him and the man you're madly in love with? She often watched Elena and Cole working together, laughing, having lunch, and wished so much she and Michael could do the same. It was so hard to hide her feelings from her father and she hated deceiving him. She would get home late because once everyone left, she and Michael could finally be alone. She worshipped that time together.

One night after work, Maisy and Michael went to his house. They were sharing a glass of wine while sitting by the fire, and Maisy began a profoundly serious conversation that couldn't be put off any longer.

"I don't know how much longer I can do this," she said. "It's killing me inside. I'm deceiving and betraying a man I deeply respect and love." She said to Michael. "I can hardly look at him because he always looks at me with such love and concern in his eyes, and I feel horrible inside." Maisy was in tears as she held Michael close.

"I know, Maisy, but I don't think Eric would be pleased with our union," Michael responded. "In fact, I think he would oppose it with every fiber of his being. He often talks to me about you and hopes you meet a wonderful man who will love you as you deserve to be loved and, in those times, I just want to tell him that she has, but I stop short of doing that because I know that if I did, I would never see you again." Tears ran down his face. "He's happy that things are progressing well with Elena and Cole and often calls them a power couple, and he's told me that Cole has intentions of proposing to Elena at Christmas. He talks about how hard you work and how he wishes you could meet someone like Cole, a young and vibrant man with the whole world ahead of him." Michael looked at Maisy with pain in his eyes.

"Just hold me, Michael," Maisy said, "and never let me go."

Michael reached for his Maisy and held her close. "Maisy, I can't stand to watch you suffer like this. Our relationship has blossomed into a love I only dreamed of, one that I never thought I would experience. You know I was married before and about the tragic accident that took my family from me. My little girl, I miss her so much, Maisy. What I have come to understand, however, is that although I loved my wife dearly, I did not love her as I love you. You're an amazing person, Maisy, always looking out for everyone, putting everyone's needs above your own. You work with your father and the man you love, never betraying your feelings about one for fear of hurting the other. I can only imagine how difficult it must be for you to sit at the dinner table with your siblings and their significant others, watching your parents enjoy the fullness of their table, and knowing that I cannot be a part of that. That although I can sit at the table, Eric would never accept me as his son-in-law because he wants someone you can spend your life with, not someone who may die before you even reach sixty. If he does anything, it's because he loves you, Maisy, and I cannot continue to love his daughter knowing how much the deception of this relation- ship would hurt him. He was there, as the brother I never had. He never gave up on me, and when I was able and asked for my job back, he didn't give me something easy, just to make me feel good about being there. He gave me the most difficult portfolio he had to show me he believed in me. When my father passed away, it was Eric who made sure I got through it. When my mother died, he never left me alone. He stayed with me here in this house and invited me into his home as if I were another son. This relationship we're in is a double-edged sword, my love."

"Michael, I can't be with anyone else," Maisy replied."I can't live without you in my life. Please don't tell me this is your breakup speech, because I really can't deal with that, not now, not ever." Maisy was hysterical.

"Maisy, there's no resolution to this problem that will not involve people being hurt," Michael replied.

"Then let's run away, let's go somewhere else and live our lives. We can change our names and get jobs. We both have excellent business skills and if we can't find jobs then we can start our own company. We can do anything together. Apart, I won't survive," she said. "There will be nothing to live for, Michael. You are my love and my world. Without you, I have nothing."

Michael held her in his arms, "I don't deserve you Maisy." He gently kissed her lips. "Make love to me, Michael."

"No. It's not because I don't want to, believe me, I'd like nothing more than to make passionate love to you and never stop, but it wouldn't be right. You're not making a rational decision right now," Michael said to her tenderly.

"Since when is love rational?" She smiled and began to kiss him, intending to stay the night. Michael couldn't control himself any longer. He loved her and loved her passionately until they both fell asleep in each other's arms.

Maisy awoke the next morning to find Michael's arms around her, and she felt so blessed, so happy.

"Good morning, my love," he said. "While you were sleeping, I've been thinking. Marry me, Maisy. I don't want to wait; I don't want to wake up tomorrow morning without you. I've learned from the very hard lessons life has taught me that we don't have all the time we think we do, and I'm not wasting one more minute. He got up from the bed and walked over to the dresser. He looked for his mother's ring and put it on her finger. "We will have to talk to Eric, and he's not going to make it easy. Just be prepared for that." Maisy hugged her man and could not contain how happy she was to be Maisy Barrett-Jones.

35

Eric sat at the dinner table and noticed that Maisy was missing. "Where's Maisy?" he asked?

"At work, I believe. She didn't say she was going anywhere, not to me at least," replied Jenny.

"This late?" Eric asked.

"I think she was going to have dinner with a friend," replied Elena. She was covering for her sister, and it wasn't the first time. Just then, Zain, Christopher, and Maryam came in for dinner.

"You don't have a romantic bone in your body," Zain said to Christopher.

Eric looked at his boys as they came in and said, "What's this about?"

"Dad, you will not believe this story," Zain said. "Christopher needs some serious help with social skills, particularly in the women department." Zain laughed as he looked at his brother. "Listen to this, Dad," Zain said. "I went to pick up Maryam at the hospital and as we're waiting for her, this nurse is reading something, not looking at where she's going, reaches to put her coffee cup down directly where Chris is standing and ends up pouring it all over him. He screams because it's hot, and she of course says she's sorry. He answers with 'Why you don't watch where you're going,' and as he looks at the nurse, he gets hit by lightning! The look on his face, I wish you had been there to see it. She's trying her best, and is apologetic, he doesn't say a word. Looks at her and says, 'What's your name?' She responds Sarah. He gives her his card and says to call him when her shift is over. She asks him who he is, and he says it's on the card. She reads it and says, 'Well, Mr. Barrett, you may be used to having your way, but I don't roll like that.' Are you ready for this response, Dad?" Zain asked with a smirk on his face. "Chris says, 'If I want sex, I can have it anytime, anywhere I want. This isn't about that. Call me when your shift is over.' He turns to me and says we're done here, then leaves."

"He's a lot like his grandfather," Eric responded laughing.

"This isn't about that, Dad. We need an intervention here," said Zain. "Do you think she'll call him after that! He was so smug."

Eric laughed heartily. "I don't think it's that serious."

Throughout dinner, Christopher checked his watch a few times. It was about 9 p.m. when his phone rang. Christopher checked the phone number and it said unknown caller. He had a smile from ear to ear.

"Guess who, big brother," Christopher said with a smirk on his face as he left the room to take the call. When he came back, they all looked at him. "I have a date," he said with a big grin on his face. Then he looked at Maryam. "What can you tell me about her?"

"Well," Maryam replied, "she's kind and a hard worker. We've had several dinners together at two in the morning during graveyard shifts. She takes her job very seriously and it looks like she may be promoted to head nurse."

"Did you hear that, Chris? She's being promoted to head nurse," Zain said with a huge grin on his face. As he looked over to his father, Eric, Christopher, and Zain all laughed.

"Oh, stop that," said Maryam. "That's disgusting! It's a very important role and she will be responsible for a whole unit. It's not an easy job! "

Zain looked over at Christopher. "You have a date with the head nurse and it's not an easy job," he said laughing.

Maryam just shook her head. "I think it's time I go home," she said as she gave Zain a nasty look.

Zain pulled her close to him. "You upset? I'm just playing around," he said smiling.

"No, I have an early morning shift and should be going now," she replied.

Zain was certain, something else was bothering her but now didn't seem to be the time to address that.

"I love you, Mary," he said as he looked at her with kindness.

"I know, Zain. I should just be going," she said. Zain had a driver take Maryam home but was sure something else was bothering her. Something in the conversation sparked anger, of that he was certain. What Zain didn't know was that Maryam had been receiving information about him that she was not happy about. She knew she would have to speak with him about it but hadn't figured out how or when to have that discussion.

36

Eric wondered why Maisy hadn't come home last night. This was the second time she did not come home, and it wasn't like her, which concerned him. He asked Jenny if Maisy had said anything at all about where she was going yesterday. Jenny said no, nothing specific, but she knew she was dating someone.

"Who is she dating?" he asked.

"Well, she hasn't given me a name, but the way she describes him, he walks on water," she said smiling. "She is so in love with him, and he seems to make her happy. I asked her what he looks like, where he works, and how long they've been seeing each other, trying to gauge if this new romance is something serious. Her responses were rather vague, to say the least. She told me he was tall, had dark hair, worked in business, and that they had been seeing each other for a while," Jenny explained.

Eric listened intently to what Jenny was saying. "That's not like her at all," he replied. "She's usually so bubbly and talkative. Why is she being so secretive? Why does she feel like she can't tell us about him? She sees her brothers and sister bring their love interest's home. What is it that she feels she can't tell us?"

"I don't know," Jenny responded. "But I do know that she loves this man and that he makes her unbelievably happy. Listening to her talk reminded me of how I felt when I was seeing you. You were the only man in the world for me, and Maisy feels the same about her man."

"Jenny, do you think she spent the night with him last night?" Eric asked. "Do you think it might be someone just trying to find their way into this family, for money, power, or influence? Maisy is such a gentle soul. She's like you, Jenny, and she has your gentle nature and soft voice, not to mention her beauty. If someone is playing with my daughter, I will destroy him!" Eric said angrily.

"Eric, I think you're jumping to conclusions and getting upset without having any information to base your anger upon."

Eric looked at his wife with a stern look in his eyes. "I want her to bring this guy home and I want to see him tonight. Now, do you want to tell Maisy or shall I?"

"I'll do it. I don't think you should talk to her right now. Whoever he is, he's already been judged before he's had a chance to say hello. Just calm down, it's probably not what you're thinking at all."

Eric left for work and was unhinged over the situation. He thought about it the whole ride into the office. As he walked in, Eric saw Michael.

"Good morning, Eric," Michael said with a smile.

"Good morning, Michael. Missed you at dinner last—" Eric stopped in mid-sentence.

"Are you alright, Eric?" Michael asked.

"Why don't you come into my office. I'd like to discuss something rather delicate with you," Eric said as he began walking towards his office. Michael followed, and as they walked by Eric's secretary, Eric leaned towards her. "Hold all my calls until I'm finished with Michael," he said in an ominous tone.

"Sit down, Michael. Can I get you a drink?" Eric asked

Michael smiled nervously and said, "It's 9 a.m. Eric, a little too early for me." Michael immediately sensed Eric was angry but wasn't sure if this was related to Maisy or business.

Eric poured himself a scotch, leaned himself on his desk, and stared intently at Michael.

"I noticed you haven't been coming by the house as often as you used to. I notice that you keep very late hours here at the office. Do you need some personnel support? I can allocate more staff because I also notice that my daughter is working those same late hours and she didn't come home last night." Eric's anger was visible. "Would you have anything to do with that?"

Michael knew Eric was astute and sharp. Just as he was about to respond, Maisy came into the office.

"Good morning, dad, Michael. I wanted to go over a few things with you, do you have some time now?"

Eric looked at his daughter and rather icily asked if the secretary had told her, he was in a meeting.

"Yes," she replied, "but she said you were with Michael so I thought it wouldn't be a problem if I just walked in." Maisy tried to be as natural as possible, but she knew there was nothing natural in her father's tone.

"I'm glad you're here," he said to her. "Shut the door. Is Michael the tall businessman you've been seeing for some time?" Eric asked in the coldest tone she had ever heard come out of his mouth.

Michael took a breath to answer, but Maisy responded with an incredibly quiet and feeble, "Yes, dad." She mustered all the strength she had and said, "I love him, dad, and I will not leave him."

Eric noticed a tremble in her voice and her hands shaking, as did Michael, who immediately took her in his arms.

"Eric, I know this is not what you wanted for your daughter," Michael said. "However, you did want someone who would love her the way she deserves to be loved and I am doing just that."

"Really? Was that what happened last night? Did you take advantage of my little girl? After everything I've done for you, you would deceive me and stab me in the back like a common criminal!" Eric said furiously. "I treated you like my brother, and I was there for you when there was no one else. I hid so many things you did from your father because I knew how much David would be hurt. And you repay me by screwing my daughter! I told you what my hopes were for her and the whole time you were doing this? I should have left you for dead, none of this would be happening right now! I want you gone, take whatever you want, except my daughter, and leave!" Eric was practically screaming at Michael. "The only reason I'm being lenient is that your father was a man I respected. You, I never want to see again."

"Dad, don't do this please!" Maisy said. "If you love me, please don't do this. I will find him, and I will be with him. There is nowhere you can send him that I won't follow."

With pain in his eyes, Eric looked to his daughter. "How could you deceive me like this, Maisy? Have I not been a good father to you?"

"Dad, I am in the unfortunate position of having to choose between the father I love and the man I cannot live without," Maisy responded crying. "I didn't deceive you, dad; I was trying not to hurt you." She took the ring out of her pocket. "We didn't just have sex, dad. We're engaged and we want to get married right away." Maisy showed her father the engagement ring with pride.

Eric recognized Marie's ring. David and Eric's father had gone together to the jewellers to pick it out. It was a priceless sapphire that David had designed just for Marie. Its value, immeasurable. He looked up at his daughter.

"It's a wedding I will not condone," he replied. "You do realize you are half his age? You do realize that this love you supposedly feel for him can only be short-lived. He could be your father!" Eric yelled at Maisy angrily. Maisy started to tremble, her father had never yelled at her like that, ever.

Michael put his arms around Maisy. "Listen, Eric, I know there is nothing I can say that you will hear right now. We had no intention of hurting you. We fell in love, and as that love grew, it transformed my life in a way I never dreamed possible. Do you remember, years ago, when Jenny took your hand and you danced to a song? At the end of it, I remember saying that I hoped I would find that kind of love someday? Well, I have, and there is nothing I wouldn't do to make sure that Maisy is happy every day of her life," Michael said, trying to quell Eric's anger.

Eric looked at Michael and said, "I want you gone! I want you to allow my daughter to find love, a love that will be long and lasting. She doesn't need another father, she has one, and right now, he is looking after her. Maisy, to you it may feel like I'm doing something very wrong, but in time, you'll come to understand that it was the right decision." He turned his attention back to Michael. "You have forty-eight hours to make arrange-ments, after that, I'll have you arrested." Eric took Maisy's hand. "You come with me, right now!" He called for his car to be ready and took his daughter home.

Before Eric and Maisy arrived home, Jenny had calls from Zain and Elena informing her of what had happened. They let Jenny know that although they had not heard the entire conversation, Eric was screaming at both Maisy and Michael. He was extremely angry with Michael and told him he had forty-eight hours to leave. That was what they were able to overhear of the conversation. Jenny waited patiently for her husband and daughter to arrive. She knew that Maisy was not equipped in any way to handle Eric's wrath. She had seen Eric in action in business and he seemed to adopt a different persona. He was not the caring and under- standing father she was accustomed to dealing with and could be very cold. Eric had never behaved this way with his family, so this was disturb- ing, to say the least.

The car ride home was quiet. Eric did not say a word to Maisy, who cried all the way home. Eric arrived and asked Jenny and Maisy to meet him in the library. He poured himself a double scotch and called the office to let them know that, although he had intentions of returning, he would realistically be in tomorrow. Any issues of any kind were to be delegated to Zain, Christopher, Elena, and Cole. He sat down and began drinking his scotch. Maisy went directly to her mother and cried in her arms. Jenny held her tightly and comforted her.

"Maisy, do you want to tell me what's going on before we sit with your father? At least give me some of the basic details?" Jenny asked gently as she wiped the tears away from Maisy's face, feeling the pain that her daughter was in.

"Mom," Maisy said, barely able to speak through her tears. "The person I've been seeing is Michael. Dad somehow figured it out and his anger just went through the roof. He was so upset, and I tried to explain that I was put in the impossible position of having to choose between the love I have for my father and the love I have for Michael. It was an impossible choice, Mom, you have to believe me. Look, Mom, we're engaged." Maisy showed her mother her engagement ring and smiled feebly.

Jenny held her daughter close and said, "Let's go talk to your father."

As they arrived in the library, Eric said, "Shut the door and sit down." He looked directly at Jenny and began his angry tirade. "The mystery man is Michael. They've been seeing each other for quite some time, and they've been sleeping together as well. Michael has been screwing my daughter and for how long, I can't be sure! This is why she couldn't bring him home and this is why he wasn't coming to the house for dinner. They were in the office for late-night activities or at his place, who knows at this point," Eric was screaming in anger. "He's twice your age; he manipulated your feelings for him!" Eric yelled as he spoke to Maisy. "You are so much smarter than this. How did this happen? I treated him like my younger brother and loved him like my sons, how could he do this?"

"Eric, stop!" Jenny said as she tried to calm the situation. "I know you're angry right now, but yelling at Maisy isn't going to resolve the situation."

"Oh, I've taken care of that! Michael has forty-eight hours to pack and leave, and if he doesn't, I will make him regret the day he was born," Eric replied.

"Is that what you would have done if someone had tried to separate us? I believe someone did and your reaction was not to walk away, Eric. They love each other." Jenny continued addressing her husband in a firm but soft voice, using his own experience to help him understand.

"Jenny, stop right there, this is different," Eric replied. "He is old enough to be her father. I confided in him about what I hoped Maisy would find in a man. He never once said anything. Does that sound like a decent man to you?"

"Eric, Michael loves you and I'm sure this wasn't easy for him," Jenny said. "You would send him to different parts of the world at a moment's notice, never once did he refuse. He did your bidding day in and out, and I'm sure he worked very hard on everything you put before him. He never let you down. He is the honest, intelligent man that you count on. Michael hasn't changed, Eric. He is still the man of integrity he ever was and one that you can trust. He is the same! What you don't like is that he's in a relationship with your daughter and he's twice her age. That's the problem here."

"Do you hear yourself?" Eric responded. "How can I trust someone who deceived me in the worst way? How can you not be upset about this whole thing, Jenny? He deceived me and he did that by using my daughter. How am I supposed to react to that, Jenny?" Eric looked at Jenny, confused by her reaction.

"Eric, Michael and Maisy were put in the position of choosing to love you or choosing to love each other. You, my love, did not provide another avenue. They both knew that you would not approve of this union for no other reason than his age," Jenny said calmly, trying to help Eric see reason.

"Michael was so torn over this dad," added Maisy. "Neither one of us meant to hurt you or deceive you. We had no choice. We started seeing each other over dinner for work and we began to talk. I so enjoy his intelligence, and that's what I was drawn to at first. Michael and I began to discuss a wide variety of topics and found we had a lot in common. We went to see plays, Broadway shows, the opera, symphonies, concerts, and even went to the circus," she said with a smile. "We connected in a way that I can't explain. From there, we became more romantically involved, and now we're engaged. Dad, Michael and I want to get married right away. If this had been anyone else, with Michael's character, you would be helping me plan a wedding. We did not deceive you, Dad. Our relationship just blossomed. I'm not leaving him, Dad, and he won't leave me."

"He hasn't been given a choice," Eric responded. "You think I'm being harsh. If Michael can deceive me, using my daughter, after everything I've done for him. How much will he deceive you with another woman? Have you thought about that? This is the man you put your trust in."

"He loves me, dad, and Michael wouldn't do anything you're suggesting. I know you understand what love is because you and mom have an incredibly powerful love between you. You are one body, one soul, and one life. Michael and I are the same, dad. Don't you want me to be happy? Or is my happiness defined by your terms? I don't think there's anything else to discuss here. I'll be in my room if you want to discuss this further, but my mind is made up, dad. If I have to live in squalor to be with Michael, sharing a piece of bread for dinner, then so be it. I'll be fine. I don't need anything else as long as he's with me." With that said, Maisy left the room.

Jenny looked at Eric. "Be careful what you do, Eric, because in your zeal to destroy Michael, you are destroying Miaisy. Michael makes her happy. I have never seen her look so beautiful, confident, radiant, and accomplished. You cannot deny that what they've successfully worked on together, the work they have produced, has been nothing short of outstanding. They are powerful together, as are we, Eric," Jenny said. While Jenny continued to try to calm Eric down and help him to see reason, Elena walked into the library.

"You can't do this, dad!" Elena said. "You can't pull them apart when you haven't seen them together!"

"And you have?" replied Eric, astonished. "You've known about this and said nothing?"

"Yes, I've known about them for a while and I've covered for her when she didn't come home," Elena replied. "He worships the ground she walks on, dad. The love those two share is storybook material, and you want to destroy that? If you saw how well Michael looks after Maisy, you would understand. All she has to do is mention something, and he already has it in his hands. They're connected in a way that I wish Cole and I were, but we're not. Sure, Cole and I love each other, but their love, well, it's nothing short of enviable." Elena turned to her mother and said, "Where is Maisy now?"

"She went to her room. She's emotionally exhausted, tired, and in a lot of pain. She could use some comfort," Jenny said to Elena kindly.

"I'll go check on her," Elena responded.

A few moments after Elena left the room, Eric and Jenny heard a bone-chilling shriek. They rushed upstairs to find Elena trying to wrap Maisy's wrists. She looked at her mother and screamed to her for help before it was too late. Eric immediately called for his pilot to take Maisy to the hospital by helicopter. While onboard, he called Steven, Brian's son, who had taken over since Brian's retirement, and explained what had hap- pened. Steven replied that he would be ready to receive Maisy as soon as they arrived. Elena called Michael.

Jenny, holding her daughter's hand, looked at her husband and said, "Is this better? Is this what you were hoping for? She's your daughter and behaved the same way you did when you thought you lost me. She loves Michael, Eric. Maisy loves Michael." She stressed the last three words of her sentence.

Once at the hospital, Steven was waiting to take care of Maisy. Michael arrived in utter despair. Jenny ran to meet him to explain that Steven was looking after her and they were waiting to hear from him. She took his hand and brought him into the room Maisy would be taken to and where

Eric was waiting. In his rage, Michael lunged at Eric.

Michael grabbed him and said, "I don't care how powerful you are, you will not keep Maisy away from me. You will have to kill me for that to happen and Maisy would never forgive you".

Eric took Michael's hands off him and said, "Never do that again. You'll regret it. Right now, my only concern is ensuring my daughter is going to be okay. Once this ordeal is over, we will discuss your situation."

Steven came in and said she was stable but in a coma. She would be brought in soon.

"I would like to start a course of antibiotics. This may be an awkward question, but I have to ask," Steven said. "Is there any chance Maisy might be pregnant?"

Michael looked at Steven and said, "There may be, I can't be sure."

Steven nodded. "I'll just run a quick test then, to be sure." He instructed the nurse to take a blood sample and get the information to him stat. Then he smiled and left the room. Maryam and Sara arrived with Christopher and Zain.

"Is she going to be alright?" Zain asked in horror.

"She'll be fine, she's a fighter. If I know my Maisy, she won't leave me," Michael responded, tears streaming down his face. They all stood quietly in the room waiting for Maisy to be brought in.

Cole finally came in and took Elena in his arms. "How are you holding up?" he asked.

She smiled and said she was okay, just really worried right now.

Cole looked at her and said, "I hear you're the one that found her. It must have been pretty traumatic." Steven was just entering the room and overheard Cole.

"If it hadn't been for Elena's quick thinking, Maisy might not be here. If anyone saved her life it was Elena." Then he asked, "Okay, well who do I give the good or bad news to?"

"What are you talking about?" Eric responded.

"Maisy is pregnant, so I will prescribe amoxicillin, which is a light antibiotic we give safely to children. I will do my best to keep her comfortable. Hopefully, she'll come out of it soon," Steven said. "I don't know what's going on and don't want to know, but this young lady is utterly exhausted and extremely stressed, that's why she's in a coma. Her body has shut down to help her stabilize. People that come into the hospital in this condition normally do not go into a coma. If they do, it's primarily for the reasons I've mentioned." Steven looked at everyone in the room before leaving.

A smile came to Michael's worn, distraught face. He was overjoyed with the news and couldn't wait to tell Maisy. Eric closed his eyes and squeezed Jenny's hand. She put her arms around him and held him tight. Eric looked at his wife and tears streamed down his face.

"I need to get some air," Eric said and left the room. Jenny immediately followed. Eric put his head in his hands and cried.

"God has a way of teaching us difficult lessons through our children," he said to Jenny. "When I found out we were having the boys, I was so happy. Do you remember what you said to me?" Eric asked.

Jenny smiled and wiped the tears from his face. "Yes," she said. "You told me that our love was so strong, we made life, the very first time we made love. Well, my guess is that's what happened here."

"Jenny, I didn't want this for her, I wanted something more, so much more," he said crying. "She's my amazing Maisy, and I did this to her by not giving her a choice."

"We don't choose who we fall in love with, Eric. God joined them and they love each other. You could not have wished for a better man to look after your daughter, and you know that. Yes, he's older but so are you."

"Yes, but I'm not twice your age. It doesn't matter. I won't come between them. If this is what makes Maisy happy, then so be it," Eric replied.

Eric came back into the room and said nothing. Maisy had been brought in and the antibiotics had been connected to her. She was so   pale, she reminded him of Jenny after she gave birth to her and her sister. Michael walked toward Eric.

"Eric, I don't want to fight with you anymore," Michael said. "Maisy and I will leave. We have a family now and I need to think of them. I can restart anywhere. I wish I could make you understand. Maisy is my Jenny. She saved me." He turned away from Eric and took Maisy's hand, holding it tight while everyone in the room wept.

"I think it's time we gave these two some privacy," Eric said. "Why don't we go home. I'm sure Michael will let us know if there are any complications."

Before he left, Eric took Maisy in his arms and cried. "My beautiful Maisy, can you ever forgive me? You should have never had to choose between Michael and me. I love you so much, Maisy, and I promise to give you the biggest wedding you can imagine. Just come back to me honey, just come back," Eric said tearfully as he lay Maisy down and made sure she was comfortable. He looked to Michael, "Take good care of my daughter, make sure she has everything she needs. I'll be back in the morning." Eric took Jenny's hand and called for a few cars to pick everyone up.

Once home, Eric went to Maisy's room. The blood had all been cleaned and it looked as if nothing had happened. But Eric remembered standing at the doorway and seeing his daughter limp and bleeding. How could he not have seen the love she felt for him and Michael? How could he have been so blinded by his rage that God saw fit to show him in the most painful of ways? He would never be able to forgive himself for causing his beautiful, sweet daughter so much pain. He made her choose and rather than making that choice, she tried to take her life because she loved them both. Eric lay in Maisy's bed and cried uncontrollably. Jenny laid down with him, held him close, and they wept together until they fell asleep from exhaustion.

37

Eric and Jenny arrived at the hospital at 6 a.m. the next morning. Looking very strained and fatigued, they came into the room to find Michael asleep with Maisy in his arms. Eric had brought Michael a fresh cup of coffee and woke him with it. Michael's eyes were so swollen, he could hardly see. He had spent the night crying and praying that Maisy would come out of it. He thanked Eric for the coffee and said there had not been any change in her condition. Jenny asked Michael if he wanted to go home, maybe get changed, take a shower, and come back. They would stay with Maisy until he returned. Michael would not leave her side.

"Thank you, Jenny," Michael said, "but I'll go home when I can take my family with me," Eric smiled. They stayed for most of the morning, then Eric asked Michael to notify him if there was any change.

"I'm at the office and not far. I can be here at a moment's notice," Eric said. He took Jenny's hand and left.

After an exceedingly difficult night, Jenny thought it best to stay at the penthouse for a while, get some distance from the house that now had a very painful memory in it. She worked downtown at the Centre and Eric drowned himself in work. It was his distraction; work was the only way he could cope with what was happening in his life right now. Eric worked twelve- to fifteen-hour days, only stopping to drop in and check on Maisy. Jenny could not stand to see him this way and decided enough was enough. She walked into the office and had the secretary inform Zain, Christopher, Elena, and Cole to meet her in Eric's office. Once they arrived, she told the boys she was taking their father upstairs as he needed to rest. Eric refused to leave. He had been working on Michael's 5.2-billion-dollar deal and was nowhere near prepared for the meeting on Wednesday. Zain let his dad know that he and Chris could take that on and be ready for Wednesday. Eric admired his confidence and asked if he knew anything about it, to which Zain said yes.

"Dad, you have four of the best minds in the country right here. Do you think we can't get this done?" Zain asked.

"These people are shrewd and business savvy, Zain. It won't be an easy deal," Eric replied.

"Shrewd? Bring it on, Dad. I was born for this and it's not my first rodeo," replied Zain laughing. "Mom, take dad upstairs and do him right. Nothing like a good afternoon in bed to recharge the batteries," he said with a huge smirk on his face.

"Zain!" Elena replied "That's your mother you're talking to. Have some respect."

"Well, if anyone can fix Dad, it's Mom, just saying!" He replied. "We've got this, Dad. Nothing will get past Chris and me. Is everything we need here?"

"No, some of it's still in Michael's office. I've mapped out a plan of attack and was just looking for details," Eric said, so tired he could hardly speak.

"Perfect," Zain responded. "Although once Chris and I get through with your plan, I'm sure we'll find holes in it, old man. C'mon, disappear, we have work to do. Elena, Cole, how about you give us a hand, the more minds on this deal the better. Looks like we'll be having dinner here tonight."

"I'll call Arthur and let him know," replied Elena.

"I'll get the files from Michael's office," said Christopher.

They worked incessantly together, creating an airtight plan. Elena ordered dinner and they took a break.

"Dad's in pretty bad shape," Zain said, "but I don't think he should beat himself up about it. He was doing what any father would do to protect his little girl. Unfortunately, he learned a painful lesson."

"Yeah, that you can't push people too far and that you should listen when they're trying to tell you something, especially family," replied Christopher.

"No, I don't think that's it at all," Zain said. "Dad felt betrayed by both his daughter and Michael. He didn't expect that his daughter would be manipulated by an older man, one that he trusted completely."

"She wasn't being manipulated," responded Elena. "Cole and I had dinner with them several times. He worships her. The love between those two is so strong, I'm not surprised that Maisy did what she did. Dad forced her to choose between himself and Michael. Maisy couldn't do that, so she decided to solve the problem in the worst way."

"No, little sister, Dad was blinded by rage," responded Zain. "He needed some time to calm down and then he would have thought things through, and Mom would have helped him. He didn't get that chance. He had no idea Maisy would do what she did. And now he's completely distraught. Do you realize how he must be feeling right now? His daughter could die and take his only grandchild with her because of a decision he made. But I don't think he needs to feel that kind of guilt. Dad's a shark in business because he makes sure he has every shred of information. He works hard to get that information and he's successful because he's prepared. He had no idea what was going on. He was completely blindsided by two people he loves. It was a punch in the gut he did not see coming and he reacted in rage, especially thinking that Michael, being twice her age, took advantage of his little girl. I don't blame Dad one bit. Any father would have reacted the way he did."

"Dad learned an important lesson, I think," Christopher said. "He learned that family is all you have, and it is both precious and fragile. How a man deals with his family requires careful handling of the facts you know and responding to those you don't. It's his response that Dad is strug- gling with right now, not whether Maisy and Michael love each other or whether they deceived him or not. It's the fact that he made her choose without foreseeing the results of his actions. I think Dad is struggling with the fact that he didn't know his daughter as well as he thought, and that's why he couldn't anticipate that she would try to kill herself. The shark completely miscalculated his move."

"Maybe there's some truth to that," replied Zain as he picked at his food, "but I think he acted in a blind rage, and that all of this would have ended very differently if he had just been given time. I don't see any fault in Dad's decision, maybe it's because I'm so much like him that I understand him. This whole situation has got me thinking about my relationship, and I think I want to marry Maryam. What am I waiting for exactly? We're both thirty, both ready for a family, and I don't see my life without her in it. Chris, you know I've been building a house not far from Dad's, and it's almost ready. A few more days as the furniture is just coming in. I'm going to give it to her as a wedding present," Zain said smiling. Just then, his phone rang.

"Mary, calm down, what's going on?" Zain said. "I'm here at the office with Chris, Cole, and Elena." He paused before hanging up and letting everyone know that Maryam was on her way and was upset. "I can't tell if she's angry or hurt," he said. They continued working until she arrived. Maryam walked into the office, visibly hurt, and upset. She walked directly over to Zain and asked who Janet was.

"I don't know," Zain replied.

"I've been getting messages about all kinds of things you've done. It's been going on for a while and I never said anything to you because I thought there are probably so many women who want to be with you and are jealous," Maryam said. "But this, Zain Barrett, is the last straw.

This was sent to me today. A clear message that I can't trust you." She passed him her phone, which showed a video of him having sex with a woman named Janet.

Zain looked at it carefully. "Look at this video, Mary, but don't look at what I'm doing, look at the windows in behind me. What do you see?" he asked. Maryam refused to look at it again. Zain passed the phone over to Chris. "What do you see?" he asked.

Christopher looked at the video and said, "Christmas lights? There are Christmas lights on the window."

"Exactly! See?" Zain said looking at Mary. "Please, Mary, look beyond what I'm doing, look at the window."

Maryam looked and realized Christopher was right. "Christmas lights," she whispered.

"This was long before I met you, and this girl, I don't remember who she is, because she meant nothing to me. I may have been completely drunk," he said. "I know this was tough to watch, and I've done things in my past I'm not proud of, but one thing I know is true, there is no one in my life but you. You probably won't believe me if I say this, so I won't. Would someone tell Mary what I was just talking about before she came?" Zain asked.

"Are you sure you don't want to tell her yourself?" said Christopher. "I mean this is milestone shit."

"She will never believe me right now, little brother," Zain said.

"Zain was telling us that he wanted to marry you," responded Elena.

Maryam looked at him. "Just so that you can have sex?" she asked.

"No," he responded, "just so that I can have it with you, every day of my life. I love you, Mary. I have been faithful to you from the first day we met. Do you think I'm stupid enough to jeopardize the only thing in my life that makes it worth living? I would never do that! I need you Mary, and I want to marry you."

Maryam couldn't stay angry at him. She realized he was right; the video had been used to pull them apart and it had almost worked. She loved him so much and jumped into his arms, ecstatically happy.

"There we go, just like that, come to daddy," Zain said smiling. "So, I was thinking tomorrow, unless you want to have a big wedding," he said as he held her in his arms.

"Zain, tomorrow is Tuesday. Who gets married on a Tuesday?" she asked.

"Does Friday work for you?" Zain asked. "Do you think you can clear your schedule to marry me on Friday? I don't want to wait anymore."

"Friday is perfect, Zain," she said. "Just the family and my parents, that's all I want."

Zain looked at his siblings. "I'll be right back, and we'll keep working. I just want to tell Mom and Dad," Zain said as he and Maryam went to the penthouse.

38

It would be two more days before Maisy showed any signs of improvement. Eric held her hand and whispered in her ear.

"Maisy, I know you can hear me, honey. I was so angry, so wrapped in my rage that I didn't hear what you were trying so desperately to tell me. You should have never been put into the position of having to choose. I am so sorry, Maisy. Please give me a chance to make it up to you. I love you, my precious, precious little girl."

He saw tears stream down the side of her eyes and realized she had heard him. "Fight, Maisy, fight whatever is holding you down. Fight for Michael, my grandchild, and me Maisy, because I would never be able to forgive myself for what I did to you," Eric said as he held his little girl close to him, tortured by his own emotions. Jenny came in with coffee for everyone and looked over at her husband.

"She may have her mother's heart, but she has her father's determination. She's a fighter and she'll come out of this," Jenny said. "It's going to be okay," she said reassuring her husband. Exhausted, worried, and unable to focus on anything else, they spent the day at the hospital and then went home.

The next morning, Eric arrived with Jenny, looking ragged and exhausted, at 5 a.m. Maisy's situation had taken its toll on Eric, and it was noticeable. Eric touched Michael on the shoulder, and Maisy opened her eyes.

"Please dad, let him sleep," Maisy said. "He's so tired."

At that moment, the joy that Eric felt in his heart at seeing Maisy out of the coma, was overwhelming. His little girl was awake, and he was so grateful.

"It's so good to see those beautiful eyes of yours," Eric said as he kissed her forehead. "Did Michael tell you the news?" Eric asked.

"No, Dad, you did. Are you upset? I never meant to hurt you," she said crying.

"Why would I be upset, princess?" Eric said smiling at Maisy. "I'm going to be a grandfather! You've given me the greatest joys of my life, with your love, and with my grandchild."

"So, I can marry Michael?" she asked smiling.

"I'll throw the wedding of the century, even David and Marie will hear about it," Eric replied. "Michael is a good man. He will be a good father, and he loves you Maisy. Of that, I am now certain."

Just then, Michael stirred. "Thank God for that, because the thought of having to move and get a new job was stressing me out," he said laughing, and they all laughed with him.

"I have some good news to share," Jenny said. "Zain and Maryam have decided to get married, and they're doing it this Friday at the house followed by a nice dinner, just our family and her parents. Do you think you can muster the strength to be there with Michael?"

"Even if I have to sit in a wheelchair, Mom, I'll be there for Zain and Maryam," Maisy replied with a smile.

Jenny wiped the tears from her eyes and said, "Well, there's a lot to do before Friday. I think I'll start by sending Mary Anne over. You can choose a nice dress to wear. Under the circumstances, she'll most likely bring a catalog but I'm sure you'll look beautiful no matter what you wear." Jenny held her daughter close to her and cried, both relieved and happy her daughter was out of danger. Jenny and Eric left Maisy in Michael's capable hands. Jenny went home to attend to preparations for the wedding.

After his visit at the hospital, Eric went straight to the office. He was stressed about the meeting the boys were having today. Specifically, the 5.2-billion-dollar deal on the table at today's meeting. *7at deal has to be airtight*, Eric thought, *and they're up against some of the sharpest minds in the world.* Eric arrived at the office around noon. He had spent a little more time with Maisy, but it was well worth it. Once he arrived, he asked the secretary to let Zain and Christopher know he would meet them in his office. The boys came in with profoundly serious looks on their faces, and Eric asked for an update. Were they ready for this meeting?

"Dad, there was a lot of work to do and the plan you mapped out wasn't going to cut it for the scope of this deal. We had to start from scratch and a few days wasn't exactly enough time for us to get it together," Zain said with an austere look on his face.

Eric's face went pale. "So where are we?" he asked as he looked at his sons anxiously.

Zain gave Christopher a worried look. "Do you want to tell him?"

"Yeah," Christopher replied as he took a deep breath. "Dad we're 5.2 billion dollars richer as of 11:30 today," he said with a huge smile on his face.

"What? How?" Eric said with a smile wider than the St. Lawrence River.

"The meeting started at seven and by eleven-thirty we were done," Zain explained. "Together, the Barrett brothers are a force to be reckoned with, old man. We hammered out the plan and worked nonstop along with Elena and Cole. Michael helped too. I had to call him to get some information, and he insisted on participating. So, we connected with him via a video conference. The group came together with Michael's help, and we ensured that all aspects of this deal had been addressed and any weaknesses exposed. We came in ready, guns blazing, and four and a half hours later; we were done," said Zain.

"That's why Michael kept staring at his watch all morning," Eric said smiling. "I have to say, I'm pretty impressed. Maybe it's time I retire or at least take on consultative tasks. I don't think I could ever leave this place," he said proudly as he looked at his sharks.

"Nah, we still need you at the helm, old man. You can come in later and leave early, but we expect you to be at work," replied Zain, appearing to give an order.

"Don't you have wedding plans to take care of?" Eric asked "Friday is only a few days away. Did you get a tux?"

"We're Barrett's, Dad," Christopher replied. "Everything we need comes to us."

"Exactly," Zain replied. "All I had to do was make a few phone calls, and if you ask Mom, the house is full of plans in the making as we speak," Zain said with a conceited smirk on his face.

Christopher and Zain left the office and Eric put his feet up on his desk and leaned back. There was a lot of truth to what the boys were saying. They were definitely a coveted family, and any event would most likely yield many takers. Eric Barrett had accumulated a staggering fortune of 2.5 trillion dollars. His children had inherited an empire they were fully capable of running and expanding. Eric was pleased with what he and Jenny had been able to do together, and as he thought of Zain's wedding, he remembered his own. How he couldn't wait, got married in the hospital, and how Jenny transformed his life from that day forward. Teaching and showing Eric that the things most valuable and precious in life could not be bought; his greatest joys didn't cost him a cent. Jenny's unconditional love, the boys' birth, then his precious girls, the countless birthdays, anniversaries, family gatherings that filled his heart with so much joy, he often thought it would burst. He had been favoured and blessed on so many levels and through Jenny's work at the Centre and the Foundation, he was able to give back. Worldwide programs that had been established to support children and their families, literacy and education programs, adoption centres, accommodations for teenage girls, either pregnant or abused. Programs that addressed violence against women, people suffering from mental health, and provided a haven for the most vulnerable. This is what Jenny brought to the family. Her selfless, unconditional love helped so many people worldwide. So, when a 5.2-billion-dollar deal was secured, he felt confident the money was not only benefitting his family but a myriad of people and children around the world that counted on the Barrett's for their very survival. Eric felt quite content, and with everything taken care of, at least for today, he wanted to go home and hold his wife.

39

For a small family wedding, there were shutterbugs and video cameras everywhere. It was a difficult task just to get to the gates of the house. When Eric finally got inside, he was somewhat overwhelmed. Eric looked at Jenny and she smiled.

"Our house has been a circus today," Jenny said. "I think Zain must have told every news agency and media company in the world." She laughed as she walked over to embrace her husband.

Eric smiled. "Well, it's not every day that a Barrett gets married," he said.

"It was supposed to be a quiet, family affair, remember?" Jenny said with a funny look on her face.

"There is nothing quiet about Zain," Eric replied laughing. "The guest list may be limited to twenty people, but in reality, millions are tuning in." Eric realized just how much he and Zain were alike. "Would you join me in a scotch, my love?" Eric asked.

"Sure, I think we have a few minutes," Jenny replied. Eric poured a few glasses and walked over to the living room holding Jenny's hand. He stood before his parents' portrait and began to talk to his father.

"Well, Christopher, today is a big day. Zain is getting married to his wonderful Maryam. I know you're pleased with him, he's a shark, smart, sharp, and very handsome. A little cocky, but so was I and you didn't seem to mind. I need you to look after them, Dad. Like you've looked after all of us, as we kept growing. Today Maryam becomes another Barrett and will need your protection from what we aren't able to see, but you can, from above. I love you and miss you both," Eric said proudly as he spoke of his family to his deceased parents.

Jenny held her husband close, gave him a gentle kiss, and whispered in his ear, "It's time to get dressed, my love."

Jenny took her husband's hand and went upstairs. Once in the bedroom Eric took off his clothes to get into the shower and grabbed Jenny. "Do you remember our first shower together? C'mon, Jenny," he said with a naughty but inviting smile.

She looked at Eric and smiled. "What the hell, why not? We have enough time." They enjoyed each other for a while and Eric told Jenny how blessed he felt. He loved her dearly, and over the years, that love had not changed. He still couldn't manage to get by one day without her close to him.

"I love you too, Eric," she responded, "but we have to get ready now!"

Eric was ready in no time. Once finished with his shower, he put on his tux and was ready. Jenny needed a little more time. Hair and makeup stylists would be at the house soon. Her Armani evening gown had been delivered last night. A beautiful strapless, heart-shaped, black lace, floor-sweeping gown. Jenny took longer than usual to get ready. She wanted to look her best for the wedding, but more so for Eric. When Eric saw her come down the stairs, he stared at her like he was seeing her for the first time.

"You look beautiful, Mrs. Barrett," Eric said as he smiled. "Why am I the only one aging in his house? You look as stunning today as the first day I met you." She took him in her arms and kissed him.

The wedding was beautiful. The solarium had been transformed into a magical place, lights, flowers, lace, and veils cascading from the ceiling, lining the windows and tables. It was stunning. The family was present and there was an energy of happiness, anticipation, and love in the room. Maisy had arrived and looked stunning in a Versace gown with Michael by her side. Zain was so pleased to see them, he rushed over to give his sister a warm hug. Elena and Sarah were breathtaking in their designer gowns so much so that neither Cole nor Christopher could stop staring at them, admiring their beauty and thanking God for the blessing. For both Cole and Christopher, the thought of marriage became very real at that moment as they each pondered their happiness and bliss.

Maryam was a vision of beauty and Zain could hardly contain his emotions when he saw her. Maryam chose her dress from her mother-in-law's favourite designer, Armani, and she looked both radiant and breathtaking. Her dress had a heart-shaped, lace, tight-fitting bodice and a long sweeping gown that was lined with layers and layers of veil. The overlay was in an intricately designed lace. The lace sleeves were off the shoulders and tightly fitted around her arms. Mary looked spectacular. Zain was speechless. He took her hand and gently kissed her lips.

"My God, Mary, you're magnificent," Zain said looking at her in awe.

Mary smiled. "I'm glad you like it."

After seeing Maryam, he was glad he had allowed a few networks to come in and record the ceremony. He wanted the whole world to see his beautiful wife. It would go viral immediately. A lot like his father, Zain found it exceedingly difficult to keep his happiness a secret.

The ceremony was beautiful. The love between Zain and Maryam permeated everything in the room; a love felt by everyone in an immensely powerful way. It was precisely this love that was captured by the media and went viral in seconds. Once the ceremony was complete, the media were kindly asked to leave the premises. The dinner was shared with the immediate family, and Maryam's parents, as per Zain's request. Christopher had quite a speech prepared for his brother. He started by roasting him completely and ended in a loving and touching tone, so much so, that Christopher had tears in his eyes. Eric's turn was next.

"Well, Mary, you said I do, and God help you," Eric said laughing. "Nah, all joking aside, he's a good man, a little arrogant, conceited, and yes, downright cocky, but only because he knows his worth. In business, he is ruthless, a shark, astute, and an incredible force. As a man, he is hardworking, honest, respectable, and has his mother's heart. Zain will love you unconditionally for the rest of his life. He will be an outstand- ing father, doting on his children and making sure they want for nothing. You've been blessed with each other. The love you share today will never die. Don't listen to those who say they stopped loving one another or that they've grown apart. That's not it. When you love deeply, spiritually, with your entire being, as both of you do, that love never dies. It continues to grow as you both grow. Welcome to the family, Mary, and God bless you both. Cheers."

The dance floor was immediately opened by the bride and groom. Everyone was having a wonderful time, dancing, chatting, and joking. Eric and Jenny basked in their son's joy and happiness. Zain tapped his wine glass to gain everyone's attention and asked his mom and dad to take the dance floor for the Savage Garden song "Truly, Madly, Deeply." Eric took his lovely wife in his arms. The love in their eyes was just as magical as the room they were in.

It was about 1 a.m. when Zain asked everyone to kindly get into the limousines he had waiting outside. Everyone was confused, asking where they were going, but Zain was tight-lipped and simply showed them to the cars waiting outside. They drove about twenty minutes up the road and entered through beautiful black, wrought iron gates. Eric looked at Jenny and smiled.

"Looks familiar?" he asked. As they approached, a mansion became visible. Zain took his wife's hand, who was in utter shock. Once out of the limousine, Zain looked into his wife's eyes.

"This is my wedding present to you, Mary," he said. "Welcome home, my love." Maryam held her husband in her arms, tears in her eyes, and so much love in her heart. She kissed him, then Zain opened the door and asked everyone to come in.

The mansion was impressive. It was very much like the house Zain had grown up in with modern touches instead of antiques, except in the formal living and dining rooms, which were Louis XVI-styled rooms.

Eric hugged his son. "Well done, Zain," he said proudly. The house was fully equipped with staff and servants who served the wedding cake, various desserts, all kinds of specialty coffees and teas, and of course, scotch. Everyone was having a wonderful time, chatting and taking a tour of the incredible mansion. A few hours later; Zain tapped his wine glass to get everyone's attention.

"It is such a pleasure to have my family here with me tonight. You've made this day so exceptionally special for the both of us. I'd like to thank you all for sharing the most important day of our lives and thank you for ending the celebration in our home. However, at the risk of sounding crass, it's 4 a.m. and I've been waiting an awfully long time to make love to my wife." While everyone else laughed, Maryam was completely embarrassed.

"Zain Barrett, you don't just ask people to leave," she said.

"I did say God help you, didn't I, Mary?" Eric said laughing.

Zain and Mary said good night as the family headed home. Zain shut the door.

"Finally, alone," he said. "Let's go to bed, Mary."

"Zain, all I have is the wedding dress I'm wearing. I don't have anything to wear to bed" Mary said, looking a little disappointed.

Zain smiled at her. "I wouldn't worry too much about that. You won't need to wear anything to bed. C'mon Mary, we have a lot of lost time to make up for," he said as picked her up and carried her upstairs.

40

Maisy and Michael were married two weeks later. She decided on a small wedding and, much like Zain, used the solarium for the ceremony and only invited family. She looked stunning in her Givenchy wedding gown. The love between her and Michael was stronger than it had ever been. Once the Imam had finished the ceremony, they retired to the dining room for a lovely dinner. They had a wonderful meal, danced all night long, and enjoyed being a happy family. After a delightful evening, Maisy and Michael left for their new home; an expansive mansion of their own built by David and now housing the new Jones family, Michael and Maisy Jones.

The Barrett family continued to grow with Elena and Cole marrying the year after and Christopher and Sarah a year after that. Although the Barrett family had vast resources to host lavish weddings, all of them chose to celebrate their nuptials with a small family gathering in the magical solarium of the family home.

Time seemed to pass quickly. Eric had become grandfather to two wonderful children. Maisy had a boy and named him David. Eric was pleased with the choice and said no one deserved that honour more than David did. He knew his friend smiled from above and was well pleased with his new grandson. Zain also had a boy. The day Zain revealed his newborn's name was a day Eric would not forget. Zain had named his son Eric Michael Barrett, like his father. When Eric took his grandson into his arms, he felt both pride and gratitude and commented on the fact that he had red hair, and green eyes, as he smiled at the grandson in his arms.

"He looks a lot like you, Dad," Zain said. "So, I think the name is fitting." That day, Eric stood tall and proud.

As time passed, Zain had two more children, Dani, named after Mary's father, and Laila, his beautiful little girl. Maisy also had a little girl, who she named Marie after Michael's mother and whom Maisy loved dearly. Jenny was so proud of Maisy's choice. Marie was a wonderful woman and a dear friend. Elena had a boy, Zacharia, and a little girl named Hope, while Christopher had a little girl, named Jenna after his mother, and a boy named Matthew Michael Barrett; he used his grandfather and father's middle names. The two men he admired and respected most.

The family had grown considerably in the last ten years, and it continued to grow as both Maryam and Sarah were pregnant. Family gatherings for birthdays, anniversaries, Christmas, Eid, and all manner of life events continued to take place in the dining room, and the house was full as was Eric's heart. He enjoyed his grandchildren so much and visited with each of them daily. At night, he video-conferenced with all of them to read bedtime stories, except for Christopher's children. They lived with him, and Jenny was grateful to have them fill the house with joy. Eric enjoyed cuddling up with Jenna and Matthew, reading bedtime stories, tucking them in, and kissing each of them good night.

As the Barrett family changed, so too did the family dynamics. Eric worked closely with Zain, Elena, Maisy, Christopher, Michael, and Cole. Jenny worked with Mary and Sarah. Once they became part of the family, Jenny wanted the girls to be part of her team, if they so chose, to help her expand her programs.

"I won't miss the graveyard shift at all," Mary said, "but I will miss the children."

"Not to worry, Mary. There are plenty of children at the Centre," Jenny replied. "You won't miss them at all."

"I'm afraid we won't be much help," said Sarah. "We're pediatric nurses and know nothing of business."

"I knew nothing when I started and I can assure you, you will be an amazing duo," Jenny said.

From that day forward, Mary and Sarah received excellent training from their mother-in-law, and a new vision was created by three very ambitious ladies whose only goal was to help children in need. To that end, Mary and Sarah began to work at the Susan Barrett Centre. There they developed their business skills, and, because of their nurses' train- ing, were able to identify missing components in the pediatric units and develop much more effective services. Autism, learning disabilities, and developmental delay were identified as areas where children were grossly underfunded. Yes, the government provided some funding, but it was minimal in respect to what was required. This left many parents who could not afford private care desperate for assistance. Together, the ladies began to work on expanding the Susan Barrett Centre in order to open a wing to address this need. As they began to work on the development of a wing, it became apparent that a new Centre would have to be created to effectively address the needs identified. A new Centre was developed. It was a massive undertaking that involved residential units, treatment centres, educational facilities, and both psychological and medical personnel. Sarah and Mary had worked relentlessly on its development, construction, and architec- tural design, as did Christopher and Zain, who wanted to help their wives achieve their ambitious goals.

Opening day for the Centre arrived and Jenny was eager to see what her precious girls had created. Jenny was in awe. The girls had not designed a centre, they had created an incredible complex designed to meet the multitude of diverse needs for this very underfunded population. So many parents and children would finally be able to access professional assistance that had been inaccessible without financial means. As the girls unveiled the complex and introduced it, Jenny had tears of pride streaming down her face. The Jenny Barrett Complex for Special Needs Children was now open. Jenny rushed onto the stage, tears streaming down her face, and hugged her daughters-in-law proudly while giving thanks to God for the girls and the complex.

After this achievement, the ladies began to think on a much larger scale. Centres were opened worldwide. Where there was a Barrett office, so too would there be a centre designed to help children suffering from mental health issues, abuse, or trauma, and women who had suffered from domestic violence. Within ten years, the centres were built, and people were accessing their services worldwide. Eric and Jenny were very proud of Mary and Sarah as well as their husbands and siblings who helped make these ambitious dreams a reality. The Barrett's had worked together with countless staff to realize a dream, Jenny's dream, to help as many children as she could with what God had given her.

As Eric thought about all of these incredible achievements, he poured himself a scotch and walked toward the living room. It took him a lot longer now that he was seventy-two. The house had somehow become larger and much more difficult to navigate, especially the stairs. He stood in front of his parents' portrait.

"Well, Dad, we've built quite an empire, Jenny and I, both in busi- ness and in the family. I think you can be immensely proud of the Barrett's today."

Jenny stood next to him smiling. "I think he would be very proud, Eric, but I also think it's time for bed." She took his hand, and they made their way up the stairs.

In the morning, as they were finishing breakfast, Christopher knocked on the door.

"Dad, can I speak to you about something that's been on my mind?"

"Sure, Chris. Come in son, sit down," Eric replied with a smile. "Why don't you take the seat you used to sit in as a child."

"Do you want some coffee, Christopher?" asked Jenny.

"No, I just want to talk to you both about something that might be a little contentious with the rest of the family."

"What's on your mind son?" asked Eric intrigued.

"Dad, although I'm not privy to the information in your will, I'm quite sure you have taken care of all of your children extremely well. I was won- dering what your plans were for our home. It's the place that houses our memories, our family heritage, our ancestry, so much of who we are is right here." Christopher paused and then continued. "Have you decided whether or not to bequeath it to one of us?"

"Well, son, for all the reasons you mentioned, your mother and I thought we would leave it to the four of you. My father and his father before him only had one son, so it wasn't an issue. Do you see something wrong with that?" asked Eric.

"I do, for many reasons," Christopher replied. I suspected that you and mom would probably leave it to all of us to be fair. However, I do have some concerns that I feel need to be addressed regarding the house. So, rather than discussing them here just with the both of you, I was wondering if you would call a family meeting to address the concerns I have in this respect."

"Would you mind telling your mother and me what these concerns are before this meeting is called?"

"Sure, without going into too much detail, Zain and Elena have built beautiful mansions, and Maisy has moved into Michael's. I could have built a mansion, but I like living here, it's my home and now my children's home. I would like to continue to live here with my family and if we each own a part, me and my family would never really feel like this was our home. We would eventually have to build our own home to make it ours. Right now, it's Mom and Dad's house. Left to all of us, no one would be here to look after it. We would be involved at work and then we would all go to our respective homes at the end of the day. You see, the issue is it would be empty, just another house. The soul of the Barrett family is in this house, an identity, heritage, and soul I want to protect. Therefore, I really would prefer living in it and protecting it. To do so, I was wondering if I could present a proposal to my siblings to purchase it."

"I see," Eric said as he pondered his son's request.

"Christopher, it would be very difficult to put a price on this house for the very reasons you mentioned," responded Jenny. "Your siblings would not want to give that up."

"I know, Mom, that's why I was hoping we could discuss it together. I would identify my concerns and hope to reach a mutual agreement. It is and will always be the Barrett home."

"Alright, I think it's fair to sit down with your siblings and hash this out. I'm glad we're doing this because it will also allow me the opportunity to discuss how our family businesses will be run when your mother and I have passed on," responded Eric.

"Honey, I think this meeting will take quite some time as it is, perhaps we will deal with Christopher's situation first and hold the business conversation for another day," said Jenny.

"You're probably right, one thing at a time. Look who's telling who what to do now," Eric said with a smirk on his face as he looked at Jenny. "I'll call and set up a meeting here at home Friday night. We'll have dinner together and discuss the future of the house."

"Thanks, Dad. I wouldn't have mentioned it if it wasn't important to me and Sarah. We've discussed this for a while now and felt this was the best way to move forward. If we cannot reach consensus then I'll have to begin planning the building of my own home," Christopher said and kissed his mother on the way out.

Jenny looked over at Eric. "What do you think?" she asked.

"He has a point, with everyone involved in their own lives in their own homes, this one might be left like one of the others, and although we take good care of those homes, they are not as important as this old estate. Honestly, I wouldn't want to die knowing that this Estate would be left empty and possibly abandoned. It's too important to me. But how do we put a price on it? Let's see what our sharks have to say about it."

Eric arranged for the family to meet for dinner and told everyone that Christopher had a proposal he would like to discuss with the family. Eric wanted to make sure they were all aware that something of importance would be discussed.

Zain arrived first. Walked into the dining room and looked over at his father.

"Hey old man, how are you doing today?" He gave his father a warm hug. "I have to say I'm not comfortable with this. It can't be good if Barrett's are making proposals to each other," he said smiling.

"Zain, your brother has a proposal that he wants to discuss with all of you and there are no hard and fast decisions being made here tonight. He has mentioned his concerns to your mother and me, and I think they are valid and deserve further scrutiny. However, rest assured that no decisions have been made without consulting all of you." Eric wanted to reassure Zain that this was a discussion and nothing more.

Elena, Maisy, Cole, Michael, and all of Eric's beautiful grandchildren stormed the room.

Eric was so happy. He picked up his grandchildren and hugged them all. He enjoyed them immensely.

"Hey, Grandpa, how are you today?" said little Eric.

"I'm well, Eric. How are you?"

"I'm fine, Grandpa, just having problems with women."

"Really? What kind of trouble are these women giving you?"

"Well, I like one girl but her best friend likes me, and I don't want to tell her that I don't like her," little Eric replied.

"Why not, Eric? Don't you think you should be honest and explain how you feel?"

"Oh, Grandpa, don't you know anything about women?" little Eric asked seriously.

Zain and Eric were laughing at this point as Eric replied, "Apparently not as much as you do. Why wouldn't you tell her?"

"Well, because if I tell her, I don't like her, she'll tell her best friend what I said and then she won't like me. If I turn down her best friend and make her feel bad, she won't be nice when I talk to her. Get it, Grandpa?"

"I see. Well, you do have a problem on your hands," Eric responded. "What will you do?"

"I don't know, that's why I asked you, but you don't know either," little Eric responded frustrated.

"Well," Eric said laughing, "I have an idea. Why don't you flip it? Don't tell the girl you don't like that you don't like her and tell the girl you do like that you do. Tell her first," Eric responded.

Little Eric looked at his grandfather. "You know what, Grandpa? You might have something there. If I tell my girl, I like her, she'll tell her friend what I said, so I won't have to say anything. The other girl will get the info from her friend. I don't hurt anyone, and my girl falls in love with me. You're good, Grandpa."

Eric and Zain nearly died laughing. "Yes, I still have a few tricks up my sleeve," Eric said.

At the end of dinner, Mary and Sarah took the children to another room so the adults could discuss the proposal. While they discussed it in the dining room, Sarah would talk with Maryam and get her perspective on it.

"Anyone want a scotch?" Christopher asked.

"Will I be needing one, little brother?" replied Zain.

"No, I think we can agree to disagree if you don't like what I have to say," responded Christopher.

Eric and Jenny sat quietly and listened to their children. They had decided to only intervene if the discussion became hostile at any point. Christopher began by letting everyone know that Sarah would inform Maryam with regards to what was being discussed, everyone else was present so no one will be left out of this conversation.

"I asked dad what his intentions were for this house. He informed me that upon their deaths, the ownership of the house would be awarded to all of us; each of us owning a part. I have an issue with this, and I'll tell you why. Right now, it's Mom and Dad's house; My family and I live in it. I love this old house and my children do as well. We could continue to live in it, but it would never feel like our home. It would always feel like it belonged to all of us. Think about that for a minute. Think about how your children would feel knowing that the house they lived in was not their own. I don't want you to answer that, just think about it. This estate has our childhood memories, it has our history, ancestry, and it houses the soul of what it means to be a Barrett. If we all had our own homes, this one would be empty and we would look after it, much like we look after the homes we own worldwide, but no one would be here. At the end of the day, we would all go to our respective homes. I don't want this house to be empty and treated like the others. It's our soul, our identity that's housed in here. It's the very essence of who we are, and I would like to protect it. So, I know that we cannot put a price on the value of this home, but I would give everything that was left to me in Mom and Dad's will to all of you in exchange for the house. Provided that every Christmas, Eid, anniversary, birthday, engagement, wedding, any life event would be celebrated here in this very room as a family as we do now. This is my proposal, what do you think?" Christopher asked.

Zain looked at his brother and said, "Chris, this isn't about the money. It's about what this home means to us, you can't put a price on that. I'm not comfortable leaving you penniless for the sake of protecting what you think will be lost."

"It will be lost. We can put preventative measures in place for the first little while. We will ensure that things get taken care of, but, as our children grow, so too will we become more and more invested in their lives, and less and less invested here," replied Christopher. "The house will always be the Barrett home, that can never and will never change, but it will also be my home and as such it will be taken care of with the same care it has had over several generations. I would then have the option to pass it on to my son, in my will, to continue the Barrett legacy. The house will not be lost among all the other things we own. If this is not agreeable to any of you then I will begin making plans to build my mansion and move my family there once it's built, like you have all done."

"Christopher, you would give up everything you have to protect our family's heritage and its soul, so that who we are will continue to live for centuries, even after we're long gone?" Maisy asked.

"Yes," Christopher replied.

"Well, I know that living in Uncle David's house has meant the world to me and my children. They've been very happy in our home, and have been able to experience the grandparents, that they never met, through the stories Michael tells them. David and Marie, come alive for our children in the home that they lived in, so I understand what you mean. From what I'm hearing, the house and its use would stay the same, it would just have your name on it as its protector. The legacy would be continued in Matthew, am I right?"

"Yes," replied Christopher, "our celebrations, joys, happiness, and God forbid, our sorrows, would continue to be shared in this house as we do now. That would not change. If you would not do this or feel like you couldn't then I will begin planning my new home right away. It's a lot to think about and I don't expect an answer tonight. Please think about it and let me know."

Maisy looked at Christopher and said, "As for me, and I think Michael will support my decision, I have no problem with you assuming owner-ship of the house, Christopher. I know you'll take good care of our soul. And I know exactly what you mean having first-hand experience in my own home. Christopher, I don't want your money. I just want to spend quality time together, especially when Mom and Dad are gone. We'll need to give our kids what they gave us: love, memories, and the gift of family, togetherness right here in this very room."

Elena looked at Cole and said, "I agree with Maisy. We all have more money than we know what to do with and the house would be empty at some point, which is not what our parents ever wanted, or our grandparents. They wanted a home thriving with children, joy, and happiness. I think that's exactly what you would be doing, Christopher. I'm fine with you assuming ownership of the home and I don't want any money from you. Knowing the house is in your care is payment enough for me." She walked over and hugged Christopher.

Christopher looked over at Zain. "Well, big brother, please take some time to think about it. Regardless of Maisy and Elena's decisions, if you don't want this, I will begin to build my own home, no hard feelings."

"What everyone is saying makes a lot of sense," Zain responded, "but, I do want us to get together at my place too. So sure, we celebrate the milestones here, but I think we should celebrate family in each of our homes, together. I think that's the Barrett legacy as well. So, I too agree, and I don't want any money. Looking after our soul is payment enough. Here's to changing ownership and not changing anything at all," Zain said as he raised his glass. " We will always be here, be together, and be a close family." Zain grabbed his brother and hugged him as well.

Jenny looked at her husband with tears in her eyes and kissed him. "We've done a fine job with our children, and I can die happy knowing they will take care of each other, love each other and be close to one another."

Eric smiled at her. "The sharks have spoken and spoken well."

"Okay let's not get carried away with this death shit. Everyone is very much alive and I think we should toast to Christopher's house with a round of scotch," Zain said happily as he poured drinks for everyone. Everyone laughed and shared a drink. It was late by the time the Barrett children collected their own children and made their way home.

Eric held his wife close to him and told her how proud he was of his family. "They handled it very well," he said. "They saw into Christopher's heart and realized how important it was to him. They realized that his intention was not to take anything away, but to keep giving to future generations, that very Barrett soul that is in this house. Jenny, you taught them that. You taught them to love each other, help each other, respect each other, and always know the meaning of family. Tonight, they showed us what they learned, and I am so proud of them."

"*We* taught them, Eric," Jenny responded, "and I'm proud of the strong men and women they have become." Jenny held her husband close. "Now, let's go to sleep. It's been a long day."

41

Eric waited a few weeks and then decided to call a meeting in his office with his family. He explained to them that he had transferred the deed of the estate to Christopher as was agreed upon and that he was extremely proud of how they handled that situation. He felt relieved that the Barrett estate was in good hands and that it would continue to be the focal point of the family. This did, however, get him to thinking about how the empire that was Barrett Industries would continue in the future. He was not prepared to entertain thoughts on how it would be divided, because he had no intention of dividing anything at all. Eric and Jenny had decided to leave the business ownership to each of them without divisions. He was impressed with how they were able to work together to secure that 5.2-billion-dollar deal. It reassured him that what he and Jenny had decided was the correct course of action.

"No one in this room has any idea the value of what we have built together," said Eric. "You've secured several multimillion-dollar deals and recently a 5.2-billion-dollar deal that was quite impressive. I was exceptionally proud of each of you and assured of what you can accomplish when you work together. Barrett Industries is currently worth 2.5 trillion dollars. We are the richest people in the world." Eric stopped talking for a few minutes to watch the shock on their faces, then the smiles. "This fortune," he continued, "will undoubtedly secure your lives and your children's lives long after both your mother and I have passed on. However,

I want you to understand that this money also secures the lives of many children, mothers, families, teenage girls, and people suffering from health issues and traumas. We can give them a new life and a future. This part of the industry was started by your grandmother but flourished under your mother's guidance. Her unselfish ability to love and help her fellow man, without having ever met them, is the reason why we do what we do. It's not just the money but how it is used that makes the difference. Once Maryam and Sarah came on board with your mother, these three women expanded in ways my mother had not even fathomed. Not only did they expand the current Centre, but they also built an additional Complex, and I cannot tell you how proud I was when they decided to name it after the love of my life. The Jenny Barrett Complex is a thriving endeavor dedicated to young children with learning disabilities, developmental delay, and autism. I am so impressed with what my daughters-in-law, and sons-in-law, have accomplished.

"The hard work and determination that went into building the Brian Fitzgerald hospital that focuses on cancer treatment, dedicated to Brian a man I loved and respected, was another very proud moment in my life. A project the four of you, along with your husbands and wives, worked tirelessly to bring to fruition and is now headed by Steven, his son, who is forever grateful. The work ethic in this family is strong, something my grandchildren will undoubtedly learn from all of you. Aside from the luxury and opulence we live in, the focus has always been on helping the underprivileged. This is the empire that your mother and I created and hope you continue when we are unable.

"When we were first married, we were all over the news and your mother was astounded that people were talking about us. At the time, they called us a power couple who were going to change the world. I remember saying to your mother that it was a little exaggerated but a kind thought. Your mother said she didn't think so. She thought that we would change the world together." Eric smiled at his wife and then continued. "I have been blessed my entire life with an incredible love that has opened my eyes to the value of what is important in life. Everything your mother gave me over the years I could not have bought, even with 2.5 trillion dollars. What she taught this privileged man she met in a coffee shop was that warm, selfless acts of love provide a joy and peace that is unimaginable. Every joy I have experienced in my life never cost a cent. The incredible joy I felt when I learned I was to be a father; I thought my heart would burst that day. It had never felt so full. This is why we do what we do, every day. These are the reasons we come to work and work as hard as we can to acquire as much wealth as possible. We offer new life to desperate children and their families, to desperate women who suffer trauma from abuse." Eric looked very seriously at each of his children as he spoke.

"Therefore, I have decided not to divide the wealth in my will. I have left Barrett Industries to all of you equally. What you continue to build together is what you will enjoy, with the understanding that the more you expand, the more lives can be saved. I've already drawn up the papers and they will need to be signed here today. Does anyone disagree with what your mother and I have decided?" he asked. There was a unanimous no. Eric responded, "I didn't think so!"

As everyone was beginning to sign the forms, Zain became a little concerned.

"Dad, in the last little while you and Mom have settled a lot of your affairs, and I have to say, I'm rather worried," Zain said. "Is there something going on with either one of you that we should know? All this talk of settling things while you're alive, to ensure it's done after your death, has got me worried."

"No, Zain," responded Eric. "These are things that have to be done and I want to do them together. I don't want you to be listening to an executor read a will someday, wondering what your mother and I decided to do. I want to do it as a family, together, as we have always done things." Eric smiled lovingly at his son. "The truth is, Zain, I'm seventy-two and while both your mother and I are healthy, it's just natural to do these things at our age."

Jenny felt the need to break the somber atmosphere in the room as everyone seemed to be thinking about the day when the family would be forever changed with their deaths.

"So," Jenny said with a smile, "how about we sign these papers and have a round of scotch. The family that drinks together stays together."

"I'll drink to that, Mom," responded Christopher, laughing as he began pouring the scotch.

"We'll all drink to that," said Maisy with a smile on her face.

42

———————————

Eric felt at peace. He sat in his library and thought about all of the wonderful things he and Jenny had accomplished together and how they had changed the world. But his peace was about to be shattered. He noticed that for the past few weeks, Jenny had been sleeping in a little longer and going to bed a bit sooner. One night as he climbed into bed and took her in his arms, he asked her if she was okay and noted his observations. She replied that she was feeling a bit sluggish, fatigued, and thought she was probably coming down with a cold. He waited for her to fall asleep then called Steven.

"Hello, Eric. It's a little late. Is everything okay at home?" Steven asked.

"Sometimes you remind me of your father, Steven," Eric said with a chuckle. "I'm a little concerned about Jenny. She's feeling sluggish, fatigued as she says, and I was wondering if you could—" before Eric could finish his sentence, Steven replied.

"I'll be there at 8 a.m. tomorrow, Eric," Steven said. "I'll collect a blood sample and should have some idea of what's going on by eleven. In the meantime, Eric, get some sleep," Steven said.

"Thank you, Steven. See you in the morning. Good night." Eric said.

At 7 a.m., Eric woke Jenny for breakfast. She looked at him intently.

"So, what time will Steven be here?" she asked with a smile.

Eric looked at Jenny. "You know I called him? I thought you were asleep?"

"I was asleep," she laughed. "I just know you that well."

"He should be arriving in an hour," Eric said concerned. "I thought you might want to have breakfast and get ready. Unless you would rather stay in bed, that's fine too. I'll just have him come up."

Jenny shook her head and laughed. "It's probably just a cold, my love. No need to panic."

"Jenny, it's who I am. When it comes to you, I won't take any risks. It's you we're talking about, and you are my life. I need to know that you're okay and I won't have any peace until I can be sure of that, okay?" Eric said as he held her closely in his arms.

"Yes, my love, it's okay," Jenny answered as she kissed him. "I think I'll take a quick shower and sit with you for breakfast."

"Okay, I'll just check messages and emails and wait until you're done," Eric responded with a loving smile.

"Why don't you just have breakfast?" she asked.

"Because I haven't eaten alone since the day we were married and don't intend to start now. So, get in the shower. I'm famished," he responded with a smile.

As they sat for breakfast, Steven arrived and took a blood sample. He said he would call them both, to which Jenny replied that she realized he was very busy, and it would be fine if he just called Eric.

"Steven, thank you for coming to our home and I apologize for Eric.," Jenny said. "I know he must have called late last night while I was asleep. He just worries about me and loves me so much. I hope you understand."

"It's no problem, Jenny. Eric has done quite a lot for my family, the clinic, and the hospital. A phone call in the middle of the night is nothing. More importantly, you're not a patient, Jenny, you're family," Steven replied and left.

Eric took Jenny in his arms. She could see the worry in his eyes. "It's going to be fine, please don't worry," she said. "Now, I have work to do, so I'll be in my office."

"Okay," he said. He kissed her gently and headed to work in the library. He called the office and told them that he would work from home and could be reached there if necessary. Within five minutes, he got calls from Zain and Christopher wondering what was wrong. Eric explained and told them that he preferred to be close to home while he waited for the results.

Both boys became concerned and asked that he keep them informed. They would not have peace until they learned the results.

It seemed to be taking quite some time to get the results. Eric was on pins and needles and had unusually nervous energy about him. He had taken Jenny a cup of tea, twice, and insisted she get rest if she was feeling tired. Jenny threatened to throw him out of her office and lock the door if he didn't let her work. When she noticed the hurt look on his face, she smiled, walked over, and held him in her arms.

"It's going to be fine, Eric," she said. "Please don't worry." With that, he smiled at his Jenny and left to go to the library. He tried to focus but he had this dreadful sense that something was wrong. It was after 11 a.m.

* * *

Steven had the results in front of him and tears rolling down his face. Jenny had somehow contracted a deadly virus that had been killing many people worldwide. He knew he couldn't tell Eric without having support for him, so he called the office and asked to speak with Zain. He explained that he needed to talk with him and his siblings concerning his mother's results. He had not yet called Eric and they would understand why once he arrived. When he did arrive, Steven didn't mince words.

"I think you're all aware that your father had me run some tests on your mother this morning," Steven said with a note of concern. They each responded or nodded, equally concerned by Steven's urgency.

"Alright," Steven paused as tears began to roll down his face. He explained that he had the tests repeated four times for accuracy and there was no mistake. "Jenny has contracted a deadly virus, the one that has been killing many worldwide. We do have treatments, medications we can start immediately and a vaccine, however, they may not be effective at this stage of the infection. We may only be able to slow it down and hope to eradicate it, but it would take a miracle. I would be lying to you if I told you that we had a vaccine that would just eliminate it," Steven said tearfully.

Maisy and Elena held each other as they cried uncontrollably. The boys were not much better. "Dad is going to need us now more than ever," said Zain, barely able to utter the words.

"This is going to consume him. Jenny is his life and the possibility that she may ... he won't be able to deal with this at all," responded Michael.

"How do I tell him?" asked Steven. "He's waiting for my phone call."

"Can you stay for about an hour Steven or come back in an hour?" asked Zain.

"Sure," he responded. "What do you have in mind?"

"I think we should get Dad out of the house, tell him there's an emergency we can't handle here, and have him come to the office. In the meantime, I'll call Mary and Chris, let Sarah know she needs to come down. We should all be here together when Dad gets the news so we can support him. He'll break down at first, and if I know Dad, he'll want to move mountains immediately. So, Steven just be ready for that reaction from him. I would do the same in his position," said Zain.

"That sounds like a good plan, big brother. It will also give us time to absorb this and try to be there for Dad," Christopher said, trying not to let his emotions get the better of him. Christopher had always been very close to his mother and had a connection with her that he did not have with his father.

Maisy walked over to Christopher. "It's okay to cry. Let it out. It will help you to deal with this," she said. Christopher hugged his sister and began to cry uncontrollably as she held him close.

Elena, the voice of reason as Eric had always called her, wiped her tears and said, "I'll make arrangements for our kids to be looked after. It will be a long and painful night for all of us."

Cole rushed to hold her in his arms. "Tell me what you have in mind, and I'll make the arrangements," he said to Elena.

She nodded in tears. "Just hold me, Cole, please just hold me!" she said as she sobbed in his arms. The richest family in the world was also the most close-knit. They each felt the other's pain; a pain Eric would soon come to know, that would undoubtedly destroy him.

An hour later, everyone was assembled. As Eric arrived, Christopher poured a scotch for his father and one for himself.

"Hey, Dad, I was just about to have a drink. Why don't you join me as we get down to the matter at hand?" asked Christopher.

"Sure son, but I'm not certain I know what this is about," Eric said bewildered. "There's nothing the six of you can't handle, and I'm still waiting for a very important call from Steven. I don't know what's taking so long, but I'm done waiting. I think I'll just go see him at the clinic once we're done here." As he was talking, all his children, daughters-in-law, sons-in-law, and Steven walked into the office and shut the door. Eric's face went pale as he closed his eyes.

He looked at Christopher and said, "Make it a double, son. I'm not sure I can hear this." Tears streamed down his face as Christopher passed him the scotch and gave him a tight hug.

"Steven, how bad is it?" Eric asked.

Steven explained that Jenny had contracted a deadly virus and while they had medication and a vaccine, it would be difficult to eradicate it as the virus was in a progressive state.

"Tell me what you can do, Steven," he said with a very cold tone in his voice.

"We can slow it down for sure, give her more time, and we can try the various vaccines and hope for the best," Steven replied.

Eric had his head in his hands and was completely distraught. As he cried, everyone in the room could feel his agony. They were all in tears, including Steven. Zain grabbed his dad and cried with him until Eric pulled away.

"Steven, how many labs will you need to get people working on something that will cure my Jenny?"

"We have labs working on it already, Eric," Steven replied

"No, you don't!" Eric responded angrily. "I want you to get in touch with at least four labs, buy them today. Then I want you to get the best minds in the world, offer them anything and everything they want to come here and work in these labs. Put them to work on a cure for my Jenny. Do you understand?"

"Yes, Eric. I will get on it right away," Steven replied.

"Christopher, Zain, Cole, and Michael, work with Steven to get the labs and get a hold of these people, get them over here! We don't have time to lose. The more we wait the less time Jenny has, and I will not lose her while I am still alive. Do you hear me?" He was yelling at everyone in the room as tears streamed down his face. "This is your top priority," Eric said.

"Whatever you're working on, delegate it to other personnel. We pay a lot of people and if we don't have enough, hire them. Our time will be spent finding a way to save your mother. There is nothing more important right now." Pain, anger, and desperation hung in the air.

"We're on it, Dad. She means a lot to us too," Zain said as he grabbed Christopher, Cole, Michael and left the room with Steven.

Eric sat in the office with his girls and cried uncontrollably. "She is my life. I can't be without her. I am nothing without my Jenny. I can't be without her. God don't take her from me, I cannot. I cannot." Maisy and Elena held him tight in their arms.

"Dad, you have to be strong for Mom," Elena said. "If we're going to help her through this, we have to be strong. You have to get control of yourself, Dad, and we have to work hard to find ways to help Mom and to support her through this. I know how painful this is for you, we can all feel it, but this pain, you must harness it into action, positive action to help Mom. These medications may be brutal, and she needs to be able to count on you, okay?"

Eric looked at his daughter. "Always the voice of reason. I love you, Elena, and I will be everything your mother needs. I just need to figure out how," he responded.

"With love, Dad. That's the only way," responded Maisy. "You will hold each other and cry together and once you've done that, you'll be stron- ger together."

Eric reached for his daughters and daughters-in law held them close. "I don't know how to tell Jenny in a way that doesn't sound so terminal, and that's what I need to figure out; how to give her hope," Eric replied. Each of his children sat with him and tried to provide comfort. Eric finally explained to them that it was okay to leave him to his thoughts and go home to their families. He needed time alone to absorb the news. They each hugged him and left the office.

Eric stayed in his office for quite some time, trying to figure out how to give his wife the dreadful news. He stayed there until about 10 p.m. and had had a few drinks. Christopher called, his father wondering if he was okay. He explained to Eric that he was making up excuses to his mother who had been asking why he was not home. Eric told Christopher that he was on his way now and should be home soon. Once he arrived, Christopher and Zain met him at the door.

"Dad are you alright?" asked Christopher.

"Yes, son, I'm okay. Is your mother still awake?"

"No, I think she's gone to bed," replied Zain. "She still doesn't know; in case you were wondering whether or not we said anything to her about the results."

"Thanks, son, I appreciate it. You should get going to that wonderful family of yours. I'm sure your wife is waiting for you," Eric replied.

"I just wanted to see you and reassure you that we're doing every- thing humanly possible, Dad. The labs have been bought and several of the world's best minds have accepted our offers. They should be arriving within the week," replied Zain

"I knew neither of you would let me down and I appreciate you stepping up when I was too broken. Only a Barrett can do that," responded Eric with a smile. He put his arm around his son and said, "Thank you, now go home."

Once Zain left, Eric turned his attention to Christopher. "How are you feeling, son, and how is Sarah?"

"We're doing better than you are, Dad, but not by much," responded Christopher in tears. "Do you think we can stop this, Dad?"

"We're going to do all we can, and we can do a lot. So, pray and have faith and we'll all get through this. I know that you and your mother have a very special relationship and I know this is hitting you very hard, son, but rest assured, we will find a solution," Eric responded as he hugged his son tightly. "I need to get upstairs, and you need to get some rest. I'm sure Sarah is waiting up there with open arms, so go to her. Good night, son." Christopher gave his dad a warm hug and said good night.

Once upstairs, Eric took off his clothes and climbed into bed. Jenny welcomed him with open arms.

"You're awake," Eric said. "I thought you would be asleep by now."

"You know I can never sleep unless you're beside me," Jenny said smiling at her husband, but she sensed something was wrong the minute he turned towards her. "How bad are the test results that you couldn't come home to tell me?" Jenny asked. "You were hoping I would be asleep.

You've been both drinking excessively and crying. Do you want to tell me why everyone here is so sad, Eric, or do I ask the kids?"

Eric drew a deep breath. With tears rolling down his face he began to explain the test results and that she would begin treatment in the morning. He explained to Jenny that there were medications that would slow the progression of the virus and that although they had vaccines, the virus had multiplied extensively and there was no guarantee they would be able to eradicate it. As he explained, he could not hold back the tears streaming down his face, and Jenny gently wiped them away. She held him tightly, close to her, and let him cry. Then she kissed him gently.

"Eric, it's going to be okay," she said. Then, trying to lighten the mood, she spoke to him rather playfully. "So which lab did you hijack to have them come up with a miracle cure?" she asked with a smile.

"I didn't," Eric responded almost in a whisper. "I bought four labs." Jenny just shook her head and laughed. "I had to buy them, sweetheart, because I'm flying in some of the best minds in the world to work on finding a cure for you," Eric responded as he cried.

Jenny now had tears in her eyes. "Oh, Eric, I love you so much and I love what you're trying to do for me. I hope we find a cure for this and I'm sure many will benefit from what you're doing for me, but you must entertain the possibility that we may not. It may be that God has decided it's my time," Jenny said to him, gently trying to help Eric come to terms with a reality he did not want to face.

"Don't say that Jenny, please. I need you to fight this right now, not give up. Please fight for your kids and grandchildren who still need your endless, boundless love. Please, Jenny, fight for me! I can't be here without you," he said, sobbing in her arms.

"Eric, listen to me. I will fight and fight as hard as I can to stay with you. Just prepare yourself for the worst and hope for the best. Can you do that for me?" Eric nodded as she continued. "I want to enjoy my children and grandchildren, laugh, and have fun. I want to enjoy you, Eric. I want you to love me like—"

He interrupted her. "Like it's the last time," he said in tears. She gently wiped the tears from his face and held it in her hands.

She kissed him gently and said, "No, Eric, like it's the first time, like it has been every night since I married you. I don't want that to change. I want to feel alive, not waiting for my death. Do you understand?"

Eric held her close and said, "You know, you sound a lot like Thomas."

Jenny laughed. "Well, that's because Thomas was right. Do the kids know about this?"

"Yes," Eric whispered.

"Okay, then tomorrow we'll have a fun, family dinner and we will not talk about this again," Jenny said.

"I don't think that's a good idea, Jenny," Eric said. "The kids were devastated by the news, and I think they just want to see you, talk to you, hold you. They need to cry with you to help them work through this. Does that make any sense?" he asked.

"Yes, it does, Eric. A lot of sense," Jenny responded. "I'll meet with them separately. It's probably a good idea."

"Jenny," Eric said, "you will not die as long as I'm alive. I won't let that happen. We will slow this down, and, in the meantime, find something that will kill this virus. You hear me, Jenny?"

Jenny smiled. "Just hold me, Eric, and never let me go. I love you." They held each other close and fell asleep.

43

Steven was over at the house early the next morning. He sat down with Jenny and explained what each medication was, what it would do, the side effects, and how she was to take them. He gave her a great big hug and said they were all working extremely hard because she was an amazing person and very precious to all of them. He then left and said he would check in on her daily.

Jenny made her way to her office. She had work she wanted to get done and wanted to schedule meetings with each of her children. As she was working, two beautiful, very ornate recliners were moved into her office. Jenny was puzzled as she knew she had not ordered any furniture. Just then, Eric walked into the office with his computer and phone in hand.

"I thought they would match your décor. Do you like them?" Eric asked.

"Yes, they're beautiful, but why do I need a recliner?"

"I thought that if you felt tired, you could just recline the chair and rest."

"That's very thoughtful, Eric, thank you, but why do I need two?"

"The other one is for me. I'm not leaving your side, Jenny, and I know you will want to continue working and so will I, right here," he responded smiling.

Jenny gave her husband a huge hug and kissed him. "How did I get so lucky?" she asked.

"I'm the one that got lucky, Jenny. You showed me what life was about and you loved me unconditionally, with all my faults and shortcomings. I have never deserved you, my love."

"Okay stop it! You're going to make me cry and I have work to do," she said.

"Then let's get to work," Eric responded with a smile.

Jenny could feel the effects of the medications she was taking and noticed that they did make her very tired. Eric monitored her every move without making it look like that's what he was doing. Jenny left her desk and sat in the recliner.

"I think I'll take a little nap," she said. "These medications are making me tired." Eric watched Jenny recline her chair as he reached for a blanket. He covered her, reclined his own chair, held her hand, and watched her. As she slept, Eric called Steven, who let him know that this was a very normal response as the medications were quite strong.

"The more rest Jenny gets the better it will be for her," Steven said. Eric thanked him and apologized for the trouble.

"Call me whenever at whatever time. I'll be there," Steven replied.

44

Seeing how the medications affected her, Jenny decided to meet with Maisy, Michael, Elena, and Cole together. She would have to meet with them early in the morning to have enough strength to talk to them. Once they arrived, Jenny met them in the library.

"Give your mother a warm Barrett hug," she said with a smile. The girls ran up to hug her and immediately broke down in tears.

"What is this?" Jenny asked. "I'm not dead yet and I don't want any tears at my funeral. I have had a wonderful life, was blessed with amazing children, and have the love of an incredible man. What is there to cry about? Stop this nonsense," Jenny said as she held her girls close.

"Mom, I'm glad you're taking this so well," said Elena. "I wasn't sure what to expect really. I don't want to think of you out of my life, Mom. I want you in it, for as long as we can—" Elena couldn't finish her sentence as she began to cry.

"That's exactly it, Elena. We've taken care of each other always and we will get through this too. I love you and Cole and my grandchildren so much. I just want to have fun, go sailing, the kids love that, maybe take a family trip if I can," Jenny responded.

"Jenny," responded Cole, "let me check with Steven and if he says we can sail, how about we do that this weekend. It would be a lot of fun."

Jenny nodded, "I agree Cole."

Maisy had not stopped crying as her mother held her close. "I should have called you Erica," Jenny said as she laughed.

"Mom, how am I supposed to do this? How can I not think about the possibility that I may not have you for long? I don't know what to do." Maisy said in tears.

"She doesn't eat, or sleep and I can't blame her, Jenny. She's a mess," Michael responded. "We all are. The office is not a happy place right now and we're all supporting each other as best we can," Michael continued, tears rolling down his face.

"Maisy, I will always be with you. We always knew this day would come. We, as a family, have been given the blessed opportunity to be together and help each other through this. Imagine if either your dad or I had died in an accident. We would not have had the opportunity to spend time together, talk to one another, each one saying what we want the other to know. Let's make good use of this time. Let's enjoy the time we have and love each other until we cannot. It's only for a while. Thomas once explained that to me. I'm just going first. I'll be there with Thomas, Heather, David, Marie, and I'll finally meet Christopher and Susan. I'll be there waiting to meet you when your time comes and I'll be watching over all of you," Jenny said in tears as she held Maisy in her arms.

Eric heard her talking and walked into the room. "You will not be meeting my mother and father unless I introduce you," he said. "I don't want to hear this talk. You're not dying, we are dealing with it." He hugged Maisy and Elena. "Listen, girls," Eric continued, "we will work through this, and as far as sailing goes, I think it's a great idea. Steven and his family will join us as well." Zain, Mary, Christopher, and Sarah walked into the library.

"Sailing sounds like a great plan," Zain said. "We heard that you were going to talk to these four, so we all decided to crash the party. Mom, we love you, we want to keep you forever, and we're working on it. You should know that a Barrett never gives up and I'll have you know we are making great progress. So enough of this 'I'll see you from the other side' talk because no one is going anywhere but sailing." Zain held his mother in his arms.

Jenny smiled, grabbed her sons, and hugged them. "You two are so much like your father and grandfather that it's almost frightening," she said laughing. She noticed Christopher could not look at her as was trying to control his emotions.

"Christopher, how are you digesting this news?" Jenny asked as she held him in her arms. Christopher looked at his mother and just cried as he shook his head, unable to utter even a word. Jenny held him close to her and said, "I love you, Christopher, and I will never be far from you. I will continue to hover over you just as I did when you were a child and still do on a few occasions. You won't miss me. I will make my presence known to you and you will feel me in your heart. Now, we still have time. Let's create more wonderful memories we can share." Christopher hugged his mother and held her tightly, not wanting to let her go.

Sarah put her arm around her husband and held him. Knowing how hard Jenny worked and wanting so much to lighten her load, she said, "Jenny, I hope you feel confident enough with Mary and me taking over some of your workload while you continue to work from home. I think we've learned from the best."

"I am confident, my precious Sarah. I was just preparing what I've been working on so that it made sense to the both of you when I redirect my work to your very capable hands," Jenny responded. "I don't know what I would have done without the two of you. You helped me realize so many of my dreams and those of so many worldwide. For this, I thank you." She hugged them and tried not to cry.

"I think it's almost time for dinner," Eric said. "Why don't you have all of my grandchildren driven here and we'll have a family night," Eric said cheerfully.

"Okay, we can set up a games night. The kids will love it," responded Sarah.

"Perfect," replied Eric. "I'll let the kitchen staff know we'll need the dining room set up for tonight."

"How about we set up the solarium instead?" Jenny responded. "It's a beautiful night, stars are shining, and all my stars are here with me." Jenny tried to fight back her tears.

Eric took her in his arms. "I thought we agreed that we were not going to do that. I can't bear to see a single tear drop from those beautiful eyes. The solarium it is, my love," Eric said as he left the room.

45

With the tension and fear somewhat under control, the Barrett family had a wonderful evening, full of fun and laughter. Their sailing trip was an incredible success and just what the family needed to start living and forget what was happening in the background. Jenny loved spending time with her children and grandchildren, who always enjoyed sailing on their yacht. Steven and his family also enjoyed the many sailing days they spent together.

The medications Jenny was taking, and the new ones being developed, seemed to be working for the time being. Jenny felt tired because they were so potent, but once she rested, she seemed to be doing well. Four months had gone by, and Jenny was living her life quite normally. Eric had started going back to the office and Jenny tried to get to the Centre a few days a week. The developments being made by Barrett Industries in new medications to fight this horrible virus were making headlines. Many people being treated with the drugs were making incredible improvements and, in many cases, the virus was eliminated.

This was encouraging news for the Barrett family, but it was not to last. Jenny began to feel very weak, and the situation escalated quickly. It was the beginning of the fifth month from her diagnosis that Jenny started to feel very tired. She stopped going to the Centre and found that she slept much more than usual. As Jenny began to feel weakened, she decided she would write a letter to her children. She wrote only one as she didn't think she had the strength to write four; the sadness in trying to write them would deplete any energy she had to fight the virus.

My Dear and Darling Children,

I want you to know just how much joy you have brought to my life, from the moment you were born until the time I take my last breath, know that you have filled my heart with so much love every day of my life. I don't want any tears at my funeral or any day after because I will always be with you and will be guiding you from above, protecting you and warning you of things that you cannot see, but I can. I want you to take care of each other, never break the family bond of unconditional love that you now share and teach my grandchildren the strength of that family bond. I ask that you guide my grandchildren as I and your father have guided you to be part of an amazing empire that provides so much to so many and that you continue to care for the most vulnerable. Never forget that if you use your wealth for good, God will give you so much more. I ask that when I am no longer with you, please watch over Eric, who will be so distraught and in so much agony. We are one body with one soul, and I fear that he might harm himself as he did in the past when we were apart. Please never leave Eric alone. It would break my heart to know that he was alone at any time. Someone, please watch over him at night until he can deal with my loss. He is my life, the meaning of my very existence, and if I could change anything, it would be to find some way to be together in life and death. I understand that I can't do this, as things will be the way that God intends. My whole life, I have always trusted that God would help me in my most difficult of times. This is one of those times and I pray for his guidance daily. Please take care of your father, take care of each other, and love each other always, unconditionally, fully, and completely as I have loved you my whole life. That is the Barrett legacy, and what guides our intentions and actions.

I will love you always,

Mom

Jenny completed her letter and felt extremely tired. *It must be the raw emotions I felt writing it that has taken my strength, Jenny thought. It might be a good idea to take a nap. I'll speak to Arthur tomorrow about making sure that Eric gets this letter once I've passed on.* She left the letter on the desk and went to take a nap.

Eric came into Jenny's office looking for her and realized she was probably in their bedroom. What caught his attention was the paper on the desk. It was Jenny's stationery, which she only used in special situations. She had it made especially for this purpose. It had pink roses as a back- ground and the paper was scented to smell like roses. Eric knew Jenny rarely used it unless she wanted to write something incredibly special. She often left him beautiful notes on that exact paper. He walked over to the desk and saw the first sentence. His heart sank knowing she was writing a letter to leave to the children. As he read the letter, Eric was in so much pain. He sat and cried as he read each line trying not to let his tears stain the page.

"Oh, Jenny," Eric said out loud, "how will I ever live without you, my love. We are one body and one soul and you're right, I will not be able to live without you by my side. You are my life. How I wish God could see that he cannot take you without taking me too. I know I have never deserved you, but I have spent my life trying to change that and I hope God finds it in his heart to take me too like he did my parents. Together!" Eric put the letter back on the desk and cried uncontrollably, alone. Jenny woke up from her nap, almost as if she could feel his pain. She heard Eric crying and went to her office.

"You weren't supposed to see that," she said looking at her husband, who was in so much anguish. She took him in her arms. "I love you, Eric, and I will always be with you," she said to him. They held each other and cried together. Jenny took Eric to their bedroom and held him in her arms until, exhausted from the pain and sadness, they both fell asleep.

As Jenny continued to feel weak and fatigued, Eric began to fear the worst and spoke with Steven about what he was noticing. Steven did not mince words and explained to Eric that despite all efforts being made, the possibility that Jenny would succumb to the virus was very real. Eric stopped going to the office and remained with Jenny every waking moment. In his face, Jenny could see the stress, worry, and the hurt that was in Eric's heart. She tried to reassure him that things would be fine and that he shouldn't worry, and although Eric smiled every time she said it, he could not deal with the pain.

A few weeks later Jenny's condition declined rapidly, and she was bed-ridden. She did not have the strength to stand or sit. The hospital was now in their bedroom. Every detail, piece of machinery, medical equipment, or medication that could make a difference had been brought to the house. Although he had medical staff in the house and two daughters-in-law that were nurses, Eric refused to have anyone touch Jenny and preferred to bathe her and brush her hair himself every morning. Each day, Eric put Jenny into a warm bath and gently washed her body, then washed her hair. As she sat in her white plushy robe, he brushed her hair and styled it the way she liked it. Jenny smiled, and always gently kissed her husband as he caressed her. He held her close in his arms for as long as possible, talking to her about their children and grandchildren. He would let her rest while he watched her sleep. While she could eat, he fed her, and of course, never left her side. At night, Jenny would tell him how much she loved him, how incredible her life had been with him, and how she was so blessed to have the four amazing children he had given her. Not to mention the joys of their grandchildren.

"Jenny, stop, please, don't talk like that," Eric said painfully. "Don't talk like you're going to leave me please," Eric begged. "I love you so much and I can't bear the thought of you leaving me."

"No, Eric," Jenny said in a whisper. "I was just looking back on my life and thanking God for all the blessings he has given me, and I realized that they all came from you. From the day I met you, my life was transformed. My life with you has been magical, incredible, and my heart so full of gratitude. God has given me so much, Eric."

"No, Jenny, it is I that was blessed with you," Eric said. "I have never deserved the love you've given me. The joys my heart has felt, it was so hard to contain it from just rupturing open. I was blessed with so much love, unconditional love, a love that most people never find, a love that is the stuff dreams are made of a love that is so rare. Even the most difficult times of my life were made easy because I have you, because your love feeds my very soul and heals the pain. Oh, Jenny, that fateful day when I decided to go to a coffee shop, something I would never have done, was the day I began to live, to see the world through a very different lens, to experience a love that I never thought existed. I cannot lose you, Jenny. I am nothing without you, my love."

"Eric, you have children that love you and that need you. You are their guide, their teacher, the person they look up to. If and when I am no longer here, they are your solace, your comfort, because we made them with so much love, Eric. So much love that we created life, four times," she said with a smile as she gently kissed his lips.

"I can't lose you, Jenny. Please, honey why don't you just get some rest? I'll be right here holding you and watching over you all night," Eric replied. Jenny fell asleep as Eric wept.

It was around 5 a.m. when Jenny opened her eyes and reached for her husband who was holding her. She could feel her strength leaving her as she desperately clung to him.

"Your eyes are so beautiful, Eric, and your hair now snowy white. I'm not sure which one I prefer best, red hair or white," she said to him playfully, but unable to speak above a whisper.

"Well, I think the freckles are a lot more pronounced with the white hair, don't you think?" He responded.

Jenny smiled. "My Raggedy Eric, the love of my life." She gently kissed him. "Hold me, Eric, hold me close and never let go," she said, and with that, drew her last breath.

The machines Jenny was hooked up to began making all kinds of noises.

"Jenny?" Eric said with tears forming in his eyes. "Jenny, wake up! Jenny wake up!" he pleaded. He shook her to try to wake her. "Please Jenny wake up! No! Jenny, no! Please, Jenny, wake up," he kept repeating hysterically.

He screamed in excruciating agony, "Nooo! Jenny, no! Come back, Jenny come back! Don't leave me alone, Jenny".

At this point, Christopher and Sarah were at the door in tears.

"Call Zain, my sisters, and Steven. Tell them mom is dead," Christopher said to Sarah sobbing. He rushed over to his father and hugged both him and his mother and sobbed uncontrollably alongside this father who was beside himself in pain.

"Come back, Jenny, don't leave me, honey, please. Wake up, wake up," Eric kept repeating as he held her close to him. "Please, Jenny, wake up."

In a half-hour, Steven and Zain had arrived, as had Maisy, Elena, Cole, Michael, Mary, and Sarah. Everyone was there to support each other in every and any way possible. Steven was at the bedside with tears rolling down his cheeks. He gently touched Eric.

"It's time for you to let go. Jenny's gone to a better place, and you have to let her go," Steven said as gently as he could.

"No, I will never, never let go of Jenny. No!" he said in tears. "I told her I would never let go and I won't," Eric replied.

"Oh, Eric, if anyone knows the pain you feel right now it's me," said Michael. "But I also know how much Jenny loved you and how much it would break her heart to see you cry. She would want you to do what you both did all the time, handle the pain as a family. Share the pain and heal it with love. Jenny did that so well, Eric, and it's what she would want you to do now big brother." Michael tried to pry Jenny from Eric's tight grip.

"No, Michael, I'm not leaving my Jenny. She said hold me close and never let go and I will never let her go, Jenny knows that" Eric responded in unbearable pain.

Zain put his arms around his father and mother and whispered to his father, "Dad, we have to let Mom go. She needs a proper burial now; you have to let go. Please, Dad, let's go downstairs and have a drink, right? We need to let her go now." Zain tried to pry his father away from his mother's dead body.

"Nooooooooo!" Eric yelled. "No, I will never let her go." Zain and Christopher both spoke softly to their father while they were trying to pull Jenny out of Eric's arms.

"No, I will never let go, Jenny, I will never let you go!" Eric repeated in excruciating pain as he clutched her closer to him holding on to her as if he were holding on to life itself, crying in so much pain and agony, everyone in the room crying along with him. Eric held Jenny as tight as he could. Then pain suddenly riddled his face, a pain that Eric had felt once before. His eyes wide, he looked at his wife and gently kissed her as he drew his last breath.

"What the fuck just happened here, Steven? What happened just now?"

Zain asked almost yelling.

Steven, with tears rolling down his face, put two of his fingers at Eric's neck, then took his wrist to double check, listening for a pulse. "He suffered a massive coronary. Eric most likely died in excruciating pain but within seconds of feeling it," responded Steven, barely able to get the words out as he, himself was crying. "I have heard of people dying of a broken heart, but I have never seen it happen quite like this," he continued.

"He couldn't live without her; the pain was just too much. He could not live without his Jenny," Maisy said, sobbing uncontrollably. Michael held her close as tears rolled down his face.

"Not even death could keep them apart, Maisy," responded Elena, in tears, as Cole consoled her.

"And neither will we, little sister, neither will we," responded Zain. "Steven, can you please sit down right here at this table and write their death certificates. We know how they died. I don't want the coroner doing an autopsy and pulling them apart. Christopher, we need a casket built for two. Where do we find one?"

Christopher stopped to think through the massive pain he was feeling right now. "Maybe we can pull two caskets apart and fuse them to make a large one. You know what I mean, so there is nothing in between them. So, they both fit together. You know what I mean?" he responded crying. Zain nodded.

"I'll go make a few phone calls and get it done asap," said Christopher. Sarah held her husband close. "Let me make the calls, Chris? Just tell me who to call, I'll make the arrangements, okay? I'll get it done," Sarah said. Christopher gave his wife a feeble smile as he held her close and just nodded his head through the tears.

"Little brother, we will need it in the next few hours, along with one tombstone," responded Zain. "Maisy, do you still have the phone number of the Imam that married all of us? We will need him to perform the burial service."

"Yes, I'll call him right now," responded Maisy as she sobbed uncontrollably in Michael's arms.

Zain nodded, hugged his mother and father, and sobbed like a two-year-old while Maryam held him. "Don't worry, old man," he said as he wiped the tears from his father's eyes, "no one will take your Jenny away from you. You'll be buried with your angel together as you are now in each other's arms. No one will ever pull you apart." Zain had prepared himself for his mother's death, but his fathers was painfully unexpected and all too real.

46

Media all over the world had been alerted to the deaths of Eric and Jenny Barrett. The funeral, however, was a private affair at the family cemetery. Not a camera in sight, just the Barrett's and the Imam who performed the burial. Once the ceremony was over, Zain played their song, "Truly, Madly, Deeply," as the casket built for two was lowered into the ground and covered with dirt. They let the song play out as they remembered the love in their parent's eyes as they danced to their song on so many occasions. They each cried and held each other for comfort. At the end of the song, Arthur arrived with Jenny's letter.

"Mr. Barrett," Arthur said to Zain. "I was instructed by Mrs. Jenny Barrett to make sure this was delivered to your father once she had passed on. But seeing how things have changed, I thought it best to deliver it to you. I'm sorry I could not deliver it sooner, everyone was in so much pain, but I think now might be a good time." Arthur handed Zain Jenny's letter.

"Thank you, Arthur." Zain opened the envelope and began to read it out loud for his siblings to hear. Tears streamed down his face and Christopher was unable to control his sobbing as he heard his mother's last thoughts.

As Zain reached the part where Jenny said: *"He is my life, the meaning of my very existence, and if I could change anything it would be to find some way to be together in life and death."* Zain paused and said, "God felt your pain Mom, and Dad your wish to not be separated was granted. Neither one of you could live apart and God saw that and brought you together. We will adhere to all of your requests, Mom, and live our lives as you have taught us," he said. Then, Zain pulled two roses together, intertwined them, and laid them on the grave, "Well, take care of Mom, old man. We'll take care of each other until we meet again, I promise you that."

THE END

Eric Barrett is the world's most eligible bachelor. The multimillionaire playboy can have any woman he wants, but there is only one he truly loves. Jenny Ali is young, kind, innocent, and has no idea who Eric really is. She's unlike anyone he's ever met.

After struggling with the death of his parents, Eric clings to the love and happiness Jenny provides him. But Jenny knows he's hiding something from her. When she discovers his true identity online, she feels betrayed and hurt. Fearing he may lose her forever, Eric tries to take his own life.

After realizing that Eric's intentions were not to hurt her, but to protect her from public scrutiny, Jenny stays by his side until he recovers. After an impromptu wedding, the couple get to work building a family full of love, trust, and respect.

With Eric's money and Jenny's heart, the couple set out to change the world, and what a world they create!

RITA ELENA NIMPO has an honours degree in English. As a Secondary School teacher for many years she enjoys studying literary themes and teaching her students about the transformative nature of literature. As Northrop Frye, one of Rita's favourite authors states: "Literature extends one to the heights and depths of human experience," transforming our beliefs, thoughts, and feelings.

Rita Elena Nimpo lives in Ancaster, Ontario, with her husband. She has two sons, a daughter and a cat named Felix who has a lot of cat-itude.